Published by Periplus Editions (HK) Ltd., with editorial offices at
130 Joo Seng Road, #06-01, Singapore 368357

First published by Hardie Grant Books
85 High Street, Prahran, Victoria 3181, Australia
www.hardiegrant.com.au

ISBN-10: 0-7946-0490-0
ISBN-13: 978-0-7946-0490-5

Jacket and text design by Gayna Murphy, Greendot Design
Photography by Matt Harvey
Food styling by Caroline Velik
Map on page 13 by pfisterer+freeman

Distributed by

North America, Latin America & Europe
Tuttle Publishing
364 Innovation Drive
North Clarendon, VT 05759-9436 U.S.A.
Tel: 1 (802) 773-8930; Fax: 1 (802) 773-6993
info@tuttlepublishing.com
www.tuttlepublishing.com

Japan
Tuttle Publishing
Yaekari Building, 3rd Floor; 5-4-12 Osaki
Shinagawa-ku; Tokyo 141 0032
Tel: (81) 3 5437-0171; Fax: (81) 3 5437-0755
tuttle-sales@gol.com

Asia Pacific
Berkeley Books Pte. Ltd.
130 Joo Seng Road #06-01
Singapore 368357
Tel: (65) 6280-1330; Fax: (65) 6280-6290
inquiries@periplus.com.sg
www.periplus.com

10 09 08 07
6 5 4 3 2 1

Printed in Singapore

saha

A chef's journey through Lebanon and Syria

Greg and Lucy Malouf

Foreword by Anthony Bourdain
Photography by Matt Harvey

PERIPLUS EDITIONS
Singapore • Hong Kong • Indonesia

CONTENTS

FOREWORD

For me, this is a book about possibilities.

There is, perhaps, no major world cuisine as unexplored, unsung, underexposed, unappreciated or as inexplicably under-represented as Lebanese cooking. There's simply no accounting for the fact that for most city dwellers in Western food capitals, the incredibly rich traditions and exciting colors, flavors and textures of Lebanese cooking remain—beyond shawarma—mostly a mystery. Some French and American chefs pillage those traditions for knock-off versions of classic Middle Eastern dishes, usually "updating" them—or "fixing" them, with more familiar fare. But the real thing has remained elusive. It's funny and sad, really, that having scoured France, Spain, Italy Thailand, Japan and Vietnam for inspiration, so few major chefs in the English-speaking world have fully embraced Lebanese cuisine. To ignore its enlightening and inspiring combinations of ingredients and its centuries-old cooking methods and techniques is a serious omission.

Furthermore, Lebanon's historic location at the crossroads of the spice trade, means that over the ages it's drawn on people, ingredients and influences from regions as diverse as Africa, Europe and Asia. Beirut in particular has been (at various times) a major cosmopolitan melting-pot and a jet-set watering hole—the "Paris of the Orient." All these factors, one would think, would make the country a magnet for chefs and cooks looking for inspiration.

There is no doubt that this is a country and a culinary tradition bursting with possibilities. All that's needed now, is for someone to explore them and share them with the rest of us.

Fortunately, Greg and Lucy Malouf have.

Anthony Bourdain

INTRODUCTION

IT IS EARLY EVENING AND WE ARE SITTING ON THE PATIO outside our apartment in Halat sur Mer, a small beach resort about twenty minutes along the coastal road that heads north from Beirut all the way to Syria. The evening air is soft and warm, even though it is early April and spring is yet to fully arrive. The apartment looks out onto a beautifully manicured lawn that slopes gently down to the waterfront. Ahead of us, the sun is a like a golden coin, slipping slowly into the Mediterranean.

Greg is poring over a huge map of Lebanon, steadily cracking his way through a dish of bisr—salty, dried pumpkin seeds—scattering the husks over table and floor. Over the next four weeks I will spend hours trying to perfect the technique of splitting the husks open between my front teeth and then prising the inner seed out of its shell with the tip of my tongue.

This trip has been a long time in the planning: eleven years to be exact. Greg was born in Australia, but he identifies strongly with his Lebanese heritage. His career as a chef has taken him all over the world—to France, Italy, Austria, England and Hong Kong—but never to the Middle East. When we married, eleven years ago, we came to Lebanon and Syria for our honeymoon. Those two weeks were enough for us to vow, "We must come back here. We *will* come back!"

For me, the thrill of that first trip was the usual tourist's excitement of visiting a region so different from the England where I grew up, and from Australia where I now lived. For Greg, the pull was more visceral. It was about coming face to face with a world he had previously only glimpsed in flickering black-and-white home movies of pre-war Beirut and through stories he had heard around the family dinner table. It was about exploring Zahlé, the Malouf family hometown, and meeting his Lebanese cousins for the first time.

And of course it was also about food. As is the case in expatriate communities the world over, Greg grew up in a family whose deep longing for their homeland was most often and happily expressed through the food they cooked. His childhood was filled with the noisy chatter of several generations of women sitting around the kitchen table preparing traditional Arabic dishes in the same way that they'd been made for centuries. Greg's earliest memories are of his grandmother *teta* Adèle's chicken and rice dish, roz a djejh; of his aunt Larisse's kahke bread; and of his mum's kibbeh nayeh, the famous Lebanese version of steak tartare. As a little boy, his usual after-school snack was arus bi laban, a yogurt-cheese sandwich, or a handful of leftover stuffed vine leaves. Sunday lunches were an endless array of mezze dishes followed by platters of chicken, kebabs or lamb, roasted Lebanese style, served with a mound of nut-laden rice. For Greg, as a chef, the pull towards the Middle East was a profound yearning to explore his earliest culinary influences in greater depth.

Eleven years on from that first visit, much has changed. Most significantly, perhaps, Greg and I are no longer married. Thankfully, we have both worked hard at remaining friends—good friends. We collaborate on cooking and writing projects and have co-authored two books about Greg's modern Middle Eastern food. And through it all, we have kept alive and nurtured the dream of returning to the Middle East.

Things have changed in Lebanon and Syria, too. Our visit will coincide with a particularly interesting time in the intertwined history of these neighboring countries. The brutal and repressive rule of former Syrian president Hafez Assad has given way, by birthright, to his son, Bashar. There have been tentative movements towards political and economic reform and a softening of the country's hard-line attitude to the West. Although Syria has been branded part of the "Axis of Evil" by the United States, as a visitor this "evil" is hard to see. During that first visit, local people were warm and welcoming. They were interested in finding out about us and about Australia, and were keen to share their pride in and love for their homeland.

And then there is Lebanon, a tiny beleaguered country that continues to endure the weight of its own reputation. Almost fifteen years on since the end of the relentless civil war that tore the country apart, Lebanon is still better known for bloody bombings and kidnappings than as the original "land of milk and honey," the former intellectual center of the Arab world and, in its golden years, the Paris of the Middle East. And now, at the start of the twenty-first century, Lebanon's story has become a kind of allegory for the whole benighted human condition; the very word "Beirut" is synonymous with the corrupting effect of poverty and repression, and of all that is hateful about religious and ethnic bigotry.

Aleppo

Idlib
Ariha

Dibsi Faraj

Raqqa

Sabkhat al-Jabbul

Lake al-Assad

Euphrates River

Ath-Thaura

Qala'at Saladin

Apamea
Ma'arat an-Nu'aman

Rasafa

Ugarit
Lattakia

Orontes River

Jebel Ansariya

S Y R I A

Baniyas

Hama

Qala'at Marqab
Musyaf

Salamiyya

Tartus

Safita

Krak des
Chevaliers

Homs

As-Sukhna

M E D I T E R R A N E A N   S E A

Lake Qattinah

Palmyra

Sabkhat al-Muh

Tripoli

Nahr Abu Moussa

Zgharta
Jebel el Mekmel
(Mt Mekmel)

Nahr Abu Ali

Bcharré

MT LEBANON RANGE

Nahr al-Aasi (Orontes) River

BEKA'A VALLEY

Byblos
Halat
Nahr Ibrahim

Baalbek
Jebel Sannine
(Mt Sannine)

ANTI-LEBANON RANGE

SYRIAN DESERT

Gazir
Jounieh
Ain el Kabou

Beirut
Qsaibe
Zandouqa
Chtaura

Zahlé

LEBANON

Chouf Mountains
Cedar Reserve

Sidon

Nahr al-Awali

Lake
Qaraonn

Nahr al-Litani

Damascus

Aanjar

Jebel ash-Sheikh
(Mt Hermon)

Tyre
El Qlailé

Golan
Heights

ISRAEL

GREECE

TURKEY

SYRIA

LEBANON

IRAQ

CYPRUS

ISRAEL &
PALESTINE

MEDITERRANEAN SEA

JORDAN

LIBYA

EGYPT

SAUDI
ARABIA

⊞ Historic site

♜ Historic fortress

🌲 Cedar reserve

LEBANON & SYRIA

The underlying resentments that fuelled Lebanon's civil war remain unresolved, as was evidenced by the assassination of former prime minister Rafik Hariri that sent the country into a spin just weeks before we arrived. And yet there is something irrepressible about the Lebanese spirit. As journalist Robert Fisk observes in his extraordinary account of the Lebanese civil war, *Pity the Nation*, the Lebanese have an inherent belief in happiness, "that if they believe(d) hard enough in something, then it would come true." To us, as observers, the visible groundswell of public outrage at the Hariri murder, coupled with growing resentment within Lebanon at the hegemony that Syria has exerted for the last few decades, seems to have sparked a renewed sense of national pride among the country's youth. It is almost enough to convince us that this time the people themselves might actually succeed where successive governments have failed. That Lebanon will, finally, shrug off its past, free itself from Syrian control and evolve into the syncretic society it so longs to be—truly a culture of unity and tolerance.

It is against this backdrop of political uncertainty that we are visiting Lebanon. By happy coincidence, Greg's sister-in-law is also spending some time here visiting her own family, who are scattered around Lebanon and Syria, and we have persuaded her to join us on our voyage of discovery. Amal spent her childhood and teenage years in these countries, before moving to Australia as part of the mass exodus during the civil war. Her knowledge of the region and her fluent Arabic make her the ideal candidate to be our guide, translator and trouble-shooter over the next month.

Joining us, too, is Melbourne photographer Matt Harvey who worked with us on one of our previous books, *Moorish*.

Greg's excitement about this journey has been palpable over the last couple of months, undiminished even by news of bomb scares and mass protest rallies. For him, this is to be an exploration of a cuisine—*his* cuisine—that has its origins in cultures that date back thousands of years. It is chance to recharge his imagination's batteries, to find inspiration.

So here we are, poised to start our journey. We have four weeks ahead of us of eating, drinking and exploring some of the richest historical sites in the world. I sit quietly for a few moments, watching the evening sun sink into the sea, then I open my notebook, pick up my pen and begin to write.

BIENVENUE A BEIRUT

SPICE BLENDS AND FLAVORINGS

SECTEUR 72 / ٧٢ منطقة **REMEIL** / الرميل

RUE 12 / ١٢ شارع

"BIENVENUE A BEIRUT," said the cheery immigration man. "Welcome to Lebanon."

This was a very different greeting from the one we'd received on our first visit to Lebanon. Eleven years ago, our first sight upon landing had been of surly soldiers surrounding the aeroplane, AK–47s at the ready. We'd been grilled by airport officials about the reason for our visit and Greg had received a good telling-off for his lack of Arabic.

Back then, our overriding impressions of Beirut had been of a city in complete chaos, and the devastation wrought by fifteen years of war had been grotesquely fascinating. We had driven around the shattered center of Beirut in a daze, appalled by the sight of formerly elegant hotels riddled with massive mortar holes; of office buildings whose floors had collapsed on each other, top to bottom, like a house of cards; of apartment buildings with their walls blasted completely away to expose the pitiful makeshift camp sites of the homeless who were squatting inside.

Now, first appearances suggested that things were very different. Gone was the dingy, inefficient airport, and in its place was a huge, shiny complex. The thugs with their machine guns were also nowhere to be seen, replaced by men who waved us through with words of welcome and a nod. We were met by Amal and her cousin Sami and chauffeured along the wide, newly built highway towards the city center. There were no potholes, no mounds of

uncollected garbage by the roadside, no checkpoints manned by a duo of ill-tempered Lebanese and Syrian soldiers. And then, ten minutes later, we were there.

Beirut is perched on a rocky promontory overlooking the eastern shores of the Mediterranean, set against the rugged peaks of the Lebanon Mountains. It is an ancient city—founded by the Phoenicians in around 3000 BC—and its advantageous location at the meeting point of three continents means that it has borne the imprint of many civilisations. Over the millennia, the Greeks, Romans, Byzantines, Arabs, Crusaders, Mamelukes and Ottomans all staked their claim to the city.

In the nineteenth century Beirut was a leading center of Arab learning and culture, and by early last century it had grown to become the financial and commercial center of the Arab world. In the 1950s it was famous as the most European city in the Middle East, a glittering playground for the world's beautiful people, who flocked here to sun themselves by day at chichi beach resorts and while the night away at casinos and nightclubs. All this was in the good old days, of course, before the country tore itself apart in a bloody civil war that lasted fifteen long years, ending in 1991.

The city center—or Downtown, as it is now called—is a largely pedestrianized quarter that radiates from Place d'Étoile. Devastated during the war, the city's heart has been completely rebuilt in golden sandstone, faithfully re-creating Beirut's former glory days. As we strolled through cobbled streets lined with the smooth façades of brand-new buildings that emulated the French Mandate style of the 1930s, complete with smart wooden shutters and wrought-iron balconies, it was hard not to be impressed by the results of all this industry. We passed pavement cafés and fashionable boutiques selling everything from Missoni to Mont Blancs. Families were out enjoying the warm weather, and outside an ice-cream shop we passed a group of Beiruti babes sporting designer jeans and Louis Vuitton handbags.

Of course, the cost of all this rebuilding has been massive, and the city has been effectively (and controversially) privatized to fund it. There are constant complaints about corruption within Solidere, the redevelopment company that was partly owned by Rafiq Hariri and charged with fulfilling the former prime minister's dream of a glorious new Beirut. Many residents feel that they have been cheated by the privatisation deal that involved their property being confiscated and replaced by shares in Solidere.

There are also those who believe that amidst all the rebuilding Beirut has somehow lost its soul. That with all the prettification it has become a tame, bourgeois film-set version of its former self. Certainly, there is something surreally perfect about Downtown—and things are very different in the rest of the city. You don't have to look far to see that the legacy of destruction and chaos remains, unrepaired, in the dismal shantytowns that stretch grimly and chaotically into the foothills behind Beirut.

For now, though, we were happy to be seduced by the vision of this glittering new metropolis arising, phoenix-like, from the ashes. Every other street corner was a construction site, with upmarket hotels, a gleaming waterfront marina and a massive new souk precinct in the pipeline. But the rebuilding progamme has not been solely about commerce: a proportion of the funding has been spent on excavating archaeological sites that were revealed, felicitously, during the course of rebuilding the city. On our previous visit to Beirut, work on excavating the old Roman city had just begun; now we were able to admire the magnificently restored Roman baths and *cardo maximus* (marketplace) that are tucked in amongst the city's prime real estate.

Churches and mosques are often cheek by jowl in Beirut, frequently having been built upon the foundations of the other. The massive Maronite cathedral of St George in Place d'Étoile sits right next to the al-Omari Mosque, which in turn was originally built as a Christian church in the twelfth century. To the Lebanese, however, these juxtapositions are nothing new. The entire country is an exercise in contrasts: Christian and Muslim, ancient and modern, Arab and European.

We'd wandered for several hours and now, in the late afternoon, the streets around the Place d'Étoile were eerily deserted. Some girls were playing shuttlecock underneath the square's clock tower and a few bored soldiers were leaning against a government building, smoking. It was evident that in the wake of the Hariri bombing many locals were nervously staying at home, and we were not surprised to learn that Beirut's legendary night life was much quieter than usual.

We were dining that evening with Greg's aunt Houda, who lives in the well-heeled East Beirut suburb of Achrafiyeh. It was still too early for dinner, so we wound our way up through narrow, winding streets lined with antique shops and stylish restaurants to the Hotel Albergo. A drink on its roof terrace had been highly recommended, as had the bird's-eye view of the city.

One of Beirut's prettiest boutique hotels, the Albergo is in an old Lebanese mansion, discreetly cloistered behind a high wall and an overgrown front garden. Its foyer is tiled with an exquisite mosaic of faded beige and cream, and the downstairs lounge is dimly lit and club-like—all deep red velvet and leather-bound books. We took the tiny wrought-iron elevator up to the ninth-floor roof terrace just as the city lights were twinkling into life. In summer this would be a lovely place to sit and enjoy a drink, but after shivering for a while in the cool spring evening air we retreated to the comfort of the dining room, where a middle-aged couple wearing matching Burberry shirts were sipping cocktails at the bar. The room was lushly decorated in a kind of Orientalist-Palm Court fashion, with plenty of foliage and a well-assembled collection of antique inlaid

Syrian, French and English furniture.

Later that evening we met Houda at Sultan Brahim, one of Beirut's outstanding seafood restaurants. It is located on the main Jal el Dib highway leading out of Beirut, and the passing traffic glimpsed through its large plate-glass windows gives it a rather suburban feel.

The meal was excellent: exquisitely presented food and faultless service from middle-aged waiters dressed in khaki suits. We began with silky-smooth hummus topped with diced tomatoes, parsley and a sprinkling of pine nuts; a wonderful fresh herb salad of wild thyme and rocket; a suitably smoky moutabal (eggplant dip); and, something new to all of us, kibbeh bi samak. We were familiar with lamb kibbeh, it's Lebanon's national dish after all, but we'd never tried a fish version. Finely ground fish and bulgur or cracked wheat were shaped into the customary torpedo-shaped shell and stuffed with a lightly spiced braise of tiny shrimp, pieces of white fish, tomato, onion and red pepper.

For our main course we shared a firm, bright-eyed sea bass selected from the superb display that held center stage near the front of the restaurant. It was prepared simply—with olive oil, lemon juice and a sprinkle of allspice—and was none the worse for that. We opted to fill what little room we had left with fresh seasonal fruit and chewy cubes of perfumed Turkish delight.

It was an excellent start to our culinary adventures, and as we headed off into the chilly night air I whispered to Greg, "One meal down, only another hundred-odd to go."

BAHARAT

5 tablespoons sweet paprika
4 tablespoons black pepper, finely ground
3 tablespoons cumin seeds, finely ground
2 tablespoons coriander seeds, finely ground
2 tablespoons ground cinnamon
2 tablespoons ground cloves
1 tablespoon ground cardamom
1 tablespoon ground star anise
1 teaspoon grated nutmeg

Mix all the ingredients together and store in an airtight jar for up to 6 months.

MAKES AROUND ³⁄₄ CUP (200 G)

CUMIN SPICE BLEND

7 tablespoons cumin seeds
3 tablespoons coriander seeds
2 tablespoons black peppercorns
5 tablespoons sweet paprika
3 tablespoons ground ginger

Lightly roast, grind and sieve the cumin and coriander seeds and black peppercorns. Mix with the remaining ingredients and store in an airtight jar for up to 6 months.

MAKES AROUND 1 CUP (250 G)

GOLDEN SPICE MIX

1 tablespoon ground coriander
1 tablespoon ground cumin
¹⁄₂ tablespoon ground turmeric
¹⁄₂ tablespoon ground ginger
¹⁄₄ tablespoon ground chili

Sieve all the ingredients together and store in an airtight jar for up to 6 months.

MAKES AROUND 3 TABLESPOONS

TAKLIA

3 cloves garlic, sliced
2 tablespoons olive oil
1 teaspoon ground coriander
¹⁄₂ teaspoon sea salt

Fry the garlic in the oil over a low heat, taking care not to let it color. Tip into a mortar, add the coriander and salt and pound to a paste.

MAKES 2 TABLESPOONS (30 G)

TOUM

1 whole head garlic
1 teaspoon salt
Juice of 1 lemon
³⁄₄ cup (200 ml) vegetable oil
2 tablespoons water

Peel and roughly chop the garlic cloves, then put them in a blender or liquidizer with the salt and lemon juice. Blend for 2–3 minutes, or until very smooth. Scrape down the sides from time to time to make sure that no chunks of garlic are left out of the paste.

Add the oil very slowly, as if making a mayonnaise. Make sure each amount of oil is fully absorbed before adding more. Finally, add the water.

MAKES AROUND 1¼ CUPS (300 ML)

CUMIN SALT

3 tablespoons cumin seeds
2 tablespoons sea salt

Lightly roast the cumin seeds then grind with the salt to a fine powder.

MAKES AROUND ⅓ CUP (80 G)

SPICY MARINADE

1 large bunch coriander leaves (cilantro)
2 cloves garlic, finely chopped
Grated rind and juice of 2 lemons
⅓ cup (100 ml) olive oil
1 teaspoon sweet paprika
1 teaspoon ground cinnamon
1 teaspoon ground red pepper
1 teaspoon ground cumin
1 teaspoon ground coriander
1 teaspoon salt
½ teaspoon ground black pepper
½ teaspoon ground cardamom
½ teaspoon ground allspice

Strip the hairy bits from the roots of the coriander leaves and wash the bunch well. Chop coarsely and mix with the garlic and the lemon juice and the grated rind. Stir in the spices to make a very wet paste. Use straight away.

MAKES ⅓ CUP (100 ML)

FRAGRANT SALT

½ teaspoon cumin seeds, ground
½ teaspoon coriander seeds, ground
½ teaspoon cardamom seeds, ground
½ teaspoon fennel seeds, ground
½ nigella seeds, ground
½ teaspoon sesame seeds, toasted
2 tablespoons sea salt

Put the ground spices, toasted sesame seeds and salt in a skillet and gently warm through so they merge into one fragrant powder. Store in an airtight jar for up to 6 months.

MAKES 4½ TABLESPOONS (60 G)

PAPRIKA OIL

⅓ cup (100 ml) extra-virgin olive oil
1 clove garlic, finely chopped
1 teaspoon sweet paprika
½ teaspoon caraway seeds, lightly roasted and crushed
A pinch of ground red pepper

Heat a tablespoon of the oil in a small saucepan. Add the garlic and spices and sauté gently for 5 minutes.

Add the remaining oil and heat gently until a cube of bread dropped into it starts to sizzle. Remove from the heat and allow to cool completely. Strain through a piece of muslin to remove the spices. You should be left with a vibrant orange oil. Store in an airtight jar for up to 2 weeks.

MAKES AROUND ⅓ CUP (100 ML)

A DAY IN GEMMAYZEH

SOUPS

EVERY CITY HAS THEM: DOWN-AT-HEEL NO-GO ZONES that are suddenly and surprisingly reborn as chic, ultra-desirable neighborhoods where real estate becomes "prime" seemingly overnight, changing hands for ridiculous sums of money.

In Beirut, this is Gemmayzeh, a small, semi-industrial neighborhood just east of Downtown. The suburb was close enough to the action to catch some of the sniper fire and mortar shells that rained on Beirut during the long civil war years. And here and there among the pastel-painted French-era apartment buildings, with their shutters and balconies, the occasional half-collapsed building remains, its shrapnel-scarred façade overgrown with creepers and weeds.

So far, Gemmayzeh has missed out on Solidere's prettifying ministrations, and it retains much of the flavor of Old Beirut. It's a little shabby, certainly, but hidden away in its laneways and alleys you can still spy triple-arched traditional Lebanese houses and the curved marble balustrades of ornate nineteenth-century villas.

We met Michel and Eli, the two brothers who would be our drivers for the next two weeks, and as it was getting close to lunchtime we asked them to drive us to Le Chef, a small "workers" café on Gemmayzeh's Rue Gouraud. Over its long history Le Chef has become something of a Beirut institution, renowned for its cheap and cheerful home-style cooking.

We crawled through the congested outskirts of East Beirut before hitting a traffic jam on Rue Gouraud. Cars were converging on us from every direction—sleek BMWs and shiny sedans edging down from affluent Achrafiyeh on the hillside above Gemmayzeh; from below us, delivery trucks and motorbikes honking aggressively and forcing their way through the narrow, potholed streets. All par for the course on a busy working day in Beirut.

Le Chef is halfway along Rue Gouraud, amongst roller-doored commercial premises and the moody jazz bars and French cafés that have sprung up in the Gemmayzeh in recent years. There's not an ounce of chic to be found at Le Chef, however. Small and dimly lit, with maybe ten tables, its walls are panelled with dark wood and plastered with faded newspaper cuttings and gaudy murals. Tables are clothed in plastic, and the lime-green net curtains look as if they've been there since the restaurant opened in the late 1960s. Behind the bar, the shelves are loaded with jars of pickles and dusty bottles of arak.

We arrived in the middle of the lunchtime rush and so had to wait our turn between lanky students and a group of loud businessmen, but from our position by the door we had a perfect view of the action. Regulars were greeted, tables constantly rearranged and customers good-humoredly shuffled up to make room for new arrivals. A

REGULARS WERE GREETED,
TABLES CONSTANTLY
REARRANGED AND CUSTOMERS
GOOD-HUMOREDLY
SHUFFLED UP TO MAKE ROOM.

WHAT FRANÇOIS BASSIL COOKS AND LOVES IS
COMFORTABLE, OLD-FASHIONED, HOME-STYLE FOOD,
RATHER THAN THE FUSSY LITTLE MEZZE DISHES THAT
FANCY LEBANESE RESTAURANTS OFFER.

team of waiters ducked and weaved among the diners, unloading dishes of tabbouleh and steaming bowls of chicken and rice as they hurried to and from the kitchen.

The turnover was thankfully brisk, and within a few minutes we were tightly packed into a corner table with menus in hand. Seconds later plates of bread, olives and radishes were tossed onto our table, along with our drinks order.

Le Chef has been serving home-style fare here for nearly forty years and until recently it was the only restaurant on Rue Gouraud. It's run by father and son team François and Charbel Bassil, with François in the kitchen and Charbel directing proceedings on the floor.

"*Alors, les plats du jour,*" Charbel announced, clearly spotting us as tourists and recommending the daily specials. He called the orders out to the kitchen as we made up our minds, and we were soon tucking into chiche barak, little lamb-filled dumplings in a hot yogurt soup; makloube, an upside-down dish of eggplant, chicken and rice; lamb kebabs and crisp fried fish. The food at Le Chef is definitely not haute cuisine, but nor does it have any pretensions to be so. What François Bassil cooks and loves is comfortable, old-fashioned, home-style food, rather than the fussy little mezze dishes that fancy Lebanese restaurants offer.

"Mezze is what we eat on Sundays or for special celebrations," Charbel explained. "It is not what we eat every day. The chiche barak or the chicken with rice—this is what your grandmother makes at home. It is the real Lebanese food."

The following week we had a hankering for some more comfort food. As we walked through the door of Le Chef, Charbel recognized us and, thrusting menus into our hands and briskly wiping our table, exclaimed, "*Bonjour les Australiens.* You are welcome back to Le Chef!"

Just down the street, but firmly at the other end of the style spectrum, is a hip little bistro with similar ambitions of bringing home-cooked food into a restaurant environment, although it is presented with more contemporary flair. This is La Tabkha, the latest brainchild of a trio of ambitious young entrepreneurs who already have their fingers in a slew of other pies around the city.

La Tabkha—which loosely translates as "the casserole pot"—was starting to fill when we arrived for an early lunch. The sun poured in through the bistro's large windows, making the room with its funky mustard-yellow color scheme even more bright and cheerful. We ordered a couple of cold Almaza beers while a friendly waiter explained the system: we could order from the day's specials or, for a fixed price, help ourselves to the buffet selection of cold dishes that filled a long central table.

I started at the buffet, choosing some delicious-looking fried cauliflower, vegetarian vine leaves, blanched swiss chard with tahini sauce and potato kibbeh. Greg looked up enviously from his spicy tomato and lentil soup. "We need some more laban," he announced, turning to the waiter, and a dish of creamy yogurt, drizzled with local olive oil, arrived at our table in an instant.

We had decided to pass on pudding, but changed our minds when we saw the couple at the next table tucking into a plate of aish al saraya. It's best described as like tiramisu, with a syrup-soaked base of breadcrumbs topped with thick clotted cream and chopped pistachios.

The stylish young man seated next to us smiled and nodded knowingly as he saw us fighting over the last luscious morsel. It transpired that this was Fadi Sabah, one of the co-owners of the restaurant, and he took us behind the scenes to meet his mother, the head chef.

The kitchen was a hive of industry. A bevy of white-capped women were busily packing take-away orders into neat cardboard boxes and dispatching them to a team of

"THE CHICKEN WITH RICE, THIS IS WHAT YOUR GRANDMOTHER MAKES AT HOME. IT IS THE REAL LEBANESE FOOD."

delivery boys on mopeds, as La Tabkha does a roaring take-away trade with nearby offices and apartment buildings. "I think people are sick of sandwiches," Fadi said with a smile. His mother told us she was from Falougha in the mountains. "I learnt my cooking from my mother," she told us matter-of-factly, "and she learnt it from her mother."

We definitely needed a spot of post-prandial exercise after enjoying Fadi's mother's home cooking, so we headed out for a walk around the neighborhood. The relative quiet of Rue Gouraud's bars and antique shops was broken when we passed a vacant block where a crumbling building was being demolished by an army of bulldozers. Peace resumed when we left Rue Gouraud to climb the historic Saint Nicholas steps that rise up the hill to Rue Sursock, famed for its colonial villas. The steps are flanked by crumbling apartment buildings and as we climbed we were close enough to reach out and touch their peeling plasterwork. Through an open window we saw an old man shuffling around his kitchen in his pyjamas. An old lady was watering the plants on her balcony and all around us were canaries swinging in tiny cages. Pausing to catch our breath, we looked back across the rooftops through a tangle of cabling to the Mediterranean, shimmering in the distance.

We wound our way downhill along a narrow street paved with flagstones, and arrived back on Rue Gouraud in the late afternoon. The street was quieter now, and at La Tabhka a youth was busily washing the outside windows while a group of kitchen hands hung around the rear doorway smoking cigarettes. While we watched, a take-away box appeared through a serving hatch and then the leather-clad delivery boy sped off down the road.

GOLDEN CHICKEN SOUP WITH CORIANDER, GARLIC AND PARSLEY

1 tablespoon Taklia (page 20)

1 chicken (about 2 lbs/1 kg)

1 cup (100 g) cooked rice (optional)

1 cup (40 g) flat-leaf parsley leaves,
  finely chopped

Juice of 1 lemon

Salt and pepper to taste

Chicken stock

6 lbs (3 kgs) chicken bones

1/4 cup (60 ml) olive oil

3 onions, coarsely diced

1/2 cup (125 ml) dry sherry

Up to 12 cups (4 liters) water

2 sticks celery, coarsely diced

1 medium leek, white part only,
  coarsely diced

1 medium carrot, coarsely diced

2 cloves garlic, cut in half

1 cinnamon stick

1 teaspoon white peppercorns

2 bay leaves

1/4 teaspoon ground allspice

6 cardamom pods, cracked

Peel of 1/2 lemon

Make the Taklia by following the recipe on page 20.

Preheat the oven to 400°F (200°C). To make the Chicken Stock, wash and dry the chicken bones. Heat the oil in a large heavy-based baking tray, then add the chicken bones and onions to the hot oil. Stir them around over the heat for 3–4 minutes until they start to color. Transfer the tray to the oven and roast for 20 minutes, until the onions have caramelized and the bones are a lovely deep golden brown. Take the tray out of the oven and deglaze with sherry over a medium heat.

Tip the browned bones and onion into a 5 liter stock pot and pour on enough water to completely cover. Bring to a boil then skim away any fatty scum that rises to the surface. Add the vegetables and bring back to a boil. Add the spices and lemon peel and simmer very gently for 2 hours, uncovered. From time to time you will need to skim off any scum that forms on the surface.

At the end of the cooking time, the liquid will have reduced quite substantially and you will end up with around 8 cups (2 liters) of Chicken Stock. Very carefully ladle the liquid into a fine sieve. The less you disturb the bones and vegetables, the clearer the final broth will be. If you like, you can now chill or freeze this Stock for future use.

To make the soup, cut the chicken into quarters; this will give you 2 legs (marylands) and 2 breasts on the bone. Pour the cold Stock into a large saucepan with the chicken pieces and slowly bring to a simmer. Don't allow it to boil or the soup will turn cloudy and the breast meat will toughen. Simmer gently for 5 minutes, then remove the chicken breasts from the hot liquid and put them to one side. Continue simmering gently for another 10 minutes, skimming as needed, then remove the chicken legs from the soup.

When the chicken is cool enough to handle, pull the meat off the bones and use your fingers to tear it into smaller pieces. Discard the skin and bones. Put the chicken meat back into the simmering Stock with the cooked rice (if using), chopped parsley and lemon juice. Season with salt and pepper and serve right away, topping each bowl with a small blob of Taklia.

SERVES 8

SPICY TOMATO SOUP WITH VERMICELLI

This is a gorgeously thick, spicy and comforting tomato soup that I remember well from my childhood. It's quick and easy to make. Dried vermicelli noodles are often added to Arabic soups and rice dishes to add texture, color and a lovely nutty flavor.

1/3 cup (100 ml) olive oil

1 large brown onion, finely chopped

1 leek, white part only, finely chopped

2 cloves garlic, finely chopped

1 red finger-length chili, deseeded and
  finely shredded

1 teaspoon ground turmeric

1 teaspoon ground coriander

1 teaspoon ground cumin

1/2 teaspoon ground ginger

1 teaspoon honey

1 tablespoon tomato paste

One 14-oz/400-g can chopped tomatoes

2 cups (500 ml) vegetable or chicken
  stock

Salt and pepper to taste

Small packet (3 1/2 oz/100 g) dried
  vermicelli noodles

Chopped fresh parsley (optional)

Heat half the oil in a large saucepan and sauté the onion, leek, garlic and chili until they start to soften. Add the spices, honey and tomato paste and cook for a few more minutes. Add the tomatoes and stock and season with salt and pepper. Bring the soup to a boil, then lower the heat and simmer gently for 20 minutes.

Use your hands to roughly break the vermicelli. Heat the remaining oil in a heavy-based skillet and sauté the noodles until golden brown. Tip into a sieve and drain away the oil. Add to the soup and simmer gently for 8–10 minutes until the noodles are tender. Garnish with parsley if you like and serve with chunks of crusty buttered bread.

SERVES 8

YOGURT AND BULGUR SOUP WITH SHREDDED CHICKEN, CHILI, LEMON AND MINT *kishk*

I remember my *teta* Adèle making this dish for the family when I was a child—my brothers and I used to eat it on Saturday mornings before heading off to the footy with our grandfather. Kishk, a fermented yogurt and bulgur wheat powder, is something of an acquired taste, but in the same way that one can develop a taste for the Chinese soup congee, we find it curiously addictive. You can find kishk powder in Middle Eastern grocers.

Chicken stock
2 small chicken breasts, on the bone
1 stick celery, coarsely chopped
4 pearl onions, peeled and quartered
1 red bird's-eye chili, split lengthwise
1 cinnamon stick
½ lemon
Water

SERVES 8

Kishk
1 tablespoon olive oil
2 green finger-length chilies, deseeded and finely shredded
1 onion, very finely diced
1 clove garlic, finely diced
½ teaspoon dried mint leaves
½ cup (120 g) kishk powder
4 cups (1 liter) reserved Chicken Stock
Salt and pepper to taste
Mint leaves, finely chopped
Lemon juice, to taste

To make the Chicken Stock, place the chicken breasts in a medium-sized pan with the other ingredients and pour on enough water to cover. Bring to a boil and skim away the residue that rises to the surface. Simmer gently for 5 minutes, then turn off the heat and leave the chicken to cool in the Stock. When cool, remove the chicken, reserving the Stock and pearl onions for the soup. Debone the chicken and use your hands to shred the chicken meat finely.

Heat the olive oil in a large heavy-based pot and gently sauté the chilies, onion, garlic and dried mint leaves until soft. Stir in the kishk powder and cook on a medium heat for a few minutes. Reheat the reserved Chicken Stock and add to the kishk mixture, stirring constantly. Season with salt and pepper and bring to a boil. Cook for another 5 minutes, stirring from time to time, until thick and creamy. Add the reserved pearl onions and serve garnished with the shredded chicken, chopped mint and a squeeze of lemon juice.

SPINACH, LENTIL AND LEMON SOUP, BEDOUIN-STYLE

This is a version of one of Lebanon's most loved soups, and you will find similar lentil soups all over the Middle East. We had one of the simplest and best meals of our trip at a Bedouin restaurant in the desert town of Palmyra in Syria. We were each served a complimentary cup of this tangy soup before our meal—just the thing for a chilly spring night in the desert.

2 tablespoons Taklia (page 20)
3 tablespoons olive oil
1 onion, finely sliced
1 clove garlic, finely chopped
1½ cups (150 g) dried brown lentils
4 cups (1 liter) water or vegetable stock
1 bunch spinach, stalks removed
½ cup (25 g) coriander leaves (cilantro)
Juice of 2 lemons, or more to taste
Salt and pepper to taste
⅔ cup (100 g) pine nuts, lightly toasted

SERVES 8

Make the Taklia by following the recipe on page 20.

Heat the oil in a large heavy-based saucepan and sauté the onion and garlic until they soften. Add the lentils to the pan and stir in well. Add the water or stock and bring to a boil. Simmer until the lentils are very soft—about 30 minutes.

Add the spinach and coriander leaves to the pan then the lemon juice, and season with salt and pepper. Don't add too much salt as the Taklia is quite salty. Cover the pan and cook for a few more minutes until the spinach wilts. Stir well, then tip into a liquidizer or use a hand blender to purée the soup. If necessary, thin with a little more water to lighten the consistency. It should not be too thick or sludgy.

Stir the Taklia into the hot soup and serve right away, garnished with the toasted pine nuts.

LEBANESE-STYLE DUMPLINGS IN YOGURT SOUP WITH SWISS CHARD *chiche barak*

This ancient dish has its roots in pre-Islamic Persia and is thought to have been introduced to Lebanon by the Ottomans. Traditionally, it is served with rice and makes a hearty meal. We find the dumplings quite filling, and prefer to serve them in a soup. They are partially baked in the oven, which results in a rustic, rather chewy dumpling. If you prefer a smoother, more refined dumpling, poach them in water for 5 minutes before finishing the cooking in the soup. The swiss chard isn't a traditional addition, but its earthy tang perfectly complements the richness of the lamb filling.

Lamb dumplings

1 tablespoon olive oil

½ onion, finely chopped

1 small clove garlic, finely chopped

7 oz (200 g) lean boneless lamb, finely ground

½ teaspoon ground allspice

½ teaspoon cinnamon

Salt and pepper to taste

⅓ cup (50 g) pine nuts, lightly toasted

36 round wonton wrappers (white)

Yogurt soup

2 tablespoons olive oil

1 onion, finely chopped

1 clove garlic, finely chopped

1 bunch swiss chard, leaves only, coarsely chopped

1 red bird's-eye chili, deseeded, scraped and finely chopped

½ teaspoon ground allspice

1 cup (250 ml) chicken stock

Juice of 1 lemon

2 cups (500 g) plain yogurt

½ tablespoon cornstarch

3 tablespoons water

1 egg, lightly beaten

To make the filling for the Lamb Dumplings, heat the oil in a non-stick pan and sauté the onion and garlic until soft. Add the ground lamb and continue to sauté, stirring constantly to break up any lumps. Add the spices and season lightly with salt and pepper. When the juices have evaporated, remove the pan from the heat and stir in the toasted pine nuts. Set aside and leave to cool.

Place a teaspoon of filling in the center of each wonton wrapper. Moisten the edges and fold over to make a crescent shape. Use your fingers to press the edges together and seal well. Arrange the dumplings on a lightly oiled baking tray and bake for 10–15 minutes until very lightly browned, but not cooked through.

To make the Yogurt Soup, heat the olive oil in a large pot and sauté the onion and garlic until they soften. Add the swiss chard, chili, allspice, chicken stock and lemon juice and cook over a gentle heat for about 20 minutes, until the swiss chard is tender.

To stabilize the yogurt, tip into a large bowl and stir briskly until smooth. Mix the cornstarch with the water and add to the yogurt with the egg. Stir well, then tip into the hot swiss chard mixture. Lower the heat and cook, stirring in one direction only, for about 10 minutes, or until the soup has thickened. Add the Lamb Dumplings and simmer gently for a further 5 minutes, or until they are cooked through.

SERVES 8

SHELLFISH SOUP WITH FENNEL AND SAFFRON

2 lbs (1 kg) black mussels

15 jumbo shrimp tails, split in half

3 lbs (1½ kgs), fresh crabs, shells and
    gills removed, cut in half

¼ cup (60 ml) olive oil

1 onion, finely chopped

1 leek, white part only, finely chopped

1 clove garlic, finely chopped

2 small fennel bulbs, cut lengthwise
    into wedges

⅓ cup (100 ml) white wine

6 cups (1½ liters) chicken stock

2 tomatoes, deseeded and diced

⅓ cup (15 g) flat-leaf parsley leaves,
    coarsely chopped

1 tablespoon celery leaves, coarsely
    chopped

Few sprigs of thyme

⅓ cup (100 ml) heavy cream

Juice of 1–2 lemons

Salt and pepper to taste

Extra-virgin olive oil, to finish

Spice mix

1 teaspoon ground turmeric

1 teaspoon ground red pepper

1 teaspoon ground coriander

1 teaspoon ground cumin

½ teaspoon ground ginger

½ teaspoon saffron threads

Mix all the Spice Mix ingredients together.

Scrub the mussels clean and pull away the beards. Discard any mussels that refuse to close after a sharp tap.

Heat the oil in a large heavy-based saucepan and add the onion, leek, garlic, fennel and the spice mix. Stir over a medium heat for a few minutes, then tip in the mussels, shrimp and crab, shaking the pan to move them around over the heat. Pour in the wine, cover the pan and turn up the heat. Steam for 3–4 minutes, shaking the pan vigorously from time to time.

Remove the lid and stir around well. Pick out and discard any mussels that have stayed closed, then put the lid back on and steam for a further 2 minutes. Take the pan off the heat and remove the mussels, shrimp and crab. Pick the meat from the body and claws of the crab and discard the shells. Remove the mussel meat from their shells.

Add the chicken stock, tomatoes, parsley, celery leaves and thyme to the pan and put back on the heat. Bring to a boil and simmer for 10 minutes. Pour in the cream and lemon juice and lightly season with salt and pepper. Return the shrimp, mussels and crab meat to the soup. Serve sprinkled with fruity extra-virgin olive oil.

SERVES 4–6

RAS EL MATN

MEZZE DIPS

WE WOKE TO A DINGY-GREY DAWN, made gloomier by the realisation that one of us was going to have to brave the motorway to drive to the arranged meeting place where our driver, Michel, could take over. Our final destination would be the small village of Zandouqa, deep in the hilly Ras el Matn region, directly east of Beirut.

Greg drew the short straw, and soon we were caught up in the maelstrom of morning peak-hour traffic. The road was the busiest we had seen it yet, jam-packed with commuter buses, battered service taxis, beemers and army trucks roaring around us on all sides. Greg's method of steering a direct course and simply allowing other drivers to move around him seemed to work, however, and we arrived intact, if nervous wrecks, to hand over the car keys.

We were headed for Zandouqa to meet an old school friend of Amal's called Hady Zeidan, on a mission to find out more about one of the most expensive and desirable ingredients in Lebanese cuisine: pine nuts. These resinous little kernels are native to the southern Mediterranean and are prized not just for their flavor, but for the soft crunch they add to all sorts of savory and sweet dishes. Eighty per cent of Lebanon's pine nuts come from the Ras el Matn region.

With Michel at the wheel it was a peaceful half-hour drive up into the hills, and Beirut's suburban sprawl quickly gave way to thick forest and deeply shadowed ravines. As we neared Zandouqa, the sun broke through the clouds.

Hady's house looked out across a frothy sea of pine trees and a picturesque valley, dotted here and there with the red-tiled rooftops of traditional Lebanese houses. We sat in the sunshine on the verandah, sipping coffee and munching on home-made ma'amoul biscuits, and listened as Hady told us a little about pine nuts.

"We grow the best pine nuts in the world here in Lebanon," he declared. "They have the best flavor because of their high oil content." Greg was quick to agree, pointing out his frustration at having to make do with the poorer-quality, stubby Chinese pine nuts that are most readily available in Australia.

Hady gave a sigh. "Lebanon exports pine nuts all around the world—to Europe, to Canada and to Australia, too," he said. "But we are a small country and our harvest is not as big as China's. Also, it is very labor intensive to farm pine nuts and the yield is not so large. It takes ten years before you get the first harvest and then you must collect thirty kilos of pine cones to get one kilo of pine nuts."

On the plus side, stone pine trees (*Pinus pinea*) appear to be ridiculously low maintenance: they grow wild and need virtually no water or fertilizer; they propagate themselves; and they live well over 150 years. Most of the trees we were looking at belonged to one landowner who leased his trees' crops to the highest bidder at the start

"WE GROW THE BEST PINE NUTS IN THE WORLD HERE IN LEBANON," HE DECLARED. "THEY ARE THE MOST EXPENSIVE AND HAVE THE BEST FLAVOR BECAUSE OF THEIR HIGH OIL CONTENT."

of each season. The successful bidder—in effect a kind of pine nut middleman—would then send in workers to harvest the crops and arrange for them to be shelled and processed before on-selling them, either for the export market or to local sweet and pastry manufacturers.

Suddenly our attention was caught by a stocky fellow propping a rickety ladder against the bottom of a nearby tree. As we watched, he climbed nimbly up the ladder and then shimmied up the rest of the skinny trunk, before disappearing into the green treetops. "Ah," said Hady. "You are lucky to see this. It's the last week of the picking season and most of the workers have moved on. I spoke to my neighbor this morning who needed a picker—he was prepared to pay US$40 a day, which is a very good price—but there was no-one around."

Harvesting pine nuts is dangerous work and most seasons, we learned, there are fatalities. A picker generally earns US$35 a day, compared with a mere US$12 for the less risky job of collecting and bagging up the cones that have fallen on the ground. The cones are spread out on plastic sheets in the sunshine, and as they dry they open up and the precious seeds fall out.

It was easy to believe that there were fatalities. The trees grow up to 49 feet (fifteen

meters) high and most of the lower branches are neatly clipped away, leaving impossibly long and slender trunks. The treetops bend in the wind and look far too fragile to be climbing about in. The man we were watching wasn't secured to the tree in any way and he was wielding a vicious-looking sickle-shaped knife, sending small branches crashing to the ground as he worked.

Suddenly Hady leapt to his feet. "Come" he said. "We'll go to visit my neighbor." We piled into our car and followed him around a slalom run of hairpin bends to the next village to find his friend and neighbor Georges Neaimeh.

Georges' main work was making carob molasses (known as dibs), but he and his cousins also harvested and processed pine nuts during the season. His face and hands were blackened, his clothes dusty and he looked weary, but he shook our hands and greeted us with a polite "As'salaam aleikum." Hady translated his welcome for us. "He welcomes you to his home and apologises that he is very tired. He and his cousins have been working all night, trying to finish processing the quota of pine nuts that must be delivered this afternoon."

We looked on in fascination as an antiquated husking machine took in the black-shelled nuts at one end, sent them on a bone-shaking journey through a series of graduated hammers and completed the task by spitting out a stream of golden nuts at the other end.

Nothing is wasted. The pine nuts' hard shells are gathered in buckets and sold for fuel. The precious pine nuts are soaked to loosen their papery skins and panned by hand in a large sieve to separate the creamy kernels. Georges scooped a handful from a sack propped against a wall and handed them around. We'd been longing to taste them, and found them strongly resinous yet sweet, with a soft, buttery texture.

Our snack of pine nuts had whet our appetites and it was time to get back for lunch.

HUMMUS WITH SPICED MARINATED LAMB AND PINE NUTS

This is a variation on the classic Lebanese dish lamb shawarma, which you simply can't miss if you go to the Middle East—just follow your nose. The lamb is sliced straight into Arabic bread that's smeared with hummus and topped with a few sliced onions and some pickled vegetables. You might also find a similar version of this dish on the mezze table called hummus bi lahm: hot fried ground lamb and chickpeas tipped onto a dish of hummus.

7 oz (200 g) boneless lamb loin, cut into
    thin strips
2 cups (500 g) Hummus bi Tahini (see
    recipe below)
2 tablespoons pine nuts, toasted
Extra-virgin olive oil
Parsley and Purple Onion Relish
    (page 103)

Spice marinade
½ teaspoon ground cinnamon
½ teaspoon ground allspice
¼ teaspoon crushed black pepper
¼ teaspoon ground nutmeg
¼ teaspoon ground cardamom
¼ teaspoon ground cloves
Juice of 1 lemon
⅓ cup (100 ml) olive oil

Make the Hummus bi Tahini and Parsley and Purple Onion Relish by following the recipes below and on page 103.

Combine the spices, lemon juice and olive oil to make the Spice Marinade. Put the lamb strips into a shallow dish and pour on the Marinade. Toss them around so they are well coated, then cover and refrigerate for 6–12 hours.

Let the meat come to room temperature. Heat a griddle pan as hot as you can—it should be smoking hot—and sear the lamb strips for 2 minutes or so, until they are just cooked through. Leave the meat to cool slightly while you toast the pine nuts.

To serve, put the Hummus bi Tahini into a serving dish, make a well in the middle and stack the lamb strips into a little tower. Scatter on the pine nuts and drizzle generously with extra-virgin olive oil. Serve with the Parsley and Purple Onion Relish and lots of warm Arabic bread.

SERVES 6 AS PART OF A MEZZE SELECTION

HUMMUS BI TAHINI

We make no apologies for including another recipe for hummus as this home-made version is immeasurably better than any commercially sold hummus. If you want a shortcut, use a 14-oz (400-g) can of cooked chickpeas, but make sure you rinse them well to get rid of the "tinny" flavor. Hummus is best when you take the trouble to pick out all the chickpea skins, but it's not surprising that most of us don't have the time to devote to this.

1 cup (250 g) dried chickpeas
2 tablespoons baking soda
Juice of up to 2 lemons
2 small cloves garlic, crushed with 1
    teaspoon sea salt
⅓ cup (100 ml) tahini paste, well stirred
Salt and pepper to taste

Soak the chickpeas overnight in twice their volume of cold water and the baking soda. The next day, rinse the chickpeas very thoroughly. Don't rush this step—you should take at least 5–10 minutes rinsing them under cold running water. Place the chickpeas in a large pan of fresh water and bring it to a boil. Then lower the heat and simmer for up to 2 hours, until they have disintegrated into a porridge-like mush. You will need to keep an eye on them during the cooking process, and top up with extra water every 20 minutes or so.

Tip the mush of chickpeas into a processor with the lemon juice, garlic paste and tahini and whiz until the mixture is very smooth. Taste and adjust the seasoning until you get the right balance of nuttiness, acid and pungent garlic.

As it cools, the hummus will thicken, so thin it down with a little more lemon juice or water as needed.

MAKES AROUND 2 CUPS (500 G)

HUMMUS WITH CRUSHED CHICKPEAS, PINE NUTS AND CUMIN *balila*

A simple, more rustic style of hummus that is popular in many cafés and restaurants in the Middle East.

1 cup (250 g) dried chickpeas

2 tablespoons baking soda

1 small clove garlic, crushed with 1
  teaspoon sea salt

½ teaspoon ground cumin

Juice of 1½ lemons

3 tablespoons olive oil

Garnish

3 tablespoons olive oil

2 cloves garlic, finely sliced

⅓ cup (50 g) pine nuts

Juice of ½ lemon

Soak the chickpeas overnight in twice their volume of cold water and the baking soda. The next day, rinse the chickpeas thoroughly. Place them in a large pan of fresh water and bring it to a boil. Then lower the heat and simmer for 1–2 hours, until the chickpeas are tender—the timing will depend on how old they are. Don't cook them to a mush, but you should be able to squish them easily between your fingers. When cool enough to handle, swish them around to loosen the skins and remove as many as you can. The more skins you can remove, the better.

Drain the chickpeas, and reserve ½ cup (75 g) to garnish. Tip the rest into a food processor with the garlic paste, cumin, lemon juice and oil. While still warm, blitz to a smooth purée.

To prepare the Garnish, heat the oil in a small pan and fry the garlic and pine nuts until they start to color. Remove from the heat and allow to cool slightly. Tip onto the hummus and add the reserved chickpeas. Squeeze on the lemon juice. Serve immediately with plenty of Arabic bread.

SERVES 6–8 AS PART OF A MEZZE SELECTION

RED PEPPER, WALNUT AND POMEGRANATE DIP *muhammara*

This vibrant and intensely flavored Syrian dip is especially popular in the northern city of Aleppo, where the Armenian influence is seen in the fondness for spicy flavors. There are endless versions of muhammara—some include tahini or yogurt cheese, while others omit the roasted peppers to make a nuttier, more densely textured relish. You really need to roast the peppers on an open flame to achieve the desired smokiness, and the gas burner on your stove top will work well. Otherwise, roast the peppers in a hot oven.

3 large red bell peppers

1 red bird's-eye chili, deseeded and
  chopped

1 clove garlic, crushed with 1 teaspoon
  salt

1¼ cups (125 g) shelled walnuts,
  coarsely chopped

⅓ cup (20 g) lightly toasted fresh
  breadcrumbs

1 tablespoon pomegranate molasses

Juice of ½–1 lemon

1 tablespoon hot water

½ teaspoon sugar

¼ cup (65 ml) extra-virgin olive oil, plus
  extra to serve

Roast the bell peppers directly on the naked flame of your stove burners. Set the flame to low and cook the peppers for around 10–15 minutes, constantly turning them so that the skin chars evenly all over and they start to flatten and collapse. Remove the peppers from the flame, place in a bowl and cover with plastic wrap. This allows them to continue to steam and soften further. When they are cool enough to handle, carefully peel away the blackened skin and remove the stalks, seeds and white membranes. Don't rinse the peppers as this will wash away the desired smoky flavor.

Coarsely chop the peppers and put them in a food processor with all the other ingredients, except for the oil. Process to a rough paste, scraping down the sides to ensure that all the ingredients are mixed together well. With the motor running, pour in the oil in a slow, steady stream and blend until thick and creamy. Allow to cool, then refrigerate until needed. Before serving, check seasoning and drizzle with a little olive oil. Serve with warm Arabic bread or smear onto toasted slices of French bread.

SERVES 6–8 AS PART OF A MEZZE SELECTION

WHITE BEAN PURÉE WITH OLIVES AND GOAT'S CHEESE

⅔ cup (150 g) dried white beans,
   soaked in cold water overnight
2 tablespoons olive oil
1 medium onion, finely sliced
1 large clove garlic, coarsely chopped
1 tablespoon sherry
3 cups (750 ml) water
1 small clove garlic, crushed with
   ½ teaspoon salt
2 tablespoons extra-virgin olive oil
Juice of ½ lemon
½ cup (60 g) crumbled goat's cheese
Handful kalamata olives, washed, dried
   and coarsely chopped

Strain the beans and rinse them well. Heat the olive oil in a heavy-based pot, then add the onion. Sauté for a few minutes, then add the garlic and stir over a gentle heat for a further couple of minutes. Add the beans, stirring to coat them with oil, then add the sherry. Add the water and bring to a boil. Lower the heat and simmer, uncovered, for 30–40 minutes, or until the beans are tender.

Towards the end of the cooking time, raise the heat to boil off any remaining liquid, but watch carefully to avoid burning.

Pour the beans into a sieve and strain any residual liquid, then tip them into a blender and add the garlic paste, extra-virgin olive oil and lemon juice. Blitz the mixture on high until it is reduced to a smooth purée. To serve, heat the purée through and gently fold in the goat's cheese and chopped olives.

SERVES 4–6 AS PART OF A MEZZE SELECTION

CUCUMBER AND YOGURT BALILA WITH MINT OIL

3 tablespoons bulgur or cracked wheat,
   dark, fine grade
1 head baby romaine lettuce, outer
   leaves removed, thinly shredded
2 Lebanese cucumbers, peeled,
   deseeded and diced
2 green onions (scallions), finely chopped
⅓ cup (12 g) fresh mint leaves, finely
   chopped
¼ cup (60 ml) olive oil
1 cup (250 g) firm Yogurt Cheese
   (Labneh—page 118)
½ cup (100 g) plain yogurt
Salt and pepper to taste

Mint oil
2 teaspoons olive oil
2 cloves garlic, finely chopped
1 teaspoon dried mint leaves

Make the Labneh by following the recipe on page 118.

To make the Mint Oil, heat the oil gently, then add the garlic and stir. Add the dried mint leaves and immediately remove from the heat as it will burn quickly. Allow to infuse overnight. Sieve and reserve until needed.

Cover the bulgur or cracked wheat with cold water and soak for 10 minutes. Drain it well through a sieve, then tip it into a dish towel and squeeze out as much water as you can. Reserve a tablespoon of the bulgur or cracked wheat to garnish and tip the rest into a mixing bowl with the lettuce, cucumbers, green onions, mint leaves and the olive oil. Stir to combine. Add the Labneh and yogurt and season with salt and pepper. Stir well and chill. When ready to serve, drizzle over the Mint Oil and sprinkle on the reserved bulgur or cracked wheat.

SERVES 6–8 AS PART OF A MEZZE SELECTION

MUHAMMARA LABNEH

1 cup (250 g) firm Yogurt Cheese
   (Labneh—page 118)
1 cup (250 g) Muhammara (page 46)
Extra-virgin olive oil
Salt and pepper

Make the Muhammara and Labneh by following the recipes on pages 46 and 118

Stir the Labneh and Muhammara together to form a smooth dip. Drizzle with a little extra-virgin olive oil and season with salt and pepper before serving.

SERVES 6–8 AS PART OF A MEZZE SELECTION

THE BUTCHERS OF BAALBECK

MEAT MEZZE

NOTHING PREPARES YOU FOR YOUR FIRST SIGHT OF BAALBECK. One minute you're traveling along a dusty road in the heart of the Bekaa Valley; the next, the massive columns of the Temple of Jupiter loom above you, apparently from nowhere.

The Roman remains at Baalbeck are arguably the most outstanding in the Middle East, and they're certainly the single most awesome sight in Lebanon. The Phoenicians built the original temple back in the third millennium BC to worship the sun god Baal, and it was reputedly the setting for mind-bogglingly bloody rituals and cult activities, including orgies and sacred prostitution. After the conquest of Alexander the Great the town was known as Heliopolis and it was eventually appropriated by the Romans, who grafted a massive multi-temple complex on top of the original site and dedicated it to a trio of their own deities: Jupiter, Venus and Mercury.

As you wander around the aged and weathered stone ruins you can't help but speculate about the cost of this massive undertaking, particularly in human terms. It's not just the size of the buildings—the columns of the Temple of Jupiter soar an extraordinary seventy-five feet (twenty-three meters) in height and are over six and half feet (two meters) in diameter, making them the largest in the world—it's also the staggering level of detail. At every turn there are exquisitely ornamented stone carvings: roaring lions, charging bulls, classical key designs, draping tendrils, bunches of grapes and intricately carved friezes of bacchanalian scenes.

And, of course, the cost was largely the point. The motive for building works of this scale—using the labor of more than one hundred thousand slaves over several generations—was not limited to the worship of the gods. The main purpose of Baalbeck was as an extravagant showpiece against the pagan world's swiftly advancing rival, Christianity. A final fling of defiance, if you like.

Eventually, of course, the Roman Empire embraced Christianity and in 313 AD the temples at Baalbeck were officially closed by Emperor Constantine. Over the centuries that followed, Baalbeck endured a series of sackings by waves of invaders and many of the buildings were sent tumbling by earthquakes and the ravages of war.

One of the most extraordinary things about the whole Baalbeck experience is the almost total lack of tourists. Lebanon has yet to re-stake its claim to the tourist map, so most of the country remains undisturbed by the crowds that ruin sightseeing in most other parts of the world.

We perched on an ancient lump of stone overlooking the largely intact and exquisitely decorated Temple of Bacchus and watched a small group of French visitors below us meander around the dusty ruins. Swallows dove in and around the massive columns, and our eyes were drawn to the distant vista of snow-tipped mountains. "The Acropolis has got nothing on this," said Greg.

THE ORIGINAL TEMPLE WAS REPUTEDLY THE SETTING FOR
MIND-BOGGLINGLY BLOODY RITUALS AND CULT ACTIVITIES,
INCLUDING ORGIES AND SACRED PROSTITUTION.

The small town of modern Baalbeck lies a few hundred miles down the road from the ancient ruins, and we made our way there with slight apprehension. The Bekaa Valley is notorious as the heartland of the Iranian-backed Hezbollah, and Baalbeck is its headquarters. When Greg and I were last in Lebanon, in 1994, the Hezbollah presence was far more obvious, with posters of bespectacled Iranian mullahs and the scowling visage of Ayatollah Khomeini plastered all over the town and the surrounding roads. The green and yellow Hezbollah flag, with its raised fist clutching a machine gun, hung across the streets and the walls were daubed with political graffiti proclaiming anti-American, anti-Israeli and anti-Christian slogans.

These days, however, Hezbollah maintains a fairly low profile; its most visible political activities seem to revolve around young boys shaking collecting tins asking for donations to "the resistance."

Baalbeck was bustling on the cold spring morning that we visited. It had been snowing the day before, but now the sun was out as were most of the town's inhabitants. Perhaps as a throwback to that ancient bloodlust, Baalbeck is today a butchers' town. Nearly every other shop has an artfully arranged selection of liver, lungs and sweetbreads hanging in the window. And meat was what we'd come for: specifically, Baalbeck's legendary sfiha, open-faced lamb pies.

There are so many butchers in Baalbeck that it's hard to know which one to choose, and we stood for a moment, paralysed by that familiar tourist fear of making the wrong choice. Then help was at hand as we spotted a purposeful Shiaa woman enter one of the shops, clutching a shopping list in one hand and a small child in the other. We followed her lead inside as well and selected a similar cut of lamb, which the butcher flung down onto his block with a couple of tomatoes, onions and some spices. Seizing two huge knives he proceeded to demolish the meat to a smooth, homogeneous paste within seconds.

Our helpful housewife then took us to the bakery next door, where men were busy rolling pastry, stuffing pies and shovelling enormous trays into a wood-fired oven. Ahead of us in the queue was an old man with a large beard, wearing a long white *galabeya*. He'd brought his own mutton casserole for the bakers to cook for him. The communal oven is still an important feature of daily life in rural Lebanon, and it is common for people to bring their home-prepared meals to be cooked by the local baker.

Five minutes later our pies were ready, and they emerged golden brown, steaming and fragrant from the oven. We couldn't resist grabbing a few before the baker whisked them away from us. He layered them in a cardboard box, wrapped the box in newspaper and tied it up firmly with string, and we happily made our way back to the car to share our spoils with our drivers.

THE COMMUNAL OVEN IS STILL
AN IMPORTANT FEATURE OF
DAILY LIFE IN RURAL LEBANON,
AND IT IS COMMON FOR
PEOPLE TO BRING THEIR
HOME-PREPARED MEALS TO BE
COOKED BY THE LOCAL BAKER.

FIVE MINUTES LATER OUR PIES WERE READY.

THEY EMERGED GOLDEN BROWN, STEAMING

AND FRAGRANT.

LITTLE LAMB PIES WITH YOGURT CHEESE AND POMEGRANATE *sfiha of baalbeck*

These little pies from Baalbeck are renowned across Lebanon.

Yogurt Bread Dough (page 206)
1 cup (250 g) Lahm bi Ajine filling
   mixture (page 220)
Pomegranate molasses
Yogurt Cheese (Labneh—page 118)

Make the Labneh, Yogurt Bread Dough and Lahm bi Ajine mixture by following the recipes on pages 118, 206 and 220.

To make the sfiha, dust your work surface and rolling pin with flour, then roll the pastry out as thinly as you can. Cut into 12 rounds, around 4 in (10 cm) in diameter. Place a spoonful of the mixture in the center of each round. Moisten the edges of the pastry with a little water, then pinch the corners together to form the traditional shape (page 54).

Preheat the oven to 400°F (200°C) and bake the sfiha for 8–10 minutes. Top each pie with a few drops of pomegranate molasses and a blob of Labneh.

MAKES 12 PIES

SPICY LEBANESE SAUSAGES WITH PINE NUTS *ma'ahani*

Many Middle Eastern butchers make their own version of these sausages and they are a popular addition to the mezze table. Don't buy ground lamb from the supermarket as it is far too fatty. Buy a piece of lamb shoulder or round and grind it yourself at home. Just make sure you ask your butcher for meat that isn't too lean—you do need some fat. You don't need to use casings, which is good as they can be hard to find. Simply roll the mixture into skinless sausages. Make them the day before you plan to cook them to let the flavors develop.

1 teaspoon cinnamon
1 teaspoon ground ginger
1 teaspoon sweet paprika
1 teaspoon nutmeg
1 teaspoon ground black pepper
½ teaspoon ground cloves
½ teaspoon mahlab (crushed cherry
   seeds)

1 lb (500 g) ground lamb
Splash of red wine
Salt to taste
¼ cup (40 g) pine nuts
Olive oil for frying
Squeeze of lemon juice
Lemon wedges

Stir all the spices together. Add to the ground lamb with a good splash of red wine. Mix thoroughly and season with a little salt. Pinch off a small piece of meat and fry. Taste and adjust seasoning to taste. Stir in the pine nuts so they are evenly distributed in the sausage mixture. Cover and refrigerate overnight.

To make the ma'ahani, wet your hands and roll the mixture into little even-sized chipolata sausage shapes.

To cook, fry in oil until colored. Add a good squeeze of lemon juice to the pan and toss the sausages briefly. Serve with fresh Arabic bread and lemon wedges.

MAKES AROUND 20 SAUSAGES

ALEPPO CHICKEN AND PISTACHIO SAUSAGE

We were offered tastes of a mortadella-like sausage at many of the Armenian butchers we visited in Aleppo. This is a home-made version—perhaps a bit more like a French-style boudin blanc. It's very pretty, with flecks of bright green.

2½ lbs (1¼ kgs) boneless chicken
   breasts (about 10 pieces)

3 eggs

Grated rind of 2 lemons

¼ cup (60 g) finely grated fresh ginger

1 teaspoon finely ground black pepper

3 red bird's-eye chilies, deseeded and
   finely chopped

2 cloves garlic, finely chopped

¼ cup (60 ml) extra-virgin olive oil

3 tablespoons cider vinegar

⅓ cup (25 g) fresh breadcrumbs

1⅔ cups (400 ml) heavy cream

⅔ cup (100 g) unsalted pistachio nuts,
   blanched and peeled

Dice the chicken breasts coarsely and put into a food processor with the eggs, lemon rind, ginger, pepper, chilies and garlic. Blitz to a smooth purée. With the motor running, pour in the oil and vinegar until well combined. Scrape down the sides of the bowl, add the breadcrumbs and pulse briefly. Pour in the cream and whiz until everything is thoroughly combined. You should end up with a thick paste, the consistency of mashed potato. Tip the mixture into a mixing bowl and fold through the pistachio nuts.

Tear off a big square of plastic wrap and spread it out on the work surface. Dollop on a quarter of the mixture and shape into a sausage-like log about 2½ x 6 in (6 x 15 cm). Roll it up tightly and tie each end securely. Repeat with the remaining mixture—you should get 4 sausages in total from this quantity.

Bring a large pan of water to a boil. Lower to a simmer and carefully drop in the 4 sausages. They need to be submerged in the water, so weigh it down with a plate. Poach gently in barely simmering water for 15 minutes, then turn off the heat and allow them to cool completely in the water. When cold, refrigerate until ready to eat.

Unwrap the sausages when you're ready to serve. Cut into slices and serve them as part of a mezze selection or as a starter with crusty bread and a dollop of Spicy Eggplant Relish (page 104), Muhammara (page 46) or Red Pepper Paste (page 104). The sausages are quite rich, so a few green salad leaves splashed with vinegar and extra-virgin olive oil would be the perfect accompaniment.

SERVES 8

CHICKEN LIVERS IN ZA'ATAR AND PARMESAN CRUMBS WITH YOGURT, TARRAGON AND CUCUMBER SALAD

2 lbs (1 kg) chicken livers

Pepper to taste

1 cup (150 g) flour

2 eggs, lightly beaten with a little water

¼ cup (60 ml) olive oil

Salt to taste

Yogurt, Tarragon and Cucumber Salad
   (page 119)

Za'atar and parmesan crumb mix

3½ cups (200 g) dried breadcrumbs

½ cup (100 g) finely grated parmesan

3 teaspoons za'atar

1 teaspoon ground sumac

2 tablespoons extra-virgin olive oil

Grated rind of ½ lemon

Make the Yogurt, Tarragon and Cucumber Salad by following the recipe on page 119.

Chicken livers can often be a bit stinky. Soaking them in milk helps to clean and freshen them up a bit. Put the chicken livers in a bowl, cover with milk and refrigerate for a couple of hours. Tip them into a colander and rinse in cold water. Gently pat them dry.

Prepare the Za'atar and Parmesan Crumb Mix by combining all the ingredients. Set up your little production line of a shallow dish of flour, a dish of the egg wash and a third dish of the Crumb Mix. Season the livers lightly with a few grinds of pepper, then dip them into the flour, egg and Crumb Mix.

Heat the oil in a skillet and fry the chicken livers until golden brown. They should be cooked medium-rare: test by giving them a bit of a squeeze—they should give to the touch.

Serve them hot from the pan with a sprinkling of salt and the Yogurt, Tarragon and Cucumber Salad.

SERVES 8 AS A STARTER

WARM SHREDDED LAMB'S TONGUE SALAD WITH PICKLED LEBANESE CUCUMBERS, CELERY AND LEMON MINT DRESSING

This is another salad I couldn't get enough of in Lebanon and Syria. In some versions the lamb's tongue was finely shredded, in others it was sliced. Either way, the unctuous smoothness marries brilliantly with the sharp tang and crunch of the pickles and dressing. For the best flavor, ask the butcher to pickle the tongue for 48 hours in his own special butchers' brine. It also helps keep the lovely rosy pink color.

Lemon Mint Dressing (page 133)
1 lamb's tongue
4 sticks celery, cut into chunks
2 carrots, cut into chunks
1 medium onion, quartered
1 leek, cut into chunks
3 tablespoons white wine vinegar
Salt to taste
1 small head radicchio, coarsely torn
3 pickled Lebanese cucumbers, shredded
3–4 sticks celery, from the center of a bulb
¼ cup (20 g) mint leaves, coarsely shredded
1 small purple onion, finely sliced
Salt and pepper to taste

Make the Lemon Mint Dressing by following the recipe on page 133.

Place the lamb's tongue in a large non-reactive saucepan with the celery, carrots, onion and leek. Pour in enough cold water to cover, then add the vinegar and salt. Bring to a boil then lower the heat, cover the pot and simmer gently for 1–1½ hours, or until the tongue is tender. Check the pot from time to time and top up with more water if needed. The tongue should always remain covered with water. When cooked, allow the tongue to cool in its cooking liquid. While it's still warm, carefully peel away the skin and any excess fat. Refrigerate in the cooking liquid overnight, or for a minimum of 8 hours.

Remove the cold tongue from the cooking liquid and pat dry thoroughly. Use a sharp knife to trim the back (root) of the tongue and slice away any excess fat or muscle tissue. Cut into wafer-thin slices and keep chilled until ready to serve.

This salad is best when the lamb's tongue is warm, so when you're ready to assemble it, preheat the oven to 350°F (180°C). Lightly oil a baking tray and arrange the slices of tongue on top. Put in the oven for about 2 minutes, just long enough for it to warm through.

Meanwhile, put the other ingredients in a large mixing bowl and toss together gently. Scatter on the warm lamb's tongue slices and drizzle enough Dressing to moisten the salad. Season and toss again gently to combine and serve right away with warm Arabic bread.

SERVES 4

ALEPPO-STYLE SAUSAGE ROLLS *soujok roulo*

Soujok is another spicy sausage that is particularly popular in northern Syria where there is a strong Armenian influence. Don't buy ready-ground lamb from the supermarket as it is far too fatty. Buy a piece of topside or round and grind it yourself at home. The paste needs to be as fine and smooth as possible, so grind it twice. This recipe uses mountain bread but you can also use puff pastry. Spread a thin layer of *soujok* on the puff pastry, roll it up, freeze and cut into 1-cm (½-in) slices. Bake in a hot oven for 10–12 minutes, or until golden brown.

5 sheets mountain bread
Olive oil

Soujok
1 lb (500 g) boneless topside lamb
2 cloves garlic, coarsely chopped
1 teaspoon hot paprika
½ teaspoon ground cumin
½ teaspoon ground coriander
½ teaspoon ground allspice

½ teaspoon ground nutmeg
½ teaspoon ground ginger
½ teaspoon ground turmeric
½–¾ teaspoon salt
¼ teaspoon ground red pepper
1 tablespoon olive oil

To make the Soujok, first coarsely chop the meat and put it in a large mixing bowl with all the other ingredients. Toss well then put through a mincer twice to achieve a smooth paste.

Place a piece of mountain bread on your work surface and spread a very thin layer of Soujok over it, going right to the edges. Roll it up tightly and cover while you prepare the rest of the bread.

Cut the rolls on a sharp angle into 1½–2-in (4–5-cm) rounds. Heat a little oil in a non-stick skillet and fry for a couple of minutes on each side until golden brown.

MAKES AROUND 40 SAUSAGE ROLLS

EGGPLANT "CORDON BLEU" STUFFED WITH BASTOURMA

This is a bit of a retro dish, though the mint leaves make all the difference to these fried eggplant sandwiches. They are very rich, so one will probably do you. They make a filling snack or a tasty lunch. Bastourma—Armenian air-dried beef—is available from Middle Eastern or Turkish butchers.

1 large, long globe eggplant

Salt to taste

12 mint leaves

½ cup (100 g) thinly sliced haloumi or
    mozzarella

6 slices (80 g) bastourma or air-dried
    beef, sliced paper-thin

½ cup (125 g) flour

1⅔ cups (100 g) fresh breadcrumbs

1 teaspoon za'atar (optional)

2 eggs, lightly beaten with a little water

2 tablespoons olive oil

2 tablespoons clarified butter or ghee

Salt and pepper to taste

Cut the eggplant into 12 very thin slices—no thicker than ¼ in (½ cm), then put them into a colander and sprinkle with salt. After 20 minutes, rinse them under cold water and pat dry with paper towels.

Lay the eggplant slices out on your work surface and on top of each put a mint leaf, a slice of haloumi and a slice of bastourma. Sandwich the two slices together and dust each side with flour. Repeat for the rest of the slices. Mix the breadcrumbs with the za'atar, if using. Dip each sandwich into the egg and breadcrumbs.

Heat the oil and butter in a large non-stick skillet and fry the eggplant sandwiches slowly to a deep golden brown. Drain briefly on paper towels and season to taste. Eat them with your hands, but make sure you've got a napkin handy. Serve with Tahini Sauce (page 162).

MAKES 6

LAMB'S BRAINS WITH FENNEL, LIME AND SUMAC CRUMBS *mokh makly*

Lamb's brains aren't nearly as popular as they used to be, partly due to the "yuck, offal" factor and because of their high cholesterol content. But we love them, and they're especially delicious when crumbed, with their crisp, crunchy coating and smooth, creamy interior.

6 sets of lamb's brains, soaked in milk
    for 2 hours or in cold salted water
    overnight

Salt and pepper to taste

1 cup (150 g) flour

2 eggs, lightly beaten with a little
    water

¼ cup (60 ml) olive oil

Lemon wedges

Fennel, lime and sumac crumbs

Grated rind of 2 limes

½ teaspoon ground red pepper

1 teaspoon fennel seeds, lightly roasted
    and crushed

2 teaspoons ground sumac

3⅓ cups (200 g) dried breadcrumbs

Poaching liquid

1 lemon, cut into quarters

1 cinnamon stick

4 cloves

½ onion

4 cups (1 liter) cold water

Dry the lime rind overnight or put in a very low oven for 30 minutes. This will intensify the lime flavor. Mix the rind with the ground red pepper, fennel seeds, sumac and breadcrumbs.

Place the ingredients for the Poaching Liquid in a large saucepan then add the soaked brains. Bring to a boil, then skim and simmer for 2 minutes. Remove the pan from the heat, and allow the brains to cool in the liquid. When they are cold, remove them from the pan and split each set in half. Pat dry.

Set up a production line of a shallow dish of flour, a dish of the egg wash and one of the Fennel, Lime and Sumac Crumbs mix. Season the brains lightly with salt and pepper, then dip them into the flour, egg and crumbs.

Heat the oil in a skillet and fry the brains until golden brown. Serve them hot from the pan with a sprinkling of extra salt and lemon wedges.

SERVES 8 AS A STARTER

HOT-SEARED STICKY LAMB SHANK TERRINE WITH MIDDLE EASTERN SPICES

This terrine may be served at room temperature or, just before serving, sear it in a very hot pan to bring out the rich stickiness of the meat.

3 tablespoons olive oil

6 lamb shanks

Salt and pepper to taste

2 onions, coarsely chopped

3 sticks celery, coarsely chopped

2 carrots, coarsely chopped

4 cloves garlic, coarsely chopped

3 tablespoons sherry

8 cups (2 liters) chicken stock

2 cinnamon sticks

1 teaspoon allspice berries

1 teaspoon fenugreek seeds (optional)

1 teaspoon cumin seeds

6 pearl onions, peeled and left whole

10 kalamata olives, stones removed

½ cup (25 g) coriander leaves (cilantro)

6 Lebanese pickled cucumbers

Splash of olive oil

Preheat the oven to 350°F (180°C). Heat the oil in a large heavy-based casserole dish which has a lid. Season the lamb shanks generously with salt and pepper then put them into the casserole dish and sauté until colored all over. Add the onions, celery, carrots and garlic and continue to cook for 5 minutes, until the vegetables start to color. Add the sherry and let it sizzle for a moment or two before adding the stock.

Wrap the cinnamon sticks, allspice, fenugreek and cumin in a small piece of muslin and secure. Tuck it in among the shanks. Bring the contents in the pan to a boil and skim away any fat residue that rises to the surface. Cover with foil and then the lid and put in the oven. Cook for 1¾–2 hours until the meat is very tender and falling from the bone.

Remove from the oven and strain the liquid into a saucepan. Pick the shanks out of the vegetables and, when cool enough to handle, pull the meat away from the bones, leaving it in large pieces. Set aside to cool.

Bring the cooking stock to a boil and drop in the onions. Lower the heat and simmer for 15–20 minutes until the onions are tender. Remove from the stock and leave to cool with the lamb shank meat. Continue to simmer the stock until it has reduced to about 1 cup (250 ml). It should be a glossy syrup. Leave to cool a little.

Line a 12-in (30-cm) terrine mold with 3 layers of plastic wrap. (You need the layers to be large enough to wrap the terrine.) Now, gently break the onions apart and toss them gently with the lamb meat, olives, coriander leaves and pickled cucumbers. Tip the mixture into the mold and pack it in carefully. Pour on the glaze, which will sink into the meat, then bring the plastic wrap up over the top. Seal it by cutting a piece of cardboard or polystyrene just large enough to fit into the terrine, and place it on top of the terrine. Place a weight on top and refrigerate overnight.

When ready to eat, unwrap the terrine and cut into ¾-in (2-cm) slices. If you wish to sear it, heat a heavy-based pan until nearly smoking. Add a splash of olive oil and sauté each slice of terrine for 30 seconds on each side. Serve with a leafy green salad.

SERVES 8–10

BEEF TARTARE WITH MINCED PARSLEY, MINT AND HOT ENGLISH MUSTARD *kifta nayee*

12 oz (350 g) lean beef, coarsely diced

½ cup (20 g) flat-leaf parsley leaves, coarsely chopped

½ cup (20 g) mint leaves, coarsely chopped

¼ teaspoon ground allspice

1 teaspoon salt

¼ teaspoon black pepper

¾ cup (120 g) very finely chopped white onion

1 tablespoon hot English mustard

3 ice cubes

Extra-virgin olive oil

Coarsely chop the meat and put it in a large mixing bowl with the herbs and spices. Toss well, then put it through a grinder twice to achieve a smooth paste.

Add the onion, mustard and the ice cubes and mix well with your hands. As the ice dissolves, it will bind everything together into a smooth, sticky paste. Tip onto a plate and spread into a smooth, shallow oval. Use the back of a soup spoon to make little crescent-shaped indentations on the surface and drizzle with extra-virgin olive oil. Serve with extra oil, Arabic bread, Pickled Turnips (page 103) and mint leaves.

SERVES 4–6

THE ANGEL'S SHARE

VEGETABLE MEZZE

WE'D BEEN INVITED TO HAVE LUNCH at a popular seafood restaurant on the coast near Jounieh, just north of Beirut. From the spacious upstairs dining room there was an uninterrupted view of the coastline back to the city. A storm was brewing, and waves were crashing against the shoreline but inside things were looking more promising. An array of exquisitely presented mezze dishes were spread out in front of us, and our host, Sami, decided that we should all drink arak. "It is the *only* drink to have with the mezze," he insisted.

Aniseed-flavored spirits are popular all around the Mediterranean, from Greek ouzo and Turkish raki to Italian sambucca and French pastis. But they often tend to be sickly sweet and we weren't at all convinced that this was what we wanted to drink. "No, no, no," said Sami. "Arak is quite different. The pastis and sambucca have herbs and spices in them. And sugar," he added, with a shudder. "Arak is pure. It has only two ingredients: the grapes and the aniseed. It is a fresh taste and it rinses the mouth when you eat the mezze."

A few hours later we were quite prepared to agree with him. Arak did indeed seem to be the only drink to have with mezze, where lemon, garlic and spicy flavors often compete. The spirit is fiercely alcoholic—54 per cent proof, on average—but when diluted with water it becomes a smooth, refreshing drink that clears the palate more efficiently than wine.

The arak we had been drinking was a tall and elegant blue bottle from the Massaya Vineyard in the Bekaa Valley. So the next morning we decided to drive out to the winery to become even better acquainted with Lebanon's national drink.

We bumped along a dusty track, nosing our way through a small flock of goats being hurried along by a shepherd boy. The Bekaa Valley is infamous as a stronghold of Muslim fundamentalism, and so seems an unlikely setting for a vineyard, but its sheltered, warm climate and low levels of rainfall make it perfectly suited for growing grapes. As if on cue, just as we turned off the track into the walled grounds of Massaya, the muezzin's wail started up from the minaret of a small mosque nearby.

The first of the new season's growth was just starting to appear on the neatly clipped rows of vines. We learned from our tour guide that the winery was less than ten years old. In addition to its distinctively bottled arak, Massaya also produced a successful range of table wines.

Although partly backed by French money and oenological know-how, Massaya is actually the brainchild of two Lebanese brothers, Sami and Ramzi Ghosn. Ramzi invited us into his office and he leaned earnestly across his desk when we asked him about the distinctive blue bottle.

"The Lebanese always want to be fashionable, to have the latest things," he said in flawless, American-accented English. "The quality and reputation of arak suffered a lot during and after the war, and my brother and I knew we had to find a way to make it

THE SPIRIT IS FIERCELY ALCOHOLIC, BUT WHEN DILUTED WITH WATER IT BECOMES A SMOOTH, REFRESHING DRINK THAT CLEARS THE PALATE MORE EFFICIENTLY THAN WINE.

popular again."

The Ghosn brothers are clearly a couple of smart cookies. They commissioned a designer to create packaging for their product that would make it stand out from the crowd. The blue bottle was an instant winner and sales grew steadily. In the last couple of years, arak production at Massaya has doubled and their four stills operate twenty-four hours a day, at full capacity.

"But it's more than just pretty packaging," Ramzi said. "Our arak really is very good. We wanted to expand the cellar-door idea, so that anyone could come and look around. It is important for our business to have transparency."

This focus on quality was always going to be a key factor in luring consumers back to arak. When new manufacturing machinery was introduced to Lebanon during the 1970s and '80s, some manufacturers developed shortcuts by simply blending any old neutral alcohol with artificial aniseed flavoring. "It didn't even need to be distilled," said Ramzi with a shrug of disgust. "It was cheap rubbish and gave people bad headaches."

The Lebanese desperately needed something to dull the horrors of the endless war that was raging all around them so they turned instead to whisky, and for a time

they became the world's biggest per capita consumers of the spirit.

The origins of arak are obscure, but it is manufactured and consumed all around the eastern Arab world. Palestinians, Jordans, Syrians and even Iraqis drink the stuff, but it is generally agreed that Lebanese arak is the best.

The production process is quite straightforward, and what Sami had said was true: arak needs only two ingredients—grapes and aniseed. Quality arak, such as the Massaya brand, is made from obeidi grapes, an ancient Lebanese variety that's thought to be an ancestor of chardonnay. The grapes are gently crushed and left to ferment for three weeks before being transferred to a copper still, where the magic of distillation begins. It's a process thought to have been employed in early China and Egypt, and developed further by the Greeks and Romans. But it was the Arabs who were the first to exploit the different boiling points of water and alcohol, turning weak wine into more potent "spirits."

Although the principle is simple, the technique would undoubtedly have needed some refinement in those early days, as the first distillation contains a poisonously high percentage of methanol. This first batch must always be discarded, and quality producers will distil the brew a second, third and sometimes fourth time to achieve the smooth liquor desired.

The next crucial stage is the ageing process, and arak is matured in large clay jars for at least a year. The jars have a porosity that allows for a further evaporation of alcohol, which is known as *le part des anges*—the angel's share.

The cellars at Massaya were filled, floor to ceiling, with hundreds of arak-filled clay jars, quietly waiting to be decanted. As we left, Ramzi shared his dream of seeing those blue bottles in bars around the world. Catching the determined gleam in his eye, we found it easy to believe that he might very well succeed.

We came across the premises of Boutros Kazan Pty Ltd by chance one morning as we ambled along Gemmayzeh's Rue Gouraud. Drawn to a particularly decrepit display of arak bottles languishing dustily in a window, we decided to investigate.

The shop was straight out of Dickensian London, poorly lit by a single bare light bulb swinging from a high vaulted ceiling. In the shadowy recesses of the rear of the shop we could just make out some ancient bottling machinery. Sitting behind a massive desk overflowing with paper-filled ledgers was an old man, formally dressed in a jacket and tie. He rose slowly to his feet and came round to the front of his desk to introduce himself as the proprietor, Mr Georges Kazan.

Mr Kazan had a gentle, courteous manner and was clearly pleased to see us. He was even more pleased to hear about our interest in arak, and invited us to sit while he told us his story.

The Kazan arak distillery was opened in 1919 by Georges' uncles, Girgi and Boutros, and they moved into the current premises on Rue Gouraud in 1934. Back then, Gemmayzeh wasn't the gentrified suburb that it has become over the last decade. It was an industrial area, home to large wholesalers and small family businesses—soap makers, oil merchants, chemical manufacturers, butchers and commercial bakers all operated here. Curiously, Gemmayzeh was also the location of choice for a number of other arak distillers, partly due its closeness to the city center and also because of its handy location between the port and the train station.

Boutros Kazan died childless, and so the business passed to Georges and his brother Ibrahim. By the 1970s they were market leaders, making between two and three million bottles a year. More than forty workers were employed in the Gemmayzeh operations and the company had twelve vans to distribute their precious product around the country. Georges told us proudly that Kazan arak is the oldest brand still being produced in Lebanon, and was the favorite tipple of the mother of King Farouk of Egypt.

We asked Mr Kazan if we could see the still, and his face fell. "Alas, we no longer make arak here in Gemmayzeh," he told us. As was the case with many other Lebanese businesses, long years of war changed things for Kazan arak. First there were the bombs and sniper fire, then constant interruptions to the water supply, and eventually it became impossible to continue production. So Georges and Ibrahim shifted the distillery and bottling operation to the Bekaa Valley and the Gemmayzeh premises were reduced to a mere shop front.

But worse was to come. Mr Kazan told us that by the end of the year he would probably move on from Rue Gouraud. "After more than seventy years," he sighed. "The rent for the building has become too expensive. We cannot afford to stay here." He got to his feet and reached up to a shelf behind his desk. "This," he said, producing a small, half-full bottle, "is the oldest bottle of arak in Lebanon. It was made by my father on the day I was born. He made sixty bottles to drink on my wedding day." Mr Kazan smiled. "When I got married at twenty-three years old, we opened some bottles, but it was no good. So we closed them again and kept them for another ten years. There is only this one bottle left now." Good manners restrained us from asking exactly how old the arak was, but we did ask how it tasted now. Mr Kazan's smile grew even wider. "Delicious" he declared.

There was something I was curious about, and I was sure Mr Kazan would have an informed view. I wanted to know the proportions of water, arak and ice for the perfect drink. By way of reply, he shuffled across the room and returned with another bottle of arak and a few small glasses. He disappeared again, then reappeared with a jug of water and a small bowl of ice.

"THIS," HE SAID, PRODUCING A SMALL, HALF-FULL BOTTLE, "IS THE OLDEST BOTTLE OF ARAK IN LEBANON. IT WAS MADE BY MY FATHER ON THE DAY I WAS BORN."

"It is like this that one prepares arak," he said, in his meticulous, old-fashioned French. "First, you pour in the arak." A healthy slug went into each little glass. "Next, you must add the cold water. And it should be three times the amount of arak. Now you must leave it for two to three minutes before adding any ice."

"Why?" I wondered.

"*Eh bien.* As you know, arak is very high in alcohol, which is a good conductor of heat. You leave it for a few moments with the cold water so it can adjust to the ambient temperature. This way it does not get such a shock when you add the ice." He picked up a small pair of tongs and dropped one cube carefully into each glass. "*Ça y'est.* Only one block of ice with the arak. More and it is a heresy." And with that, he passed us each a glass and lifted his own to his lips. "*Saha!*" he exclaimed, before taking a big gulp.

We stood there in the half-light, sipping slowly, savoring the smooth, cool, peppermint taste and the warmth of the arak. For a moment, it was as if time stood still in this small, cluttered shop. We were holding, if not infinity, then a man's lifetime in the palms of our hands. Outside, a horn honked. In the Rue Gouraud there was a traffic jam. Life went on as usual.

THE SHOP WAS STRAIGHT OUT OF DICKENSIAN LONDON, POORLY LIT BY A SINGLE BARE LIGHT BULB SWINGING FROM A HIGH VAULTED CEILING.

MUSHROOM-STUFFED VINE LEAVES WITH HERBS

A vegetarian version of a classic Lebanese mezze dish.

30 vine leaves

⅓ cup (80 ml) olive oil

6 shallots, finely diced

2 cloves garlic, finely diced

1 teaspoon fresh thyme leaves

1 teaspoon fresh oregano leaves

1 oz (25 g) dried porcini mushrooms,
  soaked in 1 cup (250 ml) water

1¼ lbs (550 g) fresh portobello
  mushrooms, finely diced

2 cups (220 g) cooked short-grain rice

1 tomato, deseeded and finely diced

¼ cup (40 g) unsalted pistachio nuts,
  blanched, peeled and coarsely
  chopped

2 tablespoons flat-leaf parsley, finely
  chopped

Pepper to taste

Mint Labneh (page 118)

Cooking stock

1 teaspoon ground sumac

4 whole garlic cloves

Water

Make the Mint Labneh by following the recipe on page 118.

If you are using preserved vine leaves, soak them well, then rinse and pat them dry. Fresh vine leaves should be blanched in boiling water for 30 seconds and then refreshed in cold water.

To prepare the filling, heat the oil in a large heavy-based skillet and sauté the shallots, garlic, thyme and oregano until they soften, but not turning brown.

Strain the porcini mushrooms and finely dice them, reserving the soaking liquid to add to the Cooking Stock. Add them to the pan with the diced portobello mushrooms and cook them slowly until any liquid is absorbed and you are left with a dry mushroom sludge. Tip into a mixing bowl and leave to cool. Add the rice, tomato, pistachio nuts and parsley. Season lightly with pepper and mix everything together well.

Arrange the vine leaves on the work surface, vein side up, and slice out the stems. Place a spoonful of the filling across the base of the leaf. Roll the leaf over once, fold the sides in and then continue to roll it into a neat sausage shape. The dolmades should be around the size of your little finger—don't roll them too tightly or they will burst during the cooking. Continue stuffing and rolling until you run out of filling or vine leaves.

Place the vine leaves in the bottom of a heavy-based casserole dish, packing them in tightly. Sprinkle with sumac and tuck the garlic cloves in among them. You'll probably end up with 3–4 layers. Pour in the reserved mushroom soaking liquid and enough water to just cover the vine leaves. Lay a plate over them, to keep them submerged in the liquid. Slowly bring to a boil, then lower the heat and simmer gently for an hour.

The vine leaves can be eaten hot or cold, but they are best served at room temperature. Arrange them in a pile on a serving dish and serve with plenty of Mint Labneh.

SERVES 6–8 AS PART OF A MEZZE SELECTION

CONFIT LEEKS, TOMATOES AND MUSHROOMS WITH ARAK AND ALMONDS

This dish, and the artichoke recipe on page 74, are shining examples of my favorite à la grecque style of preparing vegetables. This involves gently stewing vegetables in an oil-enriched pickling liquor that is flavored with aromatic herbs and spices. It's a great method to learn as it is easy and can be used to cook all kinds of vegetables. Leeks go particularly well with anise flavors—this recipe uses fennel seeds and a splash of arak, the famous Lebanese spirit. You can freeze and reuse the cooking liquor.

3 leeks, white part only, cut into 1½-in (4-cm) thick rounds
8 shallots, peeled
4 cloves garlic, peeled
2 bay leaves
Few sprigs of thyme
1 teaspoon black peppercorns, lightly crushed
1 teaspoon fennel seeds, lightly crushed
Juice of 5 lemons
1⅔ cups (400 ml) dry white wine
2 cups (500 ml) water
1⅔ cups (400 ml) extra-virgin olive oil
½ teaspoon salt
8 medium portobello mushrooms, trimmed

6 small vine-ripened tomatoes
⅔ cup (80 ml) arak or another anise liqueur
Freshly ground sea salt to taste
Extra-virgin olive oil
¾ cup (60 g) flaked almonds, fried golden brown

Put the leeks, shallots, garlic, herbs and spices into a large, heavy-based non-reactive saucepan. Pour on the lemon juice, wine, water and olive oil and stir in the salt.

Cut a circle of baking paper to the size of the saucepan and sit it on top of the vegetables. Bring to a boil, then lower the heat and cook at a very gentle simmer for 20 minutes. Lift up the paper and slip the mushrooms and tomatoes in amongst the vegetables. Replace the paper and simmer gently for a further 10 minutes. Remove from the heat and stir in the arak. Leave the vegetables to cool slightly in the liquid.

When ready to serve, lift the vegetables out of the stewing liquor into a serving dish, season with a little salt, drizzle with extra-virgin olive oil and sprinkle with flaked almonds. This makes a great vegetarian starter, served with plenty of hot Arabic bread or liberally buttered crusty French bread. It is also good with grilled lamb.

SERVES 6 AS PART OF A MEZZE SELECTION

ZUCCHINI AND MINT FRITTERS

These little fritters can be served at room temperature as part of a mezze selection or as a starter—that's if you can resist eating them straight out of the pan! The grated zucchini is salted to help draw out as much moisture as possible. The fritters should be made as soon as the zucchini is thoroughly dried, or they will start to seep liquid. Mixing rice flour with the plain flour is a neat trick that helps make the fritters really crispy. As for the choice of herbs, mint and dill are both delicious so it really depends on your whim on the day.

1⅓ lbs (600 g) zucchini
Salt to taste
1 small onion, grated
1 small clove garlic, finely chopped
½ cup (100 g) crumbled Bulgarian feta
2 eggs, lightly beaten
2 tablespoons flat-leaf parsley, finely shredded
2 tablespoons mint or dill, finely shredded

½ teaspoon dried mint leaves (omit if using dill)
⅓ cup (50 g) flour
¼ cup (30 g) rice flour
Olive oil for shallow-frying

Wash the zucchini, grate it coarsely and put it in a colander. Sprinkle lightly with salt, toss and set aside for 20 minutes. Squeeze well to extract as much excess liquid as you can and pat dry with paper towels.

Put the zucchini, onion, garlic, Bulgarian feta, eggs and herbs in a bowl and stir to combine. Sift the two flours onto the mixture and lightly combine.

Heat the oil in a non-stick skillet until sizzling. Drop small tablespoons of batter into the hot oil and flatten gently. Cook for 2 minutes on each side, or until golden brown. Drain on paper towels and serve with a sprinkle of salt, a squeeze of lemon or a drizzle of yogurt.

MAKES AROUND 16 FRITTERS

ARTICHOKES COOKED IN SWEET SPICES WITH PEAS, CARROTS AND POTATOES

A fragrant stewed vegetable dish that makes a delicious starter on its own or can be served as an accompaniment to all kinds of roasts or grilled meats.

8 large globe artichokes
Tub of cold water with the juice of 1 lemon
4 small kipfler potatoes, peeled and sliced thickly
1 small bunch baby carrots, scraped and trimmed
8 purple shallots, peeled
½ cup (60 g) fresh peas
4 cloves garlic, peeled
2 bay leaves
Few sprigs of thyme
½ teaspoon dried mint leaves
1 teaspoon coriander seeds, lightly crushed

½ teaspoon black peppercorns, lightly crushed
Juice of 3 lemons
1⅔ cups (400 ml) dry white wine
2 cups (500 ml) water
1⅔ cups (400 ml) extra-virgin olive oil
½ teaspoon salt
Freshly ground sea salt and pepper, to taste
Extra-virgin olive oil

To prepare the artichokes, remove the outer hard leaves and cut in half lengthwise through the stalk. Use a sharp knife to remove the choke then drop into the water.

Put all the vegetables into a large, heavy-based non-reactive saucepan. Add the herbs and spices, pour on the lemon juice, wine, water and olive oil and stir in the salt.

Cut a circle of baking paper to the size of the saucepan and sit it on top of the vegetables. Bring to a boil, then lower the heat and cook at a very gentle simmer for 15 minutes. Remove from the heat and leave the vegetables to cool slightly in the liquid.

When ready to serve, lift the vegetables out of the stewing liquor into a serving dish, season with a little salt and drizzle with extra-virgin olive oil.

SERVES 6–8

FRIED POTATOES WITH GARLIC, GREEN CHILI AND CORIANDER *harkoussa*

We love sautéed potatoes. These have a chili buzz and a tang of garlic and coriander to liven them up a bit. Use Sebago, King Edward or another type of floury potato, as they will give you the best texture—crisp and crunchy on the outside, and fluffy inside. Serve them with anything—or just eat them on their own, with a dollop of sour cream.

1 lb (500 g) potatoes, peeled and cut into ½-in (1-cm) cubes
⅓ cup (100 ml) olive oil
1 small purple onion, finely diced
2 cloves garlic, finely chopped
2 green finger-length chilies, deseeded and cut into ¼-in (5-mm) dice
1 teaspoon coriander seeds, roasted and ground
Knob of butter
Salt to taste

Blanch the potatoes in boiling water for 2 minutes, then drain and leave to steam dry.

Heat the oil in a large heavy-based skillet. When the oil is sizzling, add the potatoes and fry them for 5–10 minutes, turning them from time to time so they color evenly. As they begin to brown, add the onion, garlic, chilies and coriander.

Once the potatoes are crisp and the onions a deep golden brown, add the knob of butter. Cook for a few more minutes, then tip into a serving dish and season with salt. Serve piping hot.

SERVES 4 AS AN ACCOMPANIMENT

GREEN BEANS SLOW-COOKED WITH CUMIN AND TOMATOES *loubia bi zeit*

This is my adaptation of a home-cooked classic that every Lebanese knows and loves. It's typically served at room temperature as part of a mezze selection and, as is often the case, it's even better eaten the day after making. I prefer to use the French thin green beans as they are sweeter.

1 tablespoon Cumin Spice Blend
  (page 20)
3 tablespoons olive oil
1 small onion, finely diced
1 clove garlic, finely diced
10 oz (300 g) thin green beans
One 14-oz/400-g can crushed tomatoes
1 tablespoon tomato paste
½ teaspoon salt
Extra-virgin olive oil

Make the Cumin Spice Blend by following the recipe on page 20.

  Heat the oil in a large saucepan. Add the onion, garlic and Cumin Spice Blend and sauté gently until soft. Add the beans, tomatoes and tomato paste and enough water to just cover. Add the salt and simmer, uncovered, until the beans are tender and the liquid has reduced. Tip into a serving dish and serve at room temperature drizzled with a little extra-virgin olive oil.

SERVES 4 AS AN ACCOMPANIMENT

CHEESY MASHED POTATOES WITH CUMIN

It's rare to find potatoes as an accompaniment in Lebanon and Syria—other than the ubiquitous French fries that come with most restaurant meals and are often served at home for big family lunches. While in the Tannaïl region near Beirut we discovered a number of dairies that made a type of Gouda cheese—often flavored with cumin seeds. This recipe is a variation on a potato purée from the Auvergne in France, known as aligot. It is rich and delicious, and would make a lovely accompaniment to simple grilled or roasted meats.

2 lbs (1 kg) brushed potatoes
¼ cup (60 ml) extra-virgin olive oil
½ cup (100 g) butter
⅓ cup (100 ml) heavy cream
1 cup (200 g) grated caraway Gouda
Salt and pepper to taste

Peel the potatoes and cut them into large equal-sized dice. Put them in a large saucepan and cover with cold salted water. Bring to a boil then lower the temperature and simmer gently for 15–20 minutes, or until the potatoes are tender, but not water-logged.

  Meanwhile pour the oil, butter and cream into a small pan and bring to a boil. Lower the heat and simmer until reduced by a third.

  When the potatoes are cooked, drain them well and return them to the pan. Leave them to dry for another minute, then push them through a sieve into the hot cream mixture and beat with a wooden spoon. Leave to cool for a few minutes, then fold in the grated cheese. Return the pan to a gentle heat and leave, without stirring, until the cheese begins to melt. Use the wooden spoon to lift and turn the mixture until all the cheese has been incorporated. Don't let it boil. Just before serving, taste and adjust the seasoning and lift and turn the potato mixture once again to pull the melted cheese into strings.

SERVES 4 AS AN ACCOMPANIMENT

BRAISED SWISS CHARD WITH CRISP FRIED ONIONS AND TAHINI SAUCE

Swiss chard—or silverbeet—is very popular in Lebanon and Syria, and both the large glossy leaves and stems are used. The leaves are a little more robust than spinach, and have a unique, tangy flavor. They are often combined with fresh cheese to make stuffings for savory pastries. In this classic mezze dish they are braised in flavored oil and served with Tahini Sauce and topped with Crisp Fried Onions.

Crisp fried onions

2½ onions, finely sliced
½ teaspoon salt
½ cup (125 ml) olive oil

Braised swiss chard

1 large bunch swiss chard
3 tablespoons olive oil
½ onion, finely diced
1 clove garlic
1 tablespoon coriander seeds, lightly
  roasted
Juice of 1 lemon
⅔ cup (150 ml) white wine
⅓ cup (100 ml) chicken stock or water
Salt and pepper to taste

Tahini sauce

1 clove garlic, crushed with ¼ teaspoon
  salt
½ cup (125 ml) tahini, well stirred
⅓ cup (80 ml) lemon juice
Cold water

To make the Crisp Fried Onions, put the onions into a bowl and use your hands to break them up thoroughly. Sprinkle on the salt and toss through. Leave for 15 minutes. Rinse the onions well, then use your hands to squeeze out as much moisture as you can before drying the onions very thoroughly on paper towels. It is important that the onions are as dry as you can get them. Heat the oil in a large heavy-based skillet. When it's nearly smoking, add the onions and fry for 8–10 minutes. You'll need to move them around the pan continuously, to ensure that they brown evenly and don't burn. The onions will darken and caramelize to a deep golden brown. Drain on paper towels and reserve.

Prepare the Braised Swiss Chard by first washing the swiss chard in several changes of water then slice out the stems, reserving them for another use. Shred the leaves coarsely. Heat the oil in a large skillet and sauté the onion and garlic until they start to soften. Meanwhile, use a mortar and pestle to crush the coriander seeds as finely as you can. Tip into a sieve to remove the husks.

Add the coriander to the pan with the swiss chard, lemon juice, wine and stock. Season with salt and pepper, cover the pan and cook on a low heat for 20 minutes. Towards the end of the cooking time, remove the lid and raise the heat to allow some of the braising liquid to evaporate.

To make the Tahini Sauce, stir the garlic paste into the tahini, then gradually mix in the lemon juice and enough cold water to thin the sauce to the consistency of pouring cream. Serve the Braised Swiss Chard with plenty of Tahini Sauce and the Crisp Fried Onions. Sprinkle with paprika before bringing it to the table.

SERVES 4–6

LUNCH IN THE MOUNTAINS

PULSES AND GRAINS

THE MORNING DAWNED WET AND CHILLY after a night spent listening to the wind howling in the palm trees and the rain lashing against the windows.

Amal's cousin Véronique had invited us to share a traditional Lebanese meal with her family at their home in Zghorta, a small village in the mountains near Tripoli. Most Arab women pay great attention to their personal appearance and Véronique was no exception—she arrived on our doorstep immaculately dressed and coiffured. Like so many middle-class Lebanese, Véronique spoke fluent French. "Allons-y!" she said, click-clacking her way across the tiles to her waiting car outside.

We were soon hurtling through the downpour at a terrifying speed. Byblos flashed by and soon we were passing the industrial outskirts of Tripoli, Lebanon's second-largest city. The streets were awash and as we climbed a hill past the citadel and Sunday market, water sluiced down around us, carrying all manner of debris in its wake.

Our hosts' house was quite a surprise. Given the rural setting we had been expecting something old and traditional, but John and Marie Hammod lived in a large, spacious modern house that John had built himself. We were ushered into the formal salon to meet the rest of the family and after the usual round of handshaking, hugging and kissing, we were seated and offered warming cups of Arabic coffee and Marie's home-made biscuits.

Most Lebanese families have an exquisitely decorated formal room where they entertain. The Hammod's salon was large and airy, furnished with brocade-covered sofas and tiny gilt tables.

Early into our conversation we discovered that John was in the middle of making orange blossom water in his garden shed, and during a lull in the rain he took us out for a look. He had retired and now devoted most of his time to his beautifully ordered walled

garden, growing swiss chard, cos lettuces, broad beans, green beans, radishes, tomatoes, mint and parsley. Against the wall were two large loquats and a pomegranate tree, and the footpath was lined with gardenias. Even in the wet, the fragrant perfume of orange blossoms filled the air. John had two orange trees himself, but they were insufficient to provide the sixty pounds (thirty kilos) of flowers he required every year for making orange blossom water for his entire family.

While we were admiring his home-made still, and the pale lime-colored orange blossom water it produced, Véronique popped her head around the door of the shed and told us that Marie and her sister-in-law Dalal were about to start making kibbeh shaham.

This was what we had come for. Kibbeh may be the Lebanese national dish, but it comes in a variety of forms. At its simplest, kibbeh is a mixture of finely ground lamb and onion, bulgur or cracked wheat and spices. It can be layered in an oven tray and baked, or molded into different shapes and fried. Kibbeh shaham are the speciality of Zghorta and are found nowhere else in Lebanon. They are larger than the more familiar torpedo-shaped kibbeh—more like an oversized lemon—and they are grilled on a barbecue, which gives them a unique flavor. The other key ingredient is the stuffing of finely chopped aliya—the tail fat from a particular breed of sheep that is found all over the Middle East.

John Hammod had purchased the lamb that morning, only moments after its demise. "Zghortans like their meat fresh," he told us, smiling broadly. Two days of ageing is apparently the most any housewife will tolerate.

Marie had already prepared the meat paste, pounding it with spices, onion and bulgur or cracked wheat in her large, traditional wooden mortar. We all crammed into the kitchen to watch the two old ladies carefully shape the hollow patties and fill them with

WE ALL CRAMMED INTO THE
KITCHEN TO WATCH THE TWO
OLD LADIES CAREFULLY SHAPE
THE HOLLOW PATTIES AND
FILL THEM WITH PIECES OF
HARD WHITE FAT.

pieces of hard white fat. The shell seemed impossibly thin and Dalal passed us one to look at. "Mine are better than Marie's," she said with a cheeky smile. We held the kibbeh in our hands. It was light and with a gentle shake we could feel the pieces of fat move inside it.

As we watched the slow, measured ritual, the muezzin at the neighboring mosque started up, and so did the rain. Far from daunted, John's son Naim disappeared outside to tend to the charcoal burner, and a little while later we were seated around a table spread with an impossible amount of food. There were mounds of cucumbers, radishes and cos lettuce leaves, cut that morning from John's garden; hummus and its variation with pine nuts and cumin, balila; there was tabbouleh, eggplant dip and pickled turnips; stacks of warm Arabic bread and a tangy salad made from wild za'atar. There was also a disconcertingly large bottle of Scotch whisky on the table and a jug of John's home-made arak (60 per cent proof, he told us proudly).

We'd been peering through the window watching Naim carefully turning the kibbeh shaham on the barbecue, and now they appeared in front of us, together with huge platters of chicken and lamb brochettes. *"Yallah!* You must eat! You must drink!" John urged us from his seat at the head of the table. Somewhat gingerly, I broke open a hot kibbeh patty and the melted fat dripped onto my plate. I could feel my arteries narrowing at the sight, but popped a piece in my mouth. It was chewier than I'd anticipated, but the fat did make it tasty and moist.

By now the whisky had worked its magic and we no longer cared about the pouring rain or the thought of the long drive back to our apartment. The toasts were coming fast and furious: "To friendship! To family! To Australia! To Lebanon!"

QUAIL IN FRAGRANT RICE WITH DATES, GINGER AND PEARL ONIONS

This is a gorgeous, golden-hued pilaf with a touch of sweetness and a slightly peppery, ginger buzz.

8 quails (each about 7 oz/200g), cut
   into quarters
Salt and pepper to taste
3 tablespoons olive oil
1 leek, white part only, finely diced
2 cloves garlic, finely chopped
1 thumb fresh ginger, peeled and finely
   chopped
10 pearl onions, peeled and halved
½ teaspoon saffron threads
½ teaspoon ground cinnamon
½ teaspoon ground ginger
2 cups (500 ml) chicken stock
1 tomato, deseeded and diced
2 dates, pitted and diced
Juice of 1 lemon

Fragrant rice
2 tablespoons olive oil
Handful (2 oz/50 g) dried vermicelli
   noodles
2 cups (400 g) uncooked medium-grain
   rice, washed and drained
½ teaspoon ground cinnamon
½ teaspoon ground allspice
½ teaspoon ground ginger
2½ cups (600 ml) chicken stock

Heat the oil in a large heavy-based saucepan. Use your hands to coarsely break the vermicelli noodles into the hot oil. Stir vigorously, until the yellow threads deepen to a golden brown. Add the rice to the pan and stir so the grains are well coated with oil. Add the spices and stock and bring the pan to a boil. Cover and turn down the heat. Cook for 18 minutes until all the liquid has evaporated.

While the rice is cooking, prepare the quail. Trim them of their necks and wing tips then split each bird in half down the backbone and neatly slice out the breastplate (sternum) in the middle. Season lightly. Heat the oil in a large heavy-based pan, then drop in the quail pieces. Turn them around quickly in the oil until they color, then take them out of the pan and put them to one side while you make the sauce.

Put the leek, garlic, ginger and onions into the same pan and sauté for a few minutes until they start to soften. Add the spices and stock and stir everything together well. Cover the pan and simmer gently until the pearl onions are tender and everything has deepened to a golden yellow.

Return the quail pieces to the pan with the tomato and dates and season with salt and pepper. Bring the pan back to a boil, then lower the heat and simmer until the quail pieces are cooked through—it will only take a few minutes. Squeeze in the lemon juice.

To serve, pile the rice onto a large serving platter and arrange the quail pieces on top. Spoon the sauce and vegetables over and around. Accompany with plenty of yogurt.

SERVES 4

LEBANESE NUT RICE

This is a popular accompaniment to all kinds of roasts and is especially good with roast lamb.

3 tablespoons olive oil
1 onion, finely diced
5 oz (150 g) ground lamb
3 cups (650 g) uncooked rice
4 cups (1 liter) chicken stock, boiling
1 cinnamon stick
Salt and pepper to taste

To serve
½ cup (80 g) pine nuts
½ cup (80 g) shelled and unsalted
   pistachio nuts
½ cup (80 g) blanched whole almonds
⅓ cup (100 ml) olive oil
Sprigs of fresh coriander leaves (cilantro)
Ground cinnamon

Heat the oil in a large heavy-based pot and sauté the onion and lamb for about 5 minutes, until the onion is soft and the meat has browned. Add the rice and boiling chicken stock. Turn the heat down to a simmer and add the cinnamon stick, salt and pepper. Cover and cook for 16 minutes or until the rice is tender.

Fry the nuts separately in the olive oil until golden brown. To serve, turn the rice out onto a large serving platter and sprinkle with the nuts. Garnish with sprigs of coriander leaves and dust lightly with cinnamon.

SERVES 4-6

SWISS CHARD RISOTTO WITH LOBSTER AND CRISP FRIED ONIONS

1 tablespoon Golden Spice Mix (page 20)

Braised Swiss Chard (page 78)

Crisp Fried Onions (page 78)

¼ cup (60 ml) olive oil

1 small onion, quartered

2 cups (400 g) uncooked Vialone Nano
    rice

¼ cup (60 ml) white wine

Up to 4 cups (1 liter) vegetable or
    chicken stock, simmering

½ cup (100 g) butter, chilled and cut into
    small cubes

Salt and pepper to taste

12 fresh jumbo shrimp, shelled and
    deveined or 4 small lobster tails (each
    less than 7 oz/200g)

Salt to taste

Extra-virgin olive oil

Make the Golden Spice Mix, Braised Swiss Chard and Crisp Fried Onions by following the recipes on pages 20 and 78.

Heat the oil in a large heavy-based saucepan. Fry the onion for a few minutes to flavor the oil, then discard it. Add the rice and stir for a few minutes to coat each grain of rice with oil. Pour in the wine and let it bubble away until it evaporates. Next, ladle in enough simmering stock to cover the rice by a finger's width. Cook on medium heat, stirring with a wooden spoon from time to time, until most of the stock has been absorbed.

Add the same quantity of stock again, stirring from time to time, until most of the stock has been absorbed.

Add a third amount of stock (making sure you reserve around ⅓ cup (100 ml) for the final stage), and when half of the liquid has been absorbed, add the Braised Swiss Chard. Stir gently until all the stock is absorbed.

Stir in the butter and season with salt and pepper. If you find that you need more liquid, add the final ⅓ cup (100 ml) of stock and stir until the butter has melted in. Cover the pot and allow to rest off the heat for a few minutes. Taste and adjust the seasoning, if necessary.

To butterfly the lobster tails, if using, use a large, sharp knife to cut each one in half lengthwise, through the underbelly, to the shell. Pull away the intestinal tract and then open the two halves out wide. Dust the jumbo shrimp or lobster tails, if using, all over lightly with the Golden Spice Mix and a little salt.

Heat your oven broiler or barbecue, or heat some oil in a large non-stick skillet. Cook the lobster until they just turn red, turning once.

Divide the risotto between 4 bowls and stack 3 jumbo shrimp or 1 lobster tail on top of each. Sprinkle with the Crisp Fried Onions and a little extra-virgin olive oil.

SERVES 4

JEWELLED CRACKED WHEAT PILAF WITH HONEY GINGER TOMATO SAUCE

This is an absolutely fabulous, over-the-top kind of pilaf, with more "jewels" than a Lacroix bracelet. You can substitute dried cranberries for the pomegranate seeds, or to be really exotic, use dried Iranian barberries. Serve the pilaf as an accompaniment to barbecued poultry or lamb.

¾ cup (175 g) coarse bulgur or cracked
    wheat, soaked in cold water for 5
    minutes

Salt and pepper to taste

Generous knob of butter

¼ cup (30 g) currants or raisins, soaked
    in 2 tablespoons sherry for 30
    minutes

½ teaspoon ground allspice

Grated rind of ½ orange

⅓ cup (50 g) pine nuts

⅓ cup (50 g) unsalted pistachio nuts,
    blanched and peeled

¼ cup (40 g) pomegranate seeds

Honey ginger tomato sauce

2 tablespoons olive oil

2 cloves garlic, finely chopped

1 red bird's-eye chili, deseeded and
    finely chopped

One 14-oz/400-g can chopped tomatoes

Salt and pepper to taste

1 teaspoon ground turmeric

1 thumb fresh ginger, finely grated

1 tablespoon honey

Rinse the bulgur or cracked wheat well in cold water and then put in a heavy pan with 1½ times its volume of cold water. Season lightly with salt. Bring to a boil and then simmer, covered, on a low heat for 10–15 minutes, or until the liquid has been absorbed. Towards the end of the cooking time, turn up the heat to evaporate any remaining liquid at the bottom of the pan. Take the pan off the heat when you hear the bulgur or cracked wheat start to crackle and catch, and stir in the butter.

Tip the bulgur or cracked wheat into a mixing bowl, season with the salt and pepper and add the drained currants, allspice and orange rind. Fork it through well, then cover with a snug-fitting lid and leave in a warm place for 10 minutes, or until the bulgur or cracked wheat has absorbed all the liquid and is tender.

To make the Honey Ginger Tomato Sauce, heat the oil in a pan and sauté the garlic and chili for a few minutes until they soften. Add the tomatoes, salt and pepper, turmeric, ginger and honey and simmer for 10 minutes

Toast the pine nuts in a dry skillet until they color, then add them to the bulgur or cracked wheat pilaf with the pistachios. Tip onto a serving plate, pour on the Honey Ginger Tomato Sauce and scatter on the pomegranate seeds.

SERVES 4

UPSIDE-DOWN POACHED CHICKEN AND EGGPLANT PILAF *makloube*

This dish combines three of my favorite things: nuts, rice and eggplant. I like to serve it with creamy labneh.

Poached chicken

1 large chicken breast on the bone

1 small onion, quartered

1 stick celery

Sprig of thyme

2 bay leaves

1 small cinnamon stick

½ lemon

½ teaspoon white peppercorns

½ teaspoon allspice berries

Pilaf

1 medium eggplant, peeled

Salt to taste

½ cup (125 ml) olive oil

⅓ cup (50 g) pine nuts

⅔ cup (50 g) flaked almonds

1 tablespoon olive oil

1 small onion, finely diced

5 oz (150 g) lean ground lamb

½ teaspoon ground cinnamon

½ teaspoon ground allspice

Large pinch of salt

1¼ cups (250 g) uncooked long-grain
  rice, rinsed well

2½ cups (600 ml) chicken stock
  (reserved from the poached chicken)

Ground cinnamon

To make the Poached Chicken, put the chicken and all the aromatics into a small saucepan with enough water to cover. Bring to a boil, then lower the heat and simmer gently for 5 minutes. Turn off the heat and leave the chicken for 20 minutes in the hot stock. Reserve the stock for cooking the rice.

To make the Pilaf, first cut the eggplant into thin slices. Put them into a colander and sprinkle with salt. After 20 minutes, rinse them under cold water and pat them dry with paper towels.

Heat the olive oil in a large non-stick skillet and fry the pine nuts until golden brown. Remove them from the pan and drain on paper towels. Repeat the process with the almonds. In the same oil, fry the eggplant slices on both slices until golden brown, adding a little more oil, if necessary.

Heat the tablespoon of olive oil in a large saucepan and sauté the onion gently until it softens. Turn up the heat, add the lamb and sauté until all the juices have evaporated. Add the spices and salt, and stir well. Add the rice and stir again before pouring on the reserved chicken stock. Bring to a boil, then lower the heat, cover the pan and simmer gently for 20 minutes.

While the rice is cooking, pull the chicken meat off the bone and shred it coarsely into bite-sized pieces. Much of the pleasure of this dish comes from the presentation, so find a deep round bowl and lightly oil the inside. Lay the pieces of chicken inside, going three-quarters of the way up the sides. Arrange the eggplant slices on top of the chicken, then carefully spoon in the cooked rice. Pack it in fairly tightly and smooth the surface flat. Leave to stand for a few moments before inverting onto a serving platter. Garnish with the pine nuts and almonds and dust with cinnamon. Serve with a bowl of cool, creamy yogurt or Labneh (page 118), and perhaps a simple green salad.

SERVES 4

KIBBEH NAYEE WITH BASIL, MINT AND GREEN CHILIES

You can prepare this mix up to 2 hours ahead of time, keeping the meat separate from the other ingredients.

½ cup (100 g) fine bulgur or cracked wheat

⅔ cup (90 g) coarsely chopped white onion

1 green finger-length chili, deseeded and coarsely chopped

⅓ cup (12 g) basil leaves, coarsely chopped

⅓ cup (12 g) mint leaves, coarsely chopped

⅓ cup (15 g) flat-leaf parsley leaves, coarsely chopped

½–¾ teaspoon salt

Freshly ground black pepper

¼ teaspoon ground red pepper

10 oz (300 g) boneless lean lamb, coarsely diced

3 ice cubes

Extra-virgin olive oil

Soak the bulgur or cracked wheat for 5 minutes in just enough cold water to cover it. Drain it well through a sieve, then tip it into a dish towel and squeeze out as much water as you can. Tip into a mixing bowl.

Put the onion, chili and fresh herbs through a mincer—it will come through like a green slush. Add to the bulgur or cracked wheat. Stir in the salt, a few grinds of pepper and the ground red pepper.

Coarsely chop the meat, then put it through a mincer twice.

When you're ready to eat, add the meat to the bulgur or cracked wheat mixture with the ice cubes. Mix well with your hands. As the ice dissolves, it will bind everything together into a smooth, sticky paste. Tip onto a plate and spread into a smooth, shallow layer reaching right up to the rim. Use the back of a soup spoon or a knife to decorate the surface and drizzle with extra-virgin olive oil. Serve with extra oil, Arabic bread, fresh onions and mint leaves. It is delicious with a big blob of labneh, although many Lebanese would throw up their hands in horror at this unorthodox accompaniment.

SERVES 4–6

SALMON KIBBEH STUFFED WITH GROUND SHRIMP, PINE NUTS AND STEWED PEPPERS

Filling

2½ tablespoons olive oil

1 small purple onion, finely sliced

1 clove garlic, finely diced

½ cup (100 g) chopped fresh shrimp meat

Grated rind of ½ lemon

2 red bell peppers, roasted, peeled and thinly sliced

⅓ cup (60 g) fried pine nuts

½ teaspoon salt

¼ teaspoon black pepper

Kibbeh shell

¾ cup (200 g) fine white bulgur or cracked wheat

10 oz (300 g) fresh Atlantic salmon, finely ground and chilled

2 purple shallots, finely chopped

1 very small red bird's-eye chili, deseeded and finely chopped

⅓ teaspoon ground allspice

Freshly ground white pepper

1 teaspoon sea salt

1 tablespoon extra-virgin olive oil

Olive oil for shallow-frying

To make the Filling, heat the oil in a large heavy-based skillet. Sauté the onion and garlic for about 5 minutes, until they soften but do not color. Add the shrimp and lemon rind and fry until it colors a rosy pink, using a wooden spoon to break it up thoroughly. Add the peppers and pine nuts, and season with salt and pepper. Stir to mix everything together well. Remove from the heat and leave to cool.

To prepare the Kibbeh Shell, begin by soaking the bulgur or cracked wheat in plenty of cold salted water for about 10 minutes. Now, using your hands, squeeze out as much water as you can, then tip into a dish towel and twist to extract even more.

Put the bulgur or cracked wheat into a mixing bowl with the salmon, shallots, chili, seasonings and extra-virgin olive oil and mix everything together well. Put the mixture through a mincer, then refrigerate until chilled.

To make the kibbeh, put a small lump of the shell mixture in the palm of your left hand and roll it into a smooth, oval-shaped ball. Using the forefinger of your right hand, make an indentation in the ball and start to shape it into a hollow shell. Try to make it as thin and even as you can. Fill the shell with about a teaspoon of the Filling, wet the edges of the opening with cold water and pinch it closed. You are aiming for a small torpedo-shaped dumpling, with slightly tapered ends. Leave the stuffed kibbeh on a tray in the refrigerator, covered, until you are ready to cook them.

When you are ready to cook the kibbeh, heat the oil in a skillet and shallow-fry the kibbeh in batches, turning them to ensure that they're a deep golden brown all over. Drain them on paper towels and serve them piping hot.

Accompany the kibbeh with a salad.

MAKES 14–16 KIBBEH

ZGHORTA-STYLE KIBBEH PATTIES STUFFED WITH CINNAMON AND PINE NUT BUTTER

True kibbeh shaham is the speciality of Zghorta, a mountain village in the north of Lebanon. It is not terribly appealing to a Western palate as the stuffing is made from pieces of solid white fat—aliya—a product of the local breed of fat-tail sheep. This version is a twist on the traditional and incorporates a lightly spiced butter filling which keeps the shell moist, as is the intent, but is slightly less threatening to the arteries.

Kibbeh shell

1 cup (230 g) fine white bulgur or
 cracked wheat
1 onion, puréed in a food processor
¾ teaspoon ground allspice
½ teaspoon cinnamon
¼ teaspoon ground red pepper
Salt and pepper to taste
1 lb (500 g) lean lamb, coarsely diced

Cinnamon and pine nut butter

¾ cup (200 g) unsalted butter, softened
1 teaspoon cinnamon
½ teaspoon salt
½ cup (80 g) pine nuts, fried

Begin by soaking the bulgur or cracked wheat in plenty of cold salted water for about 10 minutes. Now, using your hands, squeeze out as much water as you can, then tip into a dish towel and twist to extract even more. Tip into a mixing bowl. Add the puréed onion, spices, salt and pepper to the bulgur or cracked wheat and use your hands to squeeze and mix everything together.

Put the lamb through a mincer, then add it to the bulgur or cracked wheat. Mix well with your hands, then put it through the mincer again. Place the bowl in the refrigerator for 30 minutes, which will make the paste easier to work with. While the shell mixture is chilling in the fridge, prepare the Cinnamon and Pine Nut Butter. Put the softened butter into a mixing bowl with the cinnamon, salt and pine nuts and mash together well. Scrape the filling out onto a square of plastic wrap and shape into a log about 1¼ in (3 cm) wide. Roll up tightly and refrigerate until it sets firm.

To make the patties, cut the Cinnamon and Pine Nut Butter into thin slices—no more than ¼ in (5 mm) thick. Divide the shell mixture into 16 pieces. Roll each piece into a smooth ball, and stick your thumb into the ball to create a cavity. Ideally, the shells should be as thin as you can make them. Slip in a piece of Cinnamon and Pine Nut Butter, then use a little water to moisten the open edges and seal them well. Cup your hands and smooth and shape the shells into thick, rounded patties. Leave the stuffed kibbeh on a tray in the refrigerator, covered, until you are ready to cook them.

Traditionally, these kibbeh are cooked on a charcoal grill or barbecue. Alternatively, bake them in a 375°F (190°C) oven for about 20 minutes or shallow-fry them in ⅔ cup (150 ml) medium–hot vegetable oil, turning them to ensure that they're a deep golden brown all over. Drain them on paper towels and serve piping hot with yogurt.

MAKES 16 PATTIES

ALEPPO-STYLE LAMB TARTARE WITH SMOKY CHILI AND PARSLEY

3 red finger-length chilies
1 tablespoon olive oil
½ cup (100 g) fine bulgur or cracked
 wheat
⅓ cup (15 g) flat-leaf parsley leaves,
 coarsely chopped
½ – ¾ teaspoon salt
Freshly ground black pepper
½ teaspoon ground cinnamon
¼ teaspoon smoked paprika
¼ teaspoon ground red pepper
⅔ cup (90 g) coarsely chopped white
 onion
10 oz (300 g) lean lamb, coarsely diced
3 ice cubes
Extra-virgin olive oil

Preheat the oven to 400°F (200°C). Brush the chilies with a little olive oil and roast them for 5–10 minutes, turning them occasionally, until they start to blacken all over. Remove them from the oven and, when cool enough to handle, peel away all the charred skin. Split the chilies open and scrape out the seeds. Put the chilies into a mortar and pound to a smooth paste.

Soak the bulgur or cracked wheat for 5 minutes in just enough cold water to cover it. Drain it well through a sieve, then tip it into a dish towel and squeeze out as much water as you can. Tip into a mixing bowl with the chili paste and add the chopped parsley and spices. Mix together well. Put the onions through a mincer and add to the bulgur or cracked wheat, mixing well.

Finally, put the lamb through the mincer twice, then add it to the other ingredients with the ice cubes. Mix well with your hands. As the ice dissolves, it will bind everything together into a smooth, sticky paste. Tip onto a plate and spread into a smooth, shallow layer reaching right up to the rim. Use the back of a soup spoon to make little crescent-shaped indentations on the surface and drizzle with extra-virgin olive oil. Serve with extra oil, Arabic bread, fresh onions and mint leaves. I also like to eat it with labneh.

SERVES 4–6

POTATO KIBBEH STUFFED WITH SPINACH, MOZZARELLA AND PINE NUTS

These are glorified potato croquettes, and are often served as a mezze dish during religious festivals, when people reduce their meat consumption. All sorts of cheese or vegetable fillings work well—and you could also make a tasty stuffing of spiced meat and pine nuts.

Kibbeh shell

1⅓ lbs (600 g) floury potatoes, washed but not peeled
¾ cup (200 g) fine white bulgur or cracked wheat, soaked in cold water for 5 minutes
¼ cup (35 g) flour
½ teaspoon ground allspice
½ teaspoon ground cinnamon
½ teaspoon ground cumin
½ teaspoon ground coriander
½ teaspoon salt
¼ teaspoon freshly ground black pepper

Filling

1 tablespoon olive oil
1 small onion, finely diced
1 bunch spinach leaves, stalks removed, blanched and chopped
½ cup (80 g) pine nuts, toasted
½ teaspoon ground allspice
Salt and pepper to taste
¾ cup (150 g) grated mozzarella

To make the Kibbeh Shell, begin by bringing a large pan of salted water to a boil. Cook the potatoes for 15–20 minutes, until they are tender. Remove from the heat and when they are cool enough to handle, peel them. Next, drain the bulgur or cracked wheat and, using your hands, squeeze out as much water as you can. Then tip into a dish towel and twist to extract even more. Tip the bulgur or cracked wheat into a large mixing bowl and add the potatoes. Mash the two together to form a smooth purée. Add the flour, spices, salt and pepper and knead with your hands until the mixture is thoroughly blended. Place the bowl in the refrigerator for 30 minutes, which will make the paste easier to work with.

While the shell mixture is chilling in the fridge, prepare the Filling. Heat the oil in a skillet and sauté the onion until it is soft. Add the chopped spinach, pine nuts and allspice and stir over the heat for a few more minutes. Remove the pan from the heat and leave it to cool, then season with the salt and pepper and stir in the grated cheese.

To make the kibbeh, put a small lump of the potato paste into the palm of your left hand and roll it into a smooth, oval-shaped ball. Using the forefinger of your right hand, make an indentation in the ball and start to shape it into a hollow shell. Try to make it as thin and even as you can. Fill the shell with about a teaspoon of the Filling, wet the edges of the opening with cold water and pinch it closed. You are aiming for a small torpedo-shaped dumpling, with slightly tapered ends. Leave the stuffed kibbeh on a tray in the refrigerator, covered, until you are ready to cook them.

When it comes to cooking the kibbeh, you have the choice of either baking them in a 375°F (190°C) oven for about 20 minutes, or deep or shallow-frying them in ⅔ cup (150 ml) medium-hot vegetable oil, turning them to ensure that they're a deep golden brown all over. Drain them on paper towels and serve piping hot with a dollop of yogurt.

MAKES 16 KIBBEH

PRESERVING TRADITIONS

PICKLES AND PRESERVES

MASSIVE PANS OF ORANGE
BLOSSOM JAM WERE
BUBBLING ON THE STOVES
AND ON A LONG BENCH AT
THE SIDE OF THE ROOM TWO
LAUGHING YOUNG WOMEN
WERE DIPPING PIECES OF
ORANGE PEEL IN SUGAR.

IN RURAL COMMUNITIES AROUND LEBANON the annual hands-on tradition of bottling and pickling food is very much alive and well. It's known as mouneh, which roughly translates as "provisions", and encompasses the many all-important foods that are carefully put aside every year to tide families over the long cold winters. The list includes jams, jellies and preserves, pickled vegetables, molasses, flower waters, sun-dried fruits and vegetables, home-grown herbs and spices, and kishk (a fermented yogurt and bulgur or cracked wheat powder, used to make a soupy porridge).

Two sisters, Leila Maalouf and Youmna Goraieb, have turned the production of mouneh into a highly successful business, which they run from their village of Ain el Kabou near Bskinta, in the heart of the country at the foot of Mount Sannine. Their products have become so popular that the distinctive packaging of their "Mymouné" brand is now seen on the shelves of Dean & DeLuca in New York and Bon Marché in Paris.

We met Leila Maalouf, an immaculately groomed middle-aged woman, on a sunny morning in the "tasting" room of the large stone barn that houses her company's factory. Through the glass window that separated this room from the factory floor, we caught glimpses of women in white coats and hats bustling around a kitchen. Every now and then a door opened and the heady smell of orange blossoms wafted in.

The idea for Mymouné came to the sisters in the winter of 1989, just before the end of the civil war. "People were so sick of it all," sighed Leila. "Everyone was shooting at everyone else. There was no work for the villagers here and the road was cut off so people couldn't get to Beirut to find work. We felt so isolated. We desperately wanted to find something that we could do to help give employment to locals. Especially to the women." She chuckled to herself. "The first thing we thought of was knitting. But somehow we couldn't get excited about that. And then my sister Youmna thought of food."

The full range of Mymouné's jars, bottles and boxes were arrayed on a dresser behind her. "We started with just one or two products," Leila told us in her charming Arabic-French accent. "It was springtime, like now, and the very first thing we made was rose cordial from the roses in our garden." She laughed. "We were so excited about our first batch. But really, we didn't have a clue what we were doing. We just knew that we wanted to make good-quality products that people would want to buy."

The family house had a large storage barn that wasn't being used so the sisters cleaned it out, white-washed the walls and began researching recipes. They hired local women and quizzed them for favorite family recipes. Children were put to work drawing labels and sticking them on jars. Husbands were used as taste-testers and the sisters turned to their Uncle Timothy, a nutritionist and chemist, for advice on hygiene and pasteurisation.

"We found an old still among all the junk," said Leila, "and that was the beginning of it all. We made things as they came into season, starting with rosewater and orange blossom water; jams and jellies came next. The most important thing to us was that our products would be of excellent quality. We didn't want to use any preservatives, we wanted to make our products…in good conscience." Leila paused, and when she continued her voice had become serious. "I know it all sounds very romantic, two middle-aged ladies making jams, but it was critical to us that we made it work as a business."

Leila and Youmna have certainly made a success of it. Their range now extends to nearly thirty products, including rose-petal and fruit jams, flower waters, pickled vegetables, pomegranate and mulberry syrups, kishk, apple and grape vinegars and sugared citrus peel—all the mouneh staples of the Lebanese pantry. Mymouné employs a core of fifteen local women—more at the height of the summer season—and they even employ the occasional man.

While Leila had been talking, a stream of goodies had been coming out from the kitchen for us to taste. Sweet preserved dates and pumpkin, tart mulberry jam, crystallized lemon peel and the *pièce de résistance*: "Fruits Folies," an extraordinary mixture of conserved tangerines, bitter oranges, almonds, pine nuts and pumpkin that according to Leila makes the perfect last-minute dessert spooned over ice cream.

At last we were ushered into the kitchen, a large bright room with huge picture windows looking onto the mountains in the distance. Massive pans of orange blossom jam were bubbling on the stoves and two laughing young women were dipping pieces of orange peel in sugar. The atmosphere was contagiously light-hearted and warm.

Before leaving, we stood for a moment on the verandah of Leila's family home to

gaze out over the valley. "You know," said Leila happily, "Mymouné actually has a double meaning. As well as meaning 'provisions' it also means 'blessed by God'." She swept her hand towards the horizon in a gesture of pure joy. "When I look at all this, and think about what we've achieved, I think this meaning is very true for us."

The following day we'd arranged for our drivers to take us back to the Ras el Matn region. Our destination was Qsaibe, a tiny village that was famous for its dibs (carob molasses); our contact, Georges Neaimeh, who had been busy husking pine nuts when we'd last met. It was squally weather and the pine trees that covered the hillsides were swaying violently in the wind, but as we got out of the car we could smell something sweet, unfamiliar, almost raisiny in the air.

All sorts of molasses are popular in Lebanon and they are commonly made from grapes, pomegranates, dates or carob. We were familiar with pomegranate molasses, a lusciously thick, purplish syrup that adds a tart yet sweet flavor to many Middle Eastern dishes, but neither of us had seen carob molasses before.

We asked Georges and his wife, Rita, what dibs was used for and Amal translated their answers. "I use it instead of sugar in all sorts of cooking," said Rita. "It's good in cakes and cookies and it's also lovely spread on bread with tahini. We often have that for breakfast."

"Dibs is much more healthy than processed sugar," added Georges. "And it's also used to perfume the tobacco that's smoked in nargileh pipes." He jumped to his feet. "*Yallah*! Come with me and see for yourselves."

Dibs production takes place mainly over the cold winter months between October and April. It's a continuous business of crushing, soaking, boiling and bottling, and is hot, dirty work. Georges inherited the family business from his father, who was still on hand to offer advice and help out during the busy times.

Georges stuck his hand into a sack of pods and handed a few to us. They were curious, prehistoric-looking things, like very hard, dark brown broad beans. Georges lifted one to his ear and shook it gently. "Listen," he said. We dutifully copied him and could hear the seed rattling inside. Georges snapped the pod open and handed it to me. It felt dry and tough and I found it hard to believe that it was the source of any natural sweetness.

In one room a series of terracotta sinks were full of crushed carob pods soaking in water to dissolve the natural sugars. After five hours the dibs water would be drained off and transferred to a massive pot. "This dibs water is very good for stomach problems," declared Georges. "It's much better than date water." This water would then be taken to the wood-fired furnace in the next room to be boiled for three hours to thicken and form a concentrate.

The small, dark room next door was like something from the industrial revolution.

It was lit only by a small window high in the wall, and shafts of light pierced the gloom to illuminate the sickly sweet smoke that rose in dense clouds from the bubbling pot. A wooden paddle fixed above it churned the sticky contents mechanically and Georges bent to shovel more coal onto the flames.

Despite the coolness of the day, the heat in that room was unbearable, and we were relieved to go back to the soaking room where Georges showed us the finished molasses—a sticky, thick, butterscotch-colored goo in plastic pots. "Taste!" he ordered, plunging his finger into a nearby saucepan. We followed his example and tasted the intense, almost overly sweet dibs, which had a hint of fruitiness and, yes, an almost chocolate undertone. Over time the dibs would darken to a treacly black color, and the flavor would further intensify.

I found the carob pod in my jacket pocket a week later, and put it to my nose. It smelt sweet and mysterious. The broken edge of the pod was faintly speckled with a few tiny beads of moisture. I stroked my finger along the broken edge and tasted it, and the memory of that day flooded back to me in a rush of small details: I could smell the sweet, raisiny aroma of boiling molasses and feel the heat rising from the pan. And in my mind's eye I could see Georges, bending low to shovel another load of fuel into the furnace.

ONION JAM

¼ cup (50 g) unsalted butter
5 medium purple onions, finely sliced
1 cup (250 ml) dry sherry
1 cup (250 ml) tawny port
¼ cup (50 g) dried currants or raisins, soaked in
    additional 3 tablespoons dry sherry
Salt and pepper to taste

Melt the butter in a heavy-based pan, and slowly sauté the onions until they're soft and translucent (about 5 minutes). Add the sherry and port and continue to cook for a further 45 minutes over a very low heat, stirring from time to time to ensure the jam doesn't stick to the bottom of the pan. Add the soaked currants and the soaking liquor and cook for a further 10 minutes, or until the onions have become very sticky and almost caramelized. Season with salt and pepper.

MAKES 1 CUP (250 ML)

PICKLED TURNIPS

4 turnips, peeled
3½ cups (850 ml) water
⅓ cup (60 g) sea salt
1¼ cups (300 ml) white wine vinegar
1 small beetroot, washed and cut into quarters
4 sprigs thyme
10 black peppercorns
3 bay leaves

Cut the turnips into strips around ½ in x 1½ in (1 cm x 4 cm). Put the water and salt into a large non-reactive saucepan and stir to dissolve. Add the vinegar and bring to a boil.

Pack the turnip strips and beetroot pieces into a sterilized jar with the spices. Pour on enough boiling liquid to cover the vegetables and leave to cool. Top the jar with a circle of greaseproof paper and seal. Leave for 3 days until the pickling solution penetrates the turnip strips. They will keep for up to 4 months unopened. Once opened, refrigerate. They will keep for 2 weeks.

MAKES ENOUGH TO FILL A 3½-PINT (2-LITER) JAR

PARSLEY AND PURPLE ONION RELISH

1 teaspoon ground sumac
2 purple onions, very finely sliced
¼ teaspoon ground allspice
¼ teaspoon ground pepper
1 cup (40 g) flat-leaf parsley, coarsely chopped
3 tablespoons white wine vinegar
2 tablespoons extra-virgin olive oil
Salt to taste

Soak the sumac in cold water for a few minutes and remove any husks or uncrushed berries that float to the top. In a separate bowl, soak the onions in cold water to remove some of the sharpness. Drain them and pat them dry. Mix the sumac, allspice and pepper with the sliced onions and rub in well. Add the parsley, vinegar, oil and salt, and toss together well.

Serve at room temperature with grilled or roasted poultry.

MAKES 2 CUPS (500 G)

RED PEPPER PASTE

This is a vibrant and intensely flavored, versatile paste that is especially popular in the north of Syria. It is often spread onto savory breads and pastries, added to dips, soups and stews or used to flavor marinades. All varieties of red bell pepper can be used—hot and sweet. In the Middle East the paste is dried in the open air in the hot season, and you can do the same over the summer months. It will need at least 2 days in full sunlight.

4 large red bell peppers, deseeded and
    coarsely chopped
2 red bird's-eye chilies, deseeded and
    coarsely chopped
1 teaspoon salt
1 teaspoon sugar
Olive oil

Put the bell peppers and chilies into a food processor and purée to a smooth paste. Tip the paste into a large heavy-based skillet and add the salt and sugar. Bring to a boil, then lower the heat and simmer for 40–45 minutes, stirring from time to time to make sure it doesn't catch and burn.

Preheat the oven to its lowest temperature. Scrape the paste into a large shallow baking tray and spread out evenly. Place in the oven for 5–6 hours, or overnight, until it dries to a very thick consistency. Remove from the oven and leave to cool. Spoon into sterilized jars and pour on a film of olive oil. Seal and store in the fridge or freezer.

MAKES 1 CUP (250 G)

SPICY EGGPLANT RELISH

2 globe eggplants, peeled and cut into
    ¾-in (2-cm) cubes
Salt to taste
⅓ cup (100 ml) olive oil
2 purple onions, cut into ½-in (1-cm)
    dice
1 clove garlic, peeled and finely sliced
1 teaspoon ground cumin
½ teaspoon ground turmeric
½ teaspoon sweet paprika
A pinch of ground red pepper

2 tomatoes, deseeded and diced
½ teaspoon salt
1 teaspoon sugar
Juice of 1 lemon
¾ cup (175 ml) water
¼ cup (10 g) flat-leaf parsley, finely
    chopped
¼ cup (25 g) coriander leaves (cilantro),
    finely chopped
¼ cup (10 g) mint leaves, finely chopped

Put the eggplant cubes in a colander and sprinkle with salt. After 20 minutes, rinse them under cold water and pat them dry with paper towels.

Heat the oil in a skillet and sauté the eggplant, turning the cubes from time to time, until they are light golden brown. Use a slotted spoon to transfer the eggplant to a colander to drain off excess oil. Add the onions, garlic and spices to the pan and fry in the remaining oil on a gentle heat for 5 minutes, stirring from time to time. Return the eggplant to the pan with the tomatoes, salt, sugar, lemon juice and water, and simmer gently for a further 8 minutes. Remove from the heat and stir in the fresh herbs. Serve at room temperature.

MAKES 1½ CUPS (375 G)

BITTER ORANGE MARMALADE WITH ROSEWATER AND ALMONDS

6 oranges (about 3 lbs/1½ kgs)

2 lemons

14 cups (3½ liters) water

5 lbs (2½ kgs) sugar

¼ cup (60 ml) rosewater

⅔ cup (50 g) flaked almonds, toasted in
a dry pan

Slice the oranges and lemons very thinly, reserving the pips. Put the slices of fruit in a large bowl and cover with 12 cups (3 liters) of the water. Put the pips into a small bowl and cover with the remaining 2 cups (500 ml) of water. Leave both to soak for 24 hours.

Put the fruit and its soaking water into a large pan. Scoop the pips into a small square of muslin and tie it loosely to form a little bag. Tuck it into the fruit in the pan. The pips' soaking water should also go into the pan with the fruit.

Bring the pan to a boil, then lower the heat and simmer gently for 2 hours. Remove the bag of pips and add the sugar. Stir over a low heat until the sugar has dissolved. Increase the heat and squeeze the bag of pips over the pan to extract as much pectin as you can. Stir well. Bring to a fast boil and cook for 20–30 minutes, or until the marmalade reaches setting point. While it is boiling away, place a couple of saucers into the freezer to chill them.

Test to see if the marmalade has reached setting point by placing a spoonful on one of the chilled saucers and returning it to the fridge to cool. It is at setting point if it forms a wrinkly skin when you push your finger across the surface. When it reaches setting point, remove the pan from the heat and skim the froth from the surface. Stir in the rosewater and almonds and leave to settle for 10 minutes. Skim off any more froth, then carefully ladle the marmalade into sterilized preserving jars. Seal while hot.

MAKES AROUND 9 LBS (4½ KGS)

SOUR CHERRY JAM

Sour cherries are very popular around Aleppo. In spring the orchards in the north of Syria are a mass of frilly blossoms, and by late summer the fruit begins to appear on restaurant menus in the form of the famous cherry kebabs. This preserve is also popular—not just for breakfast, but in the Arab fashion as a spoon fruit, served with glasses of icy-cold water. If you can't find fresh morello cherries then use dried sour cherries, available from Middle Eastern or Greek stores. Soak them overnight in water, then drain and pit them. Use the same ratio of soaked fruit as in the recipe.

2½ lbs (1¼ kgs) pitted morello cherries

4½ cups (900 g) sugar

Juice of ½ lemon

2 tablespoons kirsch (optional)

Layer the pitted cherries and sugar in a large bowl, and leave them to macerate overnight. The next day, tip the cherries and juice into a large pan. Bring to a boil very slowly, stirring frequently to prevent the cherries from burning. Simmer for 20–30 minutes, or until the cherries are very soft. Stir in the lemon juice. Use a slotted spoon to transfer the cherries into sterilized jars. Continue to cook the syrup until it thickens and reduces enough to coat the back of a spoon. Pour onto the cherries and seal the jars while hot.

MAKES AROUND 4 LBS (2 KGS)

DAIRY COUNTRY

DAIRY

CHTAURA, WE HAD DECIDED, WAS DEFINITELY A BIT OF A DUMP. It didn't help that we had passed through the place about twenty times, always on the way to somewhere else, or that the weather had been unfailingly bad on each of these occasions. But there was something decidedly seedy about the place.

Amal told us that she remembered Chtaura from her childhood as a summer resort, but today the inland town's main purpose was as a handy stopover point on the Beirut–Damascus road. The shops were either money exchanges or cheap and cheerful kebab restaurants, and most of the people we saw were suspicious-looking service taxi drivers on the hunt for extra passengers to fill their cars.

On this particular morning we were passing through on our way to Tanaïl, a village in the hills east of Beirut. It had been snowing and the traffic was bumper-to-bumper. We crawled along the single-lane highway trapped behind a Lebanese army truck, the soldiers inside heavily rugged up against the cold. As we climbed further up the mountain, we entered a cloud of dense, wet fog. When we finally drove out of it we pulled over to the side of the road to take in the snow-capped mountains that surrounded us.

Our destination in Tanaïl was the Massabki Dairy Shop, where we would meet Mr Bassam Hajjar, one of the co-owners. We were early and decided a mid-morning snack was in order. Perusing the glass cabinet in the front of the shop, Greg announced, "I've got to have an arus bi labneh." These sandwich snacks are standard fare for Lebanese school-children and are simply floppy big squares of sorj—mountain bread—spread thickly with yogurt cheese, drizzled with olive oil and rolled up. Extra refinements might include a sprinkling of za'atar or fresh mint leaves.

As we finished our arus, we were ushered through the back door for a tour of the dairy. My memories of visits to cheese factories in Australia always included Wellington boots and white hair-nets, but things seemed a little more relaxed here. The large white-tiled room was filled with huge troughs of warm, wobbly yogurt and the cool-room was lined with shelves stacked with neat white blocks of haloumi cheese.

Mr Hajjar offered us coffee while he gave us the dairy facts and figures. Massabki is a relatively large concern by Lebanese standards, processing four thousand liters of milk every day for cheese and yogurt production. Between April and September they also work their way through an additional three thousand liters of goat's milk a day, which mainly goes towards making labneh balls.

The large display cabinet in the shop held a bewildering array of dairy products. Familiar favorites such as ricotta, haloumi, double crème, crème fraîche, shanklish and labneh, but also other names we didn't know: ackawi, chelal, nabulsi and aricheh.

Most of the cheeses looked remarkably similar—they were all white, smooth fresh cheeses, with varying degrees of saltiness and firmness. One particularly interesting one,

chelal, looked like long strands of white fettuccine, twisted into a neat little skein.

According to legend, the Middle East was the birthplace of cheese, discovered accidentally by a nomad who was carrying a saddlebag of milk across the desert. Despite this, the region's dairy tradition is far from developed and there is nothing like the range of cheeses that we have in the West. Sheep and goats have always been the main source of dairy foods here, as cows are just not suited to the typical Middle Eastern terrain of dry scrubby hills and arid desert. Olive oil rather than butter is the primary cooking medium and milk is rarely consumed as a drink. And although fresh curd cheeses are popularly eaten with bread as a snack, cheese is mostly used in cooking.

Yogurt is a different story, however. Middle Easterners eat vast quantities of the stuff, although not the over-sweetened and artificially flavored varieties that Westerners tend to prefer. Sourness is a virtue in the Arab world, and yogurt makes an appearance at just about every mealtime. It is consumed as a refreshing drink, served as a dip or accompaniment to all kinds of savory dishes, and is also used as a cooking medium in soups and casseroles. Thick, drained yogurt and yogurt cheese (labneh) are readily available in

Lebanese supermarkets, something to be envied—in Australia, if you want labneh, you have to make it yourself.

Our next stop, the Convent Dairy, was just a short drive away. We turned off the main road and into the well-kept grounds of a large stone church, hidden from the road by tall cypresses, and we continued down the long shady driveway to the farm. Orchards in blossom lined the road and ahead of us, in the bright sunshine, were fields of newly planted corn.

We passed through an archway into a cobbled courtyard, where there was quite a collection of parked cars. Inside, a long queue of customers were waiting to stock up on supplies of butter, yogurt, cheese, eggs and freshly baked bread, for the Convent Dairy is reputed to make some of the purest-flavored and best-quality fresh cheese and yogurt in Lebanon. People obviously think nothing of making the 45-minute journey from Beirut to stock up.

As we were waiting, Father Paul, the head of the convent, came up to introduce himself. He was wearing an informal jumper and trousers rather than priestly robes. After a few fumbling attempts at conversation, half in French and half in Arabic, Father Paul put us out of our misery and chatted to us in fluent, barely accented English. As it turned out he had spent a fair portion of his youth in Sydney.

We learned that Father Paul had expanded the dairy's cheese repertoire to include boiled, pressed, Gouda-style cheeses, some flavored with caraway. Later, the head cheesemaker, Tony Rabai, took us down to the underground cellar where row upon row of shelves were stacked with round yellow cheeses at varying stages of maturity, ranging from two months to a year.

The Convent Dairy differs from most other dairies around Tanaïl in that it has its own herd of some 150 Friesian cows. The twice-daily milkings produce around one thousand liters of milk, which is piped directly from the milking shed to the dairy. As well as the Gouda-style cheeses, Tony and his offsider, Georges Farquah, make yogurt and labneh, ricotta, butter and ghee and kishk.

Tony also took us into the dairy itself, where most of the day's work had been completed. Georges had just finishing cleaning out the boiling tanks and was giving the tiled floor a quick mop. The air smelled sweet and there was a general sense of contentment to the place.

In one of the cool-rooms enormous bags of yogurt were suspended, dripping over a metal trough. "Labneh," explained Tony, waving his hand in their direction. "These have been hanging since yesterday. Soon they will be ready."

In another cool-room we came upon uneven balls of shanklish. This is a type of fermented cheese, very popular in Lebanon and Syria, and one that Greg loves for its

strong, almost blue-cheese flavor. Shanklish is something of a curiosity, and Tony laughed when we asked how it is made.

"You want to know how we make shanklish? Well, let me tell you that here at the convent we make it properly. Most of the shanklish you buy is a hotchpotch of stuff. It is just bits of cheese rejects scraped off the dairy floor or from wherever, and mashed together. They put so much spice and flavoring in it that you can't tell it's bad stuff."

We looked suitably concerned at this news and Tony continued. "You know, shanklish is actually an ancient Arabian cheese. They used to make it in the desert and keep it buried in the hot sand for a year to mature. The proper way to make it is with *arisheh*. That's a sort of whey cheese, a bit like ricotta. You boil it and drain it and then leave it in the sun to dry. It becomes a dry, lumpy powder that you press together with your hands to make these balls."

We noticed that there were several types of shanklish. "Yes. They all have spices in them, but some we roll in za'atar, and to some we add spicy red pepper. Some we leave natural."

We stocked up on tubs of yogurt, labneh and shanklish on our way out, plus a big bag of the convent's special tisane—a herbal tea concoction made from dried flowers, leaves and twigs and some rather strange vegetable matter that looked a bit like hay. It was reputed to have excellent digestive properties, and I had a feeling that over the next few weeks it would come in very handy.

FAMILIAR FAVORITES, SUCH AS RICOTTA, HALOUMI,

DOUBLE CREME, CREME FRAICHE, SHANKLISH AND LABNEH

HOME-MADE YOGURT *laban*

Laban is an essential part of the Middle Eastern diet. There are plenty of quality commercial brands around, but home-made yogurt just seems to taste sweeter and fresher. All you need is milk and yogurt. Many families have a "starter" yogurt that lasts for years—sometimes even generations. The main thing to remember is that you need to use good-quality, plain live yogurt to start things off—not a flavored, sweetened variety. Live yogurt contains the natural bacteria that cause milk to thicken and sour slightly.

4 cups (1 liter) full cream milk
1 tablespoon plain live yogurt

Put the milk in a large saucepan and bring to a boil. When the froth rises, turn off the heat and leave to cool.

As you are dealing with a living "culture" the bacteria will only grow within a certain temperature range—between 90°F (32°C) and 120°F (49°C). If you don't have a thermometer, the traditional way of testing is to dip your finger into the milk. You should be able to leave it for a count of fifteen seconds without yelling the house down.

When the milk has cooled sufficiently, remove any skin that has formed on the surface. In a glass or earthenware mixing bowl, beat a few tablespoons of hot milk into the yogurt, then pour in the rest of the milk and beat again.

Cover the bowl with a dish towel or plastic wrap and leave it in a warm place, undisturbed, for at least 8 hours—overnight is ideal. It should thicken to a custard-like consistency. Transfer to the fridge where it will keep for up to a week. If you want to keep making your own yogurt, reserve a little to make another batch within 4 days.

MAKES 4 CUPS (1 LITER)

YOGURT CHEESE *labneh*

In Lebanon and Syria people eat this fresh cheese on a daily basis. It's hard to find commercially made labneh in Australia but it is simplicity itself to make at home.

4 cups (1 kg) plain yogurt
1 teaspoon salt
3 tablespoons extra-virgin olive oil

Mix the yogurt with the salt. Spoon into a clean muslin square, cheesecloth or dish towel. Tie the four corners together and suspend the bundle from a wooden spoon over a deep bowl. Put it in the refrigerator and allow it to drain for 48–72 hours. The longer the hanging time, the firmer the result.

To serve, tip into a bowl and flatten the surface. Make a little well and fill with extra-virgin olive oil.

MAKES 2 CUPS (500 G)

MINT LABNEH

The creamy tang of fresh yogurt cheese acts as a good base for all kinds of herb purées. Try basil, oregano or dill—or even a mixture of herbs.

5 cups (1¼ kgs) plain yogurt
½ cup (20 g) mint leaves
½ cup (20 g) parsley leaves
1 teaspoon dried mint leaves
1 clove garlic, crushed with ½ teaspoon salt
1 tablespoon extra-virgin olive oil

Tip ¾ cup (200 g) of the yogurt into a blender and add the fresh herbs and dried mint leaves. Add the garlic paste and extra-virgin olive oil and blitz briefly.

Spoon the rest of the yogurt into a clean muslin square, cheesecloth or dish towel and swirl in the herbed yogurt. Tie the four corners together and suspend the bundle from a wooden spoon over a deep bowl. Put it in the refrigerator and allow it to drain for 12–24 hours.

MAKES 1⅓ LBS (600 G)

YOGURT, TARRAGON AND CUCUMBER SALAD

2 cups (500 g) natural yogurt, hung
    overnight or for 24 hours
2 Lebanese cucumbers, deseeded and
    grated (leave the skin on)
1 clove garlic, crushed with 1 teaspoon
    salt
½ cup (20 g) fresh tarragon leaves,
    roughly chopped
Juice of 1 lemon
Splash of arak or Pernod
Salt and pepper to taste

Mix all the ingredients together in a large bowl and season with a little salt and pepper. Line a sieve with muslin or a dish towel and strain for a further 4–6 hours. Chill until required.

MAKES AROUND 2 CUPS (500 G)

HOT YOGURT SOUP WITH LAMB SHANKS, PEARL ONIONS, BROAD BEANS AND RICE
laban immor

Meat dishes cooked in yogurt have been popular all over the Arab world for centuries. The name of this popular Lebanese version—meaning literally, "mother's milk"—implies that the young lamb is cooked in its mother's milk. Traditionally, this dish is served as a stew with plain rice or vermicelli noodles. I like to prepare it as a soup and to cook the rice in the full-flavored stock. As it cooks, the starch released from the rice adds a lovely creaminess to the finished soup. You can use left-over rice, if you have any.

3 tablespoons olive oil

2 large lamb shanks (about 1 lb/500 g each)

2 onions, coarsely chopped

2 sticks celery, coarsely chopped

2 carrots, scraped and halved lengthwise

1 small leek, white part only

2 cloves garlic, peeled

⅓ cup (75 ml) sherry

8 cups (2 liters) chicken stock or water

1 teaspoon cumin seeds

2 cinnamon sticks

1 teaspoon allspice berries, lightly cracked

1 red bird's-eye chili, split in half

½ cup (100 g) uncooked long-grain rice

6 pearl onions, peeled and halved

2 cups (500 g) plain yogurt

½ tablespoon cornstarch

3 tablespoons water

1 egg, lightly beaten

Salt and pepper to taste

8 broad beans, shelled, blanched and peeled

Dried mint leaves

Extra-virgin olive oil

Heat the olive oil in a large heavy-based saucepan and seal the lamb shanks until nicely browned all over. Remove from the pan and drain on paper towels. Add the onion, celery, carrot, leek and garlic and sauté over a low heat for 5 minutes. Return the shanks to the pan, add the sherry and stock and bring to a boil. Skim, then lower the heat.

Combine the cumin seeds, cinnamon sticks, allspice and chili in a small muslin cloth and tie with string. Submerge amongst the vegetables and shanks, cover the pan and leave to simmer on a low heat for 1¾–2 hours or until the lamb is falling from the bones. Remove from the heat and strain the mixture through a sieve, pressing on the vegetables to extract maximum flavor. Discard the vegetables and spice bag. Remove the meat from the bones, leaving it in bite-sized chunks, and reserve.

Return the lamb cooking liquid to the cleaned saucepan and add the rice and pearl onions. Bring to a boil then lower the heat, cover and simmer gently for 30 minutes or until the onions are tender and the rice is cooked.

To stabilize the yogurt, tip into a large bowl and stir briskly until smooth. Mix the cornstarch with the water and add to the yogurt with the egg. Stir well, then tip into the hot soup. Lower the heat and cook, stirring in one direction only, for about 10 minutes, or until the soup has thickened.

Return the meat to the pan, season to taste and gently heat through. Serve garnished with a few broad beans, a sprinkle of dried mint leaves and a drizzle of extra-virgin olive oil.

SERVES 6–8

SOFT HERB SALAD WITH GOAT'S CHEESE, CRISP BREAD, SUMAC AND PINE NUTS

1 piece Arabic bread
¼ cup (60 ml) olive oil
¼ cup (60 g) butter
1 purple onion, thinly sliced
1 teaspoon ground sumac
½ cup (20 g) parsley leaves
½ cup (25 g) coriander leaves (cilantro)
½ cup (20 g) watercress leaves
2 pickled artichokes, finely sliced
½ cup (50 g) frisée lettuce
½ cup (100 g) crumbled goat's cheese
⅓ cup (60 g) fried pine nuts
Juice of 2 lemons
⅓ cup (80 ml) extra-virgin olive oil
Salt and pepper to taste

To prepare the crisp bread, roll the Arabic bread into a tight roll and slice thinly. Heat the oil with the butter and fry the bread until it is golden. Tip onto paper towels to drain.

Place the onion in a small bowl, sprinkle over the sumac and mix gently. Tip the herb leaves, artichokes and lettuce into a large serving bowl, together with the goat's cheese, pine nuts and fried bread.

Add the lemon juice, oil and onion and lightly season with salt and pepper. Gently toss the salad and serve right away with grilled or roasted meats or seafood.

SERVES 4

SHANKLISH SALAD WITH RADISHES, CHICORY AND CUCUMBER

Look for shanklish at the dairy counter of Middle Eastern grocers.

¼ cup (50 g) crumbled shanklish or
  aged goat's cheese
1 bunch bitter chicory leaves, coarsely
  chopped
¼ cup (20 g) watercress leaves
1 purple onion, diced
1 bunch radishes, washed, topped and
  tailed and quartered
2 Lebanese cucumbers, peeled,
  deseeded and diced
2 tomatoes, deseeded and diced
Juice of 2 lemons
⅓ cup (80 ml) extra-virgin olive oil
Salt and pepper to taste

Tip the shanklish or aged goat's cheese, chicory, watercress, onion, radishes, cucumbers and tomatoes into a large mixing bowl. Add the lemon and oil and lightly season with salt and pepper. Gently toss the salad and serve right away with grilled or roasted meats or as a mezze dish.

SERVES 4

THE BEKAA VALLEY

SALADS AND DRESSINGS

OUR VISIT TO THE JESUIT-RUN CONVENT DAIRY AT TANAÏL had been educational in many ways. As well as a profitable yogurt and cheese-making business, the dairy also runs a successful model farm on its 230 hectares of land. It was here that we met its manager, Fadi Sarkis, and he was a mine of information about agriculture in Lebanon. The convent takes a very progressive approach to farming; indeed, Fadi has a master's degree in sustainable agriculture and in his spare time he is president of "Biocoop Lubnan", a dynamic organisation whose mission is to develop organic food production in Lebanon.

We had spent the last few days hurtling up and down the Bekaa Valley, the broad strip of arable land that runs down the center of Lebanon. It is flanked by two long mountain ranges: the Lebanon Mountains to the west and the Anti-Lebanon Mountains that form the border with Syria to the east.

The Bekaa Valley has always been the agricultural heart of Lebanon. In Roman times, crops of wheat, barley and millet were grown in abundance, earning the area the title of "breadbasket of the Empire". It is naturally fertile land, irrigated by two rivers, the Orontes and the Litani, and according to Fadi it accounts for 60 per cent of Lebanon's farm production.

On our drives through the region we'd seen fields of young, iridescent-green wheat, pink- and white-blossomed fruit trees and rows of frilly lettuces. The Bekaa produces a wide variety of many other crops as well, from table grapes to olives and tomatoes, as well as more prosaic crops such as legumes, sugar beet and potatoes. Fadi told us that Lebanon is famous in the Arab world for the quality of its fruit and vegetables, and it does a brisk export trade with countries such as Saudi Arabia, Syria, Jordan and Kuwait.

However, the picture was not as rosy as it first appeared. The Bekaa appeared to be much poorer than the rest of Lebanon. Farm workers were shabbily clothed and they looked weary; the roads were littered with piles of uncollected rubbish and, in contrast to the attractive traditional stone houses that dotted the mountains, accommodation in the Bekaa was often little more than crumbling concrete boxes. Even the fresh produce being sold by the roadsides looked mean and miserable.

According to Fadi Sarkis, agricultural production has yet to recover from the devastating effects of the civil war, which saw assets destroyed, livestock lost and food-growing land severely damaged. More recently, farming businesses have also had to contend with big hikes in fuel prices and with the increasing flood of foodstuffs transported illegally across the border from Syria.

Farmers resent the government's reluctance to invest in agriculture—although 40 per cent of Lebanon's population are farmers, less than 4 per cent of the country's annual budget goes to fund this sector. Neighboring countries such as Jordan and Egypt heavily

subsidize their own agriculture sectors and Lebanese farmers just can't compete. They have to make do with out-of-date machinery, ineffective water-management systems and higher labor costs.

Most of the population in the Bekaa are Shiaa Muslims who have historically been largely ignored by the government's Sunni and Christian elements. If it is this sense of marginalisation that has made locals so receptive to the fundamentalist message of religious salvation preached by the Hezbollah's "Party of God," it is also what has turned them over the years to illicit drug production for their economic salvation.

Until recently, crops of cannabis and opium reputedly generated an annual turnover of US$500 million for growers, but in the 1990s the Lebanese authorities cracked down on their production in a big way, a move that was sanctioned by the Syrian government and strictly enforced by the occupying Syrian army. Despite this ban, there are small pockets where drug crops have continued to be secretly grown around the Bekaa, but perhaps more hopefully, the area is becoming increasingly known as a wine-growing area.

There has always been something a little recherché about the idea of Lebanon as a wine country, but its viticultural roots stretch far back into early history. Historians speculate that early grapes were domesticated by Neolithic civilisations as early as 9000 BC. Certainly, there is evidence that the Phoenicians did a healthy trade in red and white wines all around the Mediterranean. And, of course, nearly two thousand years ago the Romans built a massive temple to Bacchus, the god of wine, at Baalbeck.

What might be termed the modern era of Lebanese winemaking started in 1857, when Jesuit priests planted vines at the old crusader fort at Ksara, near Zahlé in the Bekaa Valley, to make wine for Mass at the nearby Tannaïl Convent. In 1920, when the League of Nations divided the region between France and England (creating modern-day Lebanon in the process), Lebanon became a French protectorate and the influence of the French over the next twenty years helped develop the country's wine industry further.

The industry hummed along quietly until hitting a rocky patch during Lebanon's civil war. Army tanks ploughed through vineyards and the Bekaa became a battleground for Syrian and Israeli troops, but from the rubble grew a brave new world of winemaking.

Since the end of the war in 1990, the Lebanese wine industry has grown in leaps and bounds—largely as a result of the efforts of dynamic new producers such as the Ghosn brothers at Massaya—although it remains tiny by world standards. There are currently around sixteen producers—mostly located in and around the Bekaa—who produce close to seven million bottles a year. This is a mere drop in the wine ocean in global terms, of course, when one considers that the biggest players, France and Italy, produce nearly ten thousand million liters between them every year.

Lebanon is unlikely to ever be a serious wine country, largely because more than 60 per cent of its population are, ostensibly at least, Muslim non-drinkers. Local per capita consumption remains less than one liter per year, compared with the European average of twenty-six liters (the French drink fifty-six!), and on our travels we were frequently disappointed by the lack of local wines represented on restaurant wine lists. The future of Lebanese wine lies in its export markets, and these have seen a strong 75 per cent growth since 2000—mostly to the French and English, who receive the majority of Lebanon's total wine exports.

Enthusiasm among local wine producers for promoting the industry is strong, however, and there are local and international marketing campaigns and even a number of wine-tour packages starting up through the Bekaa Valley. Most wineries are keenly aware of the enormous potential to be earned from the fledgling wine-tourism sector and believe that it will be a key driver in the subsequent growth of export markets.

It's only when you drive around the region that you begin to see just how well suited it is for grape growing. The Bekaa Valley is really more of a high plain, suspended between two protective mountain ranges at a thousand feet above sea level. It offers sheltered slopes, rich brick-red soil and a climate to rival the Napa Valley. The air is soft and warm for nearly 250 days of the year, and the low summer rainfall means the grapes suffer little threat from disease. If not exactly organic, there is certainly minimal use of pesticides or herbicides.

Ksara is the oldest commercial producer of Lebanese wines, and one of the largest at around two million bottles a year. It is also one of the best known, featuring prominently on wine lists around the country and on the local wine-tour maps; it receives more than a million visitors every year. Housed in an old crusader castle, it's a well-run operation, with a vast tasting room and an extensive network of underground cellars to explore. The cellars incorporate ancient caves that were discovered by the Romans and used by them to store wine, just as they're still used today.

Rania Chammas, Ksara's charming PR executive, took us on a personalized tour of the cellars to see some of the million bottles stored there. The 80 per cent humidity and constant temperature of between 52 and 55°F (11 and 13°C) create perfect cellaring conditions, and the natural mold that covers the bottles means that re-corking is rarely required.

We were fascinated to see the massive concrete storage tanks that are so different from the shiny stainless-steel ones used in most Australian wineries. Equally intriguing to us Australians were the grape varieties—names such as cinsault, carignan, obeideh and merwah were new to all of us.

If Ksara and its close rival Kefraya are the best-known winemakers domestically, supplying around 70 per cent of the market, it is Château Musar that has the edge as far as international competition goes. It was the first local wine to succeed internationally, and for many years the name Château Musar was virtually synonymous with Lebanese wine. It had its first success on the world's wine stage at the Bristol Wine Fair in England in 1979, where it famously earned rave reviews and the Find of the Fair award with its 1967 vintage.

Château Musar was founded in 1930 by the legendary Gaston Hochar, with the objective of producing small volumes of outstanding wines for a small, sophisticated market that was already educated in the pleasures of the grape. He established his winery in an eighteenth-century castle at Ghazir, in the hills north of Beirut, and dug deep cellars to provide for long cellaring.

Today, Château Musar remains very much a family business, and is run by Gaston's two sons: Serge, who supervises the winemaking, and Roland, who manages the business. We met one morning with another Gaston Hochar, grandson of the founder, who told us that Musar's primary goal was to continue to grow its export volume. "The Lebanese don't really have a palate for wine," he said a little sadly as he led us down to the vaulted underground cellar for a spot of tasting. "They just don't have the habit of drinking wine with a meal, as is the European way." We sipped our way through a tight, fruity 2004 cinsault and then a more peppery, tannic 2004 carignan, trying to envisage the way each would develop and mature with age.

All Château Musar wines are created along traditional lines, specifically with ageing in mind. The whites are typically bottle-aged for around five years before being released, and each red variety is barrel-aged separately before being judiciously blended.

The hallmark wines are undoubtedly the powerful, complex reds that blend cabernet sauvignon, cinsault and carignan grapes. Hot-climate red wines generally age poorly, but Musar's age exceptionally well, due to careful pressing, blending and ageing in those deep, cool cellars.

The current 2004 cabernet sauvignon vintage was, as anticipated, mouth-puckeringly dry and we asked Gaston about its potential life. "Oh," he said with a little shrug of his shoulders, "around forty years or more—if the cork holds."

LEMON GARLIC DRESSING

2 cloves garlic, crushed with $\frac{1}{2}$ teaspoon salt
Juice of 2 lemons
$\frac{1}{3}$ cup (100 ml) water
1 teaspoon honey
1 cup (250 ml) extra-virgin olive oil
3 shallots, cut in half
4 sprigs thyme
Generous grind of pepper

Whisk the garlic paste, lemon juice, water and honey together in a small mixing bowl, then stir in the oil. Drop in the shallots and thyme and season with pepper. Cover and leave for 6 hours or, even better, overnight so that the flavors mingle and intensify. Taste and add extra salt if necessary. Strain through a fine sieve into a jar. It will keep, sealed and refrigerated, for a couple of weeks.

MAKES AROUND 1$\frac{2}{3}$ CUPS (400 ML)

POMEGRANATE DRESSING

$\frac{1}{2}$ cup (110 ml) red wine vinegar
2 tablespoons pomegranate molasses
1 cup (250 ml) extra-virgin olive oil
3 shallots, cut in half
2 garlic cloves, cut in half
4 sprigs thyme
$\frac{1}{2}$ teaspoon salt
Generous grind of pepper

Whisk the vinegar and molasses together in a small mixing bowl, then stir in the oil. Add the shallots, garlic and thyme and season with salt and pepper. Cover and leave for 6 hours or, even better, overnight so that the flavors mingle and intensify. Strain through a fine sieve into a jar. It will keep, sealed and refrigerated, for a couple of weeks.

MAKES AROUND 1$\frac{2}{3}$ CUPS (400 ML)

CREAMY TAHINI DRESSING

1 clove garlic, crushed with $\frac{1}{4}$ teaspoon salt
$\frac{1}{2}$ cup (125 ml) tahini, well stirred
$\frac{1}{3}$ cup (80 ml) lemon juice
Cold water

Stir the tahini into the garlic paste, then gradually mix in the lemon juice and enough cold water to thin the sauce to the consistency of pouring cream. Pour into a sealable jar and store in the fridge. It will keep for 7 days.

MAKES AROUND 1 CUP (250 ML)

WHIPPED FETA AND MUSTARD DRESSING

$\frac{3}{4}$ cup (200 g) Bulgarian feta
2 cups (500 g) plain yogurt, hung for 4 hours
1 heaped tablespoon Dijon mustard
Salt and pepper to taste
Squeeze of lemon juice

Put the feta into a food processor and whiz to a very smooth paste. Then add the strained yogurt and Dijon mustard and process until well combined. The dressing should be thick and creamy, like mayonnaise. Taste and season with salt and pepper, adding a squeeze of lemon as well, if you like. Pour into a sealable jar and store in the fridge. It will keep for 5 days.

MAKES AROUND 2 CUPS (450 ML)

LEMON MINT DRESSING

2 cloves garlic, crushed with ½ teaspoon salt
Juice of 2 lemons
⅓ cup (100 ml) water
1 teaspoon honey
1 cup (250 ml) extra-virgin olive oil
1 tablespoon dried mint leaves
1 teaspoon fennel seeds, roasted and finely ground
Generous grind of pepper

Whisk the garlic paste, lemon juice, water and honey together in a small mixing bowl, then stir in the extra-virgin olive oil. Add the mint and fennel and season with pepper. Taste and add extra salt, if necessary. Pour into a jar. It will keep, sealed and refrigerated, for a couple of weeks.

MAKES AROUND 1⅔ CUPS (400 ML)

SPICY TOMATO DRESSING

3 medium tomatoes, peeled, deseeded and diced
2 red bird's-eye chilies, deseeded and finely diced
1 clove garlic, finely diced
3 tablespoons grated ginger
2 tablespoons sugar
Juice of 2 lemons
⅔ cup (150 ml) olive oil
⅓ cup (100 ml) walnut oil
Salt and pepper to taste

Put all the ingredients, except the olive and walnut oils, into a food processor. Whiz to a fine, smooth purée. With the motor running, gradually add the oils until they are fully absorbed. Check the seasoning and add salt and pepper, to taste. Pour into a sealable jar and store in the fridge. It will keep for 5 days.

MAKES AROUND 2 CUPS (450 ML)

LEMON CORIANDER DRESSING

1 cup (50 g) fresh coriander leaves (cilantro) and roots, cleaned and trimmed
2 cloves garlic, crushed with ½ teaspoon salt
2 tablespoons water
¾ cup (200 ml) extra-virgin olive oil
1 teaspoon caraway seeds, roasted and finely ground
4 whole cardamom pods, lightly bruised
½ teaspoon black peppercorns, crushed
1 red bird's-eye chili, deseeded and diced
Juice of 1 lemon
Segments of 1 lemon

Put the coriander—leaves, stalks, roots and all—into a food processor. Add the garlic paste and water and whiz to a purée.

Put the olive oil into a large mixing bowl and whisk in the coriander purée. Add the spices, chili, lemon juice and lemon segments and stir together well. Taste and adjust the seasoning, if necessary. Pour into a sealable jar and store in the fridge. It will keep for 3–4 days.

MAKES AROUND 1½ CUPS (350 ML)

SYRIAN CHOPPED LEAF SALAD

Syrians often use chopped leaves in salads, rather than leaving them whole or coarsely broken. Substitute feta or an aged goat's cheese if you don't have any shanklish—a strongly flavored, crumbly Lebanese cheese available from most Middle Eastern grocers.

1 head baby romaine lettuce, coarsely
   chopped
1 cup (40 g) mint leaves, coarsely chopped
1 cup (40 g) flat-leaf parsley leaves,
   coarsely chopped
1 small onion, finely diced
1 Lebanese cucumber, peeled, deseeded
   and cubed

2 tomatoes, deseeded and diced
6 radishes, cut into wedges
1 clove garlic, crushed with
   $\frac{1}{2}$ teaspoon salt
2 tablespoons lemon juice
2 tablespoons extra-virgin olive oil
2 tablespoons shanklish or aged goat's
   cheese (optional)

Toss all the salad ingredients together in a large mixing bowl. Pour on the lemon juice and extra-virgin olive oil and toss together well. If you're using the shanklish or aged goat's cheese, crumble it coarsely and scatter over the top.

SERVES 4

BABY BEET AND CITRUS SALAD WITH WATERCRESS

Beetroot salads are popular in the Middle East, and the beets are often tossed in yogurt, which turns them a rather lurid pink. Simpler beetroot salads are drizzled with a little extra-virgin olive oil and perhaps topped with a few shavings of onion and chopped parsley. We like this version, full of clean, tangy citrus flavors. You might also like to throw in a handful of chopped fresh mint.

2 bunches baby beetroot (beets)
1 small clove garlic, crushed with
   $\frac{1}{2}$ teaspoon salt
Juice of 1 lemon
$\frac{1}{4}$ cup (60 ml) extra-virgin olive oil
Salt and pepper to taste
$\frac{1}{4}$ orange
$\frac{1}{2}$ lemon
1 lime
$\frac{1}{2}$ cup (20 g) watercress leaves

Wash the beetroot well and cut off the tops, leaving about $1\frac{1}{4}$ in (3 cm) attached. Trim the roots. Steam for 10–15 minutes, or until tender. While the beetroot are cooking, whisk the garlic paste with the lemon juice and extra-virgin olive oil to make a dressing. When the beetroot are cool enough to handle, peel them and cut the larger ones in half. Season them generously with salt and pepper, and while they're still warm pour on the dressing and toss gently.

   Peel the skin and white membrane from the citrus fruit. Using a sharp knife, carefully cut the membrane between each segment and flip the fruit out of its skin casing, removing the seeds as you go. Cut the segments into small pieces. Add the fruit to the beetroot with the watercress leaves and gently combine.

SERVES 4

SWEET AND SOUR EGGPLANT SALAD

This is such a versatile dish, equally happy on its own—perhaps with some Arabic bread or crusty bread and butter—or as an accompaniment to pink-roasted, garlicky lamb, grilled white fish or a humble roast chook.

1 medium globe eggplant, peeled

Salt to taste

⅓ cup (100 ml) olive oil

1 purple onion, finely sliced

1 tablespoon golden raisins, chopped

1 tablespoon pomegranate molasses

Juice of ½ lemon

A drizzle of honey

¾ cup (175 ml) hot water

Flat-leaf parsley, finely chopped

Cut the eggplant in half lengthwise then cut each half into half-moons, ½-in (1-cm) thick. Put them in a colander and sprinkle with salt. After 20 minutes, rinse them under cold water and pat dry with paper towels.

Heat the oil and fry the eggplant pieces, turning them from time to time, until they turned a light golden brown. Add the onion and raisins to the pan. Mix the pomegranate molasses with the lemon juice, honey and hot water and add to the pan. Toss well, so that everything is evenly coated. Continue to cook until the onion and eggplant are both meltingly soft. Add the parsley, toss gently and leave to cool. Taste and adjust the seasoning, if necessary. Serve at room temperature.

SERVES 4

CUMIN-SPICED LENTIL SALAD WITH WALNUT DRESSING

A fantastic earthy salad that makes a great accompaniment to simple grills, especially grilled fish. It's also a nice starter with plenty of Arabic bread.

¾ cup (150 g) Puy lentils, washed

1 small onion, peeled and quartered

1 small carrot, quartered

1 stick celery, cut into chunks

2 cloves garlic, peeled

1 cinnamon stick

1 tablespoon cumin seeds, roasted

2½ cups (600 ml) water

2 small tomatoes, deseeded and diced

1 small purple onion, finely diced

½ cup (20 g) flat-leaf parsley leaves

¼ cup (12 g) coriander leaves (cilantro)

¼ cup (20 g) watercress sprigs

Walnut dressing

⅓ cup (100 ml) walnut oil

⅓ cup (80 ml) olive oil

⅓ cup (80 ml) champagne or white wine vinegar

Juice of 1 lemon

Salt and pepper to taste

Few drops of sesame oil

Put the lentils in a saucepan with the vegetables and cinnamon stick. Wrap the cumin seeds in a small piece of muslin cloth and tie with a string. Add to the pan. Pour in the water and bring to a boil. Lower the heat and simmer for 30–40 minutes or until just tender. Tip the lentils into a sieve and drain. Remove the vegetable pieces, cinnamon stick and muslin bag, and discard.

Make the Walnut Dressing by whisking all the ingredients together and pour over the warm lentils. Stir thoroughly and leave to cool to room temperature. When ready to serve, gently fold through the diced tomatoes, onion and herbs.

SERVES 4

MONKS' SALAD WITH GARLICKY DRESSING

You'll find boiled vegetable salads all around the eastern Mediterranean. They are sometimes boiled in water and served warm with creamy dressings, or, as in this recipe, slow-cooked in oil to melting tenderness.

1 bunch baby turnips
1 bunch baby carrots
8 baby leeks
8 shallots, peeled
½ small cauliflower, broken into florets
5 oz (150 g) baby green beans
Olive oil
¼ cup (60 ml) sherry vinegar
⅓ cup (80 ml) extra-virgin olive oil
Small clove garlic, crushed with
    ½ teaspoon salt
½ cup (25 g) coriander leaves (cilantro)
Salt and lots of pepper to taste

Spice bag
1 tablespoon coriander seeds
1 tablespoon black peppercorns
1 tablespoon allspice berries
1 red bird's-eye chili, split lengthwise

Wash, dry and trim all the vegetables. Put them in a large heavy-based casserole dish and pour enough olive oil to cover them. Tuck the Spice Bag in amongst the vegetables and bring to a boil. Then lower the heat as far as possible—you just want to see the odd tiny bubble rising to the surface. Cook for about 10 minutes, by which time the vegetables should be just tender. Turn off the heat and leave the vegetables to cool down in the oil.

Remove the vegetables from the oil and put them into a colander to drain. Discard the Spice Bag. Whisk together the vinegar, oil and garlic paste to make a dressing. Tip the vegetables into a large bowl and scatter on the coriander leaves. Pour on the dressing, toss everything together, then taste and season with plenty of freshly ground salt and pepper.

SERVES 4

EGGPLANT SALAD WITH SOFT GOAT'S CHEESE AND WALNUTS

1 medium globe eggplant, peeled

3 tablespoons crumbled soft goat's
   cheese

1 tomato, deseeded and diced

1 small purple onion, finely diced

⅓ cup (15 g) flat-leaf parsley leaves,
   finely shredded

⅓ cup (20 g) coriander leaves (cilantro),
   finely shredded

⅓ cup (15 g) fresh fenugreek leaves
   (optional)

½ cup (60 g) walnuts, lightly toasted and
   coarsely chopped

1 tablespoon sesame seeds, lightly
   toasted

Salt and pepper to taste

Dressing

1 clove garlic, crushed with ½ teaspoon
   salt

¼ cup (60 ml) walnut oil

Juice of 1 lemon

Cut the eggplant into ¾-in (2-cm) cubes and steam for 10 minutes, or until tender. Tip into a colander and leave to steam dry. The eggplant cubes will have absorbed liquid as they steam, so, as they cool down, squeeze them gently to extract as much water as you can.

Combine all the Dressing ingredients in a mixing bowl and toss together gently. Whisk together the Dressing ingredients and pour on enough to coat the salad. Season, then taste and adjust to your liking.

SERVES 4

MALOUF'S CAESAR SALAD WITH ARMENIAN AIR-DRIED BEEF AND A SOFT-BOILED EGG

A twist on a great classic, using bastourma (air-dried beef) and Arabic bread instead of the traditional bacon and fried bread croutons. We also like to sprinkle the soft-boiled eggs with a version of dukkah, which adds a nuttiness to the salad. You can prepare the Dressing and fry the bastourma and bread ahead of time, but the eggs need to be boiled at the last minute and served warm.

4 slices (2 oz/50 g) bastourma or air-
   dried beef, very finely sliced

2½ tablespoons olive oil

1 piece Arabic bread

1 tablespoon (20 g) butter

4 eggs

2 heads baby romaine lettuces

⅓ cup (40 g) sesame seeds, lightly
   toasted and mixed with 1 teaspoon
   ground cumin

Dressing

2 eggs, lightly poached

1 clove garlic, finely chopped

4 anchovy fillets

Juice of 1 lemon

Splash of white wine vinegar

1 tablespoon Dijon mustard

¾ cup (200 ml) olive oil

¾ cup (200 ml) vegetable oil

Salt and pepper to taste

¼ cup (50 g) grated parmesan

To make the Dressing, put the eggs, garlic, anchovies, lemon juice, vinegar and mustard into a food processor. Blitz together then gradually drizzle in the oils, a little at a time, ensuring each amount is incorporated before adding more. Season with salt and pepper and thin with a little warm water until the Dressing is the consistency of pouring cream. Stir in the grated parmesan.

Scatter the strips of bastourma onto a lined baking tray and drizzle with half the olive oil. Grill until crisp and brown, then drain on paper towels.

Roll the Arabic bread into a tight roll and slice thinly. Heat the remaining oil with the butter and fry the bread until it is golden. Tip onto paper towels to drain.

Put the eggs into a bowl with hot tap water for 5 minutes to bring them to room temperature. Bring a pot of water to a boil. Carefully lower in the eggs and cook for 5½ minutes. Remove from the water and refresh briefly under cold running water.

While the eggs are cooking, tear the lettuce leaves coarsely and place in a large serving bowl. Scatter on the bastourma and bread and pour on enough Dressing to coat the leaves—around ½ cup (125 ml). Divide the salad between 4 bowls and place a warm egg on top. Cut the egg in half and sprinkle with the sesame and cumin mixture. Serve right away.

SERVES 4

EGG AND OLIVE SALAD

Olive salads are often found in mezze selections. This one is particularly good, as the nuttiness of the toasted sesame seeds and creamy richness of the eggs make a lovely contrast to the salty olives. Serve as an accompaniment to grills—fish in particular—and with pickled or cured meats.

1 small purple onion, peeled and finely
   sliced crosswise
4 eggs
¼ cup (65 g) green olives, pitted and
   halved
⅔ cup (100 g) pine nuts, toasted and
   coarsely chopped
2 tablespoons flat-leaf parsley, finely
   chopped
2 teaspoons sweet paprika
2 teaspoons ground sumac
½ teaspoon ground red pepper
3 tablespoons sesame seeds, toasted
Juice of 1 lemon
1 clove garlic, crushed with ½ teaspoon
   salt
⅓ cup (100 ml) extra-virgin olive oil
Pepper to taste
Paprika

Soak the onion in cold water for 10 minutes to reduce the sharpness.

Put the eggs into a bowl with hot tap water for 5 minutes to bring them to room temperature. Bring a pan of water to a boil. Carefully lower in the eggs and cook for 5½ minutes. Remove from the water and refresh briefly under cold running water.

When the eggs are cool, peel and chop 3 of them coarsely. Reserve the fourth egg for garnish. Put the chopped eggs in a large mixing bowl with three-quarters of the onion, the olives, pine nuts, parsley leaves, spices and sesame seeds. In another small bowl, whisk together the lemon juice, garlic paste and olive oil. Pour enough of the dressing onto the salad to moisten it, and toss lightly. Taste and season with pepper.

To serve, pile the salad into a small serving bowl and make a little well in the top. Fill with the remaining onion slices. Slice the top off the reserved egg to reveal the yolk and sit it on top of the onion. Sprinkle the egg and salad with a little paprika and serve at room temperature.

SERVES 4

ARMENIAN AIR-DRIED BEEF SALAD WITH SHANKLISH

This is a simple salad to throw together. If you want to make it fancier, or serve it as a heartier salad for lunch, poach some eggs and arrange them on top—perhaps sprinkled with a little za'atar or dukkah. Shanklish is a strongly flavored, crumbly Lebanese cheese available from most Middle Eastern grocers. You'll find the bastourma (Armenian air-dried beef) in Middle Eastern or Turkish butchers.

½ small ball of shanklish or aged goat's
   cheese
1 tomato, deseeded and diced
1 Lebanese cucumber, peeled,
   deseeded and diced
1 small purple onion, diced
½ cup (20 g) flat-leaf parsley leaves,
   coarsely shredded
½ cup (20 g) watercress leaves
Salt and pepper to taste
Juice of 1 lemon
⅓ cup (100 ml) extra-virgin olive oil
12 thin slices of bastourma

Crumble the shanklish or aged goat's cheese into a mixing bowl and toss gently with the tomato, cucumber, onion, parsley and watercress. Season lightly with salt and pepper, then squeeze on the lemon juice and pour on the olive oil. Toss together gently to combine.

To serve, tip onto a shallow serving dish and drape the slices of bastourma over the top.

SERVES 4

OF BOATS AND BEEHIVES

SEAFOOD

BEFORE LEAVING LEBANON we had one more trip to make: to the southern seaside towns of Sidon and Tyre. None of us had been so far south before, and a look at the map revealed that we would be frighteningly close to the still-disputed border territories.

We set off early, hoping to get to Sidon in time to see the fishermen return with their catch of the day. There were few other cars on the road, and the brand-new highway, built with money from Rafik Hariri's redevelopment fund, sped us past the airport and south along the coast.

Distances are ridiculously short in tiny Lebanon, and only half an hour later we were driving along the palm-fringed seafront and pulling up in front of Sidon's Crusader-era Sea Castle. Sidon is an ancient city, thought to have been settled as early as 4000 BC. It rose to prominence as a Phoenician trading port in the twelfth to tenth centuries BC, its wealth generated from trading murex, a shellfish that produced a rare and highly desirable purple dye. Sidon was also renowned under the Persians as a great ship-building port and its sailors played a key role in the Empire's long-running battles with the Egyptians and, later, the Greeks.

It was a bright spring morning but there weren't too many people out and about on the promenade. A solitary street vendor wheeled his barrow along the seafront selling chai. Down at the port things were busier: a few tardy fishermen were wearily rowing towards their moorings, while others were busy cleaning out their boats, mending nets and drinking coffee, the night's catch already safely delivered to the fish market a few hundred feet away on the waterfront.

Fishing is still done the old-fashioned way in Sidon. The brightly painted wooden rowing boats are passed down through the generations from father to son, and there are around four hundred fishermen left to carry on the tradition. We chatted briefly to one of the men, Jamal bil Bassi, who was happy to hand over the job of mending nets to his son while we talked.

Most of the men head out to sea at around one in the morning to set their nets, he told us. From three o'clock onwards it's constant work, checking the nets, pulling them in and re-setting them. The men are out in all weathers, sometimes fishing close to land and sometimes rowing an agonising six miles (ten kilometers) out from the shoreline. That seemed like an awful lot of rowing, but Jamal assured us that the boats carry up to four fisherman and they all take turns with the work.

It had been a quiet night for Jamal and his son, netting them a meagre forty pounds (twenty kilos) of fish. Yesterday was better though, he told us, as they'd managed to haul in about a hundred and twenty pounds (sixty kilos) of prized red mullet. We asked him about the vexed issue of over-fishing that plagues fishermen the world over, and Jamal shrugged.

"There is no shortage of fish here," he said tersely. "The main problem for us is with the nets."

Apparently, this was a long-standing bone of contention for the fishermen and they had been petitioning the government for financial assistance to purchase better-quality nets. Despite promises, they were still having to make do with poor-quality Spanish nets that strangled the baby fish rather than letting them through. "That's what will cause a problem for us in the future," he said, easing a tiny goldfish-sized red mullet from its nylon trap. "Look at this. This fish we should let go, so that, *Inshallah*, he can grow to be a big fish."

A sizeable crowd was milling around the fish market by this stage, and the quiet of the morning was broken by customers prodding and poking the goods on display as they haggled loudly with stallholders for a bargain. As well as the famous Middle Eastern red mullet, there were plenty of whiting and sea bass, sardines and cuttlefish, the occasional ray and baskets of frenetic crabs. The sweet little blue spanner crabs at one stall, we learned, were used as bait.

Many of the fish-sellers had young children at their sides, helping with the scaling and gutting. We chatted to a bright young boy who told us his name was Austin. He'd been helping his dad at the daily fish market since he was seven years old. Glancing at his watch, he told us that he worked for a few hours every morning and headed off to school at eleven o'clock.

It was now late morning and the stallholders were closing up for the day, dumping great tubs of ice onto the concrete floor. The crowd was dwindling fast, leaving behind little more than a dense cloud of cigarette smoke and the seaside smell of fish.

Our next destination lay further south, and as we put Sidon behind us the smells of the port were replaced by the increasingly strong scent of orange blossom. We passed secluded beaches dotted with picnicking families and just before the picturesque old port of Tyre the orange groves gave way to bedraggled banana plantations and the road became bumpier.

We had heard about a beekeeper called Mohammed Haidar Hassan from the proprietor of a mouneh shop in west Beirut. We hadn't been able to find a telephone number for him but knew that he was well known in his tiny village of el Qlailé. Sure enough, several villagers gave us clear directions to his house and late in the afternoon we pulled up, unannounced, in his driveway.

Mr Hassan was sitting on his front porch drinking tea with a neighbor. When we explained our interest in learning about his honey, he shook our hands warmly and was as welcoming as only Arabs can be. The table was quickly cleared and his wife and teenage daughter appeared carrying trays loaded with cake and sweet rosemary-scented tea. The southern part of the country is largely Shiaa, and more conservative than urban Beirut.

Thus, Mrs Hassan wore a *hijab* and she demurred from shaking hands with Greg, but sat next to her husband quietly while we talked about honey.

Mr Hassan is one of the top honey producers in Lebanon, his several million bees producing more than two tonnes of honey every year. He believes that his honey is the purest and best in Lebanon—if not the world. "There is no pollution here," he explained, gesturing towards the neighboring orchard. "And our honey is 100 per cent pure single-flower honey, not the cheap blends that you often find these days." We tasted the honeycomb that Mr Hassan had brought out for us to try and could well believe his claims.

Over the course of the year, Mr Hassan moves his beehives around his property according to the plants which are flowering, and so his bees feed from rosemary, thyme, citrus and a number of other flowering plants. "The best honey is orange blossom," he told us. "It's a springtime variety that fetches three times the price of other honeys." He then went on to provide a highly detailed breakdown of honey's medicinal properties. His springtime honey is exceptionally high in vitamin C and calcium, and American research has shown that it is valuable in lowering cholesterol, opening up arteries and helping blood circulation.

"This use of honey as medicine is nothing new," he told us. "The Phoenicians used it as an antiseptic and they used the bee stings to help with joint pains." Mr Hassan told us that he himself suffered from arthritis and often encouraged bee stings on an afflicted joint. "It works much better than an anti-inflammatory," he enthused.

We piled into the back of Mr Hassan's truck and he took us for a tour of his property, stopping from time to time to break off an overhanging bough or to pick a basket of sweet blood oranges for us to take away with us. We stopped in front of a little huddle of hives set on a low hill overlooking the village. "Ah, you will be interested in this," he said. "Here I have an Australian queen. I imported several of them specially. The Australian bees appear to be particularly happy in this climate."

As we bumped and jolted our way back through fields and orange groves the sky was darkening and the shadows were lengthening, spreading a soft blue haze over the surrounding hills and valleys. And from a nearby village the plaintive wail of the muezzin's call to evening prayer drifted across on the orange-scented breeze.

HIS BEES FEED FROM ROSEMARY,
THYME, CITRUS AND A NUMBER OF
OTHER FLOWERING PLANTS. "THE
BEST IS ORANGE BLOSSOM."

MIDDLE EASTERN SPICED CALAMARI WITH WARM EGG NOODLES AND VEGETABLE SALAD

If you're not confident about cleaning and preparing the squid yourself, ask your fishmonger to help you. You'll need the tentacles, head and beak to be removed, and the tube split and scraped clean. Keep the tentacles for cooking with the body of the squid.

1 bunch broccolini, blanched and
   halved lengthwise
½ cup (75 g) peas, blanched
½ cup (50 g) broad beans, blanched
   and peeled
1 small fennel bulb, finely sliced
4 tablespoons Lemon Garlic Dressing
   (page 130)
8 small calamari tubes
¼ cup (60 ml) olive oil
10 oz (300 g) fresh fettucine or Chinese
   egg noodles
A knob of unsalted butter
Juice of ½ lemon
Salt and pepper to taste

Spice paste
1 teaspoon cumin seeds
1 teaspoon coriander seeds
1 teaspoon white peppercorns
2 tablespoons olive oil
3 cloves garlic, sliced
½ teaspoon salt
Grated rind of 1 lemon, finely grated
1 tablespoon thyme sprigs, chopped

Make the Lemon Garlic Dressing by following the recipe on page 130

To make the Spice Paste, pound the cumin, coriander and peppercorns in a mortar. Heat the oil in a small skillet and sauté the garlic for a moment, just to soften it. Tip into the mortar with the ground spices, add the salt and pound to a smooth paste. Stir in the lemon rind and chopped thyme.

Prepare the vegetables and toss them in the Lemon Garlic Dressing, while still warm.

Score the inside of the calamari in a criss-cross pattern, then rub them all over with the spice mix. Heat a griddle pan or oven broiler as high as possible. Brush with oil and place the tentacles and calamari on the hottest part of the oven broiler, scored side down. After 40 seconds, turn them over. In a moment, they will curl into a tight cylinder. Cook for a further minute, then remove from the heat.

While the calamari are cooking, bring a pan of salted water to a boil to cook the noodles until al dente—it will only take a couple of minutes. Drain well, then stir through the butter and lemon juice and season with salt and pepper. Brush with olive oil.

To serve, divide the vegetables between 4 plates, arranging them in a circle around the plate. Top with pieces of calamari. Use a fork to twirl the noodles into little mounds and place in the center of each plate. Drizzle with a little more Lemon Garlic Dressing and serve while warm.

SERVES 4

CRUNCHY FRIED CALAMARI WITH TAHINI REMOULADE

Deep-fried calamari is a universally popular dish, and the golden-spice mix is a nice way to liven it up a bit.

8 small calamari tubes, quartered

Salt and pepper to taste

Vegetable oil for shallow-frying

Lemon wedges

Tahini remoulade

$^2/_3$ cup (150 g) plain yogurt

3 tablespoons tahini, well stirred

1 clove garlic, crushed with $^1/_4$ teaspoon
     salt

Juice of 1 lemon

$^1/_2$ teaspoon pepper

1 tablespoon chopped flat-leaf parsley

1 tablespoon chopped gherkins

1 teaspoon chopped capers

Crunchy coating

3 tablespoons cornstarch

3 tablespoons fine polenta

3 tablespoon fine semolina

1 tablespoon Golden Spice Mix (page 20)

Make the Golden Spice Mix by following the recipe on page 20.

To make the Tahini Remoulade, combine the yogurt, tahini, garlic paste and lemon juice in a bowl and whisk together thoroughly. Add the remaining ingredients and stir well.

Prepare the Crunchy Coating by sieving all the ingredients together. Season the calamari pieces lightly with salt and pepper, then dredge them in the crunchy coating mixture. Put the calamari pieces into the sieve to shake off any extra coating mix.

Heat the oil in a large skillet until it is nearly smoking. If the oil isn't hot enough, the calamari will "stew" rather than fry, and the end result will be soggy rather than crunchy. Add the calamari pieces to the hot oil in batches, shaking the pan to coat them with the oil and to help them color evenly. They should take less than a minute to cook. Remove from the pan and drain on paper towels. Serve them piping hot with lemon wedges and the Tahini Remoulade.

SERVES 4 AS A STARTER

GARFISH FILLETS COOKED IN VINE LEAVES WITH HALOUMI AND A CORIANDER-SHALLOT SALAD

8 vine leaves

8 garfish, whiting or any small whole
     white seawater fish

Salt and pepper to taste

Dried mint leaves

$^1/_4$ cup (60 g) finely grated haloumi or
     mozzarella

$^1/_4$ cup (60 ml) olive oil

Coriander-shallot salad

1 shallot, very finely sliced

Juice of 1 lemon

$^1/_2$ teaspoon ground sumac

1 cup (50 g) coriander leaves (cilantro)

1 red finger-length chili, seeded and
     finely shredded

$^1/_2$ clove garlic, finely chopped

$^1/_3$ cup (80 ml) extra-virgin olive oil

Salt and pepper to taste

Lemon wedges

Clean, gut and fillet the fish into butterflies, so that the two halves remain attached to each other.

Prepare the Coriander-Shallot Salad. Put the shallots, lemon juice and sumac in a large mixing bowl and toss them together. Let the mix sit for 5 minutes to marinade, while you assemble the remaining salad ingredients and prepare and cook the fish.

If you are using preserved vine leaves, soak them well, then rinse and pat them dry. Fresh vine leaves should be blanched in boiling water for 30 seconds and then refreshed in cold water.

Cut the tail ends off the garfish, then open them out and season the fish lightly with salt and pepper and a pinch of dried mint leaves. Scatter on the haloumi, dividing it evenly between the fish. Starting at the tail end, roll up each fish until you have something that looks a bit like a long rollmop herring. Don't worry, the fish will stay rolled up.

Arrange the vine leaves on your work surface, vein side up. Cut off the stalks and trim each leaf to the same width as the fish roll. Place the fish at one end and roll the vine leaf around it. Again, don't worry—it will all stay together quite well.

Heat the oil in a large non-stick skillet and fry the fish rolls in batches, for 4 minutes, turning them in the pan so they cook evenly. The vine leaves will start to darken, and the fish will be tender, white and juicy.

Finish the Salad by adding the coriander leaves, chili, garlic and oil to the shallots. Toss gently and season with salt and pepper before transferring to a serving bowl. Stack the garfish rolls on a serving platter with lemon wedges.

SERVES 4

GRILLED LARGE SHRIMP KEBABS WITH SPICY CRACKED WHEAT SALAD AND TOMATO DRESSING

Cooking shrimp in their shells intensifies the flavor and stops them drying out as quickly. Large shrimp (tiger prawns) are robust enough to serve with this highly spiced dressing and warm bulgur or cracked wheat salad. You can also sprinkle them with a little of the spice mix before cooking. The bulgur or cracked wheat salad should be served as soon as possible after it's made or it will start to go soggy.

16 fresh large shrimp
(about 1½ lbs/650 g total weight)
Salt and pepper to taste
Olive oil
2 cups (450 ml) Spicy Tomato Dressing
(page 133)

Spicy cracked wheat salad
¾ cup (200 g) fine bulgur or cracked
wheat, rinsed in cold water
1 tablespoon golden raisins, coarsely
chopped
1½ cups (360 ml) water
1 teaspoon Golden Spice Mix (page 20)
Salt and pepper to taste
1 red finger-length chili, seeded and
finely diced
1 medium tomato, seeded and finely
diced
⅓ cup (15 g) flat-leaf parsley leaves,
finely shredded
1 small clove garlic, finely chopped
¼ cup (60 ml) extra-virgin olive oil
Juice of 1 lemon

Make the Golden Spice Mix and Spicy Tomato Dressing by following the recipes on pages 20 and 133.

Cut the heads off the shrimp and use a pair of scissors to trim off their legs. To split the shrimp open, use a small, sharp knife to cut each shrimp in half lengthwise, through the underbelly, to the shell. Pull away the intestinal tract, open the two halves out and then fold them back in on themselves. Cut each shrimp in half, crosswise, and slide the pieces onto soaked wooden skewers. You should have 2 whole shrimp (4 halves) on each skewer.

To make the Spicy Cracked Wheat Salad, first put the bulgur or cracked wheat and raisins into a small saucepan and add the water. Sprinkle on the Golden Spice Mix, season lightly and stir well. Bring to a boil, then cover and simmer gently for 6–8 minutes, or until all the water has been absorbed. Tip into a mixing bowl and add the remaining ingredients. Use a fork to break up the bulgur or cracked wheat and mix everything together well.

Heat your oven broiler or barbecue, or heat some oil in a large non-stick skillet. Sprinkle the shrimp lightly with salt and pepper. Cook the shrimp until they just turn red, turning once.

To serve, mound the Spicy Cracked Wheat Salad onto a large serving platter and stack the shrimp around it. Serve a jug of the Spicy Tomato Dressing on the side.

SERVES 4

OYSTERS WITH NORTHERN LEBANESE CHILI AND HERB SAUCE *oysters harra*

A hot, spicy sauce from Tripoli that is often served with baked fish. Feel free to adjust the chili content to your own liking.

24 fresh oysters in the shell, opened

Harra sauce
¼ cup (60 ml) extra-virgin olive oil
6 cloves garlic, finely sliced
1 red finger-length chili, seeded and
shredded
1 teaspoon ground cumin
½ teaspoon ground cinnamon
½ teaspoon ground pepper

¼ teaspoon ground red pepper
1¼ cups (160 g) walnuts, finely
chopped
3 tomatoes, seeded and finely diced
Juice of 1 lemon
½ cup (25 g) coriander leaves (cilantro)
½ cup (20 g) flat-leaf parsley leaves
Salt and pepper to taste

To make the Harra Sauce, first heat the oil in a large skillet and sauté the garlic for a few seconds before adding the chili, spices and walnuts. Fry gently for a few minutes, then add the tomatoes, lemon juice and fresh herbs. Cover the pan and simmer gently for 10 minutes. Taste and season, then allow to cool.

Serve the freshly opened oysters drizzled with a little Harra Sauce.

SERVES 4

ARAK SHRIMP WITH GARLIC SAUCE AND BREAD SALAD

Matching shrimp with anise is a rather French thing to do—although the French would be more likely to use Pernod, of course.

12 jumbo shrimp (king prawns), about
    2 lbs/1 kg total weight
Salt and pepper to taste
1/4 cup (60 ml) arak
1/3 cup (100 ml) white wine
1 shallot, finely diced
2 cloves garlic, finely chopped
1/3 cup (75 g) butter, cubed
Salt and pepper to taste
Squeeze of lemon juice

Bread salad
1 teaspoon ground sumac
1 small purple onion, finely sliced
Juice of 1 lemon
1 bunch watercress
1 bunch radishes, trimmed and cut into
    wedges
1 piece Arabic bread
2 tablespoons olive oil
2 tablespoons clarified butter

Soak the sumac in cold water for a few minutes and remove any husks that float to the surface. Put the sliced onion into a small bowl with the sumac and lemon juice and rub everything together well. Place in a mixing bowl with the watercress and radishes and leave aside to the last moment.

Cut the heads off the shrimp and use a pair of scissors to trim off their legs. To butterfly the shrimp, use a small, sharp knife to cut each shrimp in half lengthwise, through the underbelly, to the shell. Pull away the intestinal tract and then open the two halves out.

Roll the Arabic bread into a tight roll and slice thinly. Heat the oil and butter and fry the bread until it is golden. Tip onto paper towels to drain.

Preheat a heavy-based skillet to high. Season the shrimp with salt and pepper and cook for 2–3 minutes until the shells turn pink and the flesh is cooked through. At the last minute, turn the heat up to high and splash in half the arak. Bubble for a moment then remove the shrimp from the pan and keep warm while you finish the sauce. Add the wine and the rest of the arak with the shallots and garlic, and let it bubble away until the liquid has reduced by three-quarters. Remove the pan from the heat and drop in the cubes of butter, whisking to make a smooth butter sauce. Season and add the lemon juice.

When ready to serve, add the fried bread to the salad and toss everything together. Divide the Bread Salad between 4 plates, arranging it in a mound. Stack 3 shrimp next to the Salad and pour on the warm sauce.

SERVES 4

RED MULLET WITH GOLDEN SPICES AND A CITRUS SALAD

12 red mullet (each about 4oz/120 g)
Salt and pepper to taste
Olive oil for frying
2/3 cup (100 g) flour
1/4 cup (30 g) rice flour
3 teaspoons Golden Spice Mix (page 20)

Citrus salad
2 medium navel oranges
2 medium lemons
2 limes
1 small purple onion, very finely sliced
1/2 cup (20 g) flat-leaf parsley leaves,
    coarsely shredded
1/3 cup (12 g) mint leaves, coarsely
    shredded
Extra-virgin olive oil
Freshly ground black pepper to taste

Make the Golden Spice Mix by following the recipe on page 20.

To prepare the Citrus Salad, first peel the skin and white membrane from the citrus fruit. Using a sharp knife, carefully cut the membrane between each segment and flip the fruit out of its skin casing, removing the seeds as you go. Toss the citrus segments with the onion, parsley and mint leaves.

To scale the red mullet, hold it under running water and use your thumb to run against the scales from tail to head—they come away very easily. Leave the fins and tail attached for presentation, but use a sharp knife to slice the fish along the underbelly. Hold the sides open and pull the insides away. Insert your finger into the reddish-colored gills and pull them out too. Rinse the insides of the fish under running water, paying special attention to rubbing away the dark blood line against the back bone. Pat dry.

Season the fish lightly inside and out. Heat the oil to 375°F (190°C) or until a little sprinkle of flour sizzles. Mix the flours with the Golden Spice Mix. Dust the fish all over with the seasoned flour. Fry the fish for 2–3 minutes on each side until they are golden brown.

To serve, tip the Citrus Salad onto a shallow serving platter, drizzle with extra-virgin olive oil and season with freshly ground black pepper. Arrange the fish on top.

SERVES 4

ARABIC FISH STEW WITH LEMON AND SAFFRON AND HOT PEPPER ROUILLE *yakhnit samak*

Another traditional fish stew popular in Lebanon and Syria. It is intensely flavored, very lemony and a deep golden color from the saffron.

Hot pepper rouille

½ lb (250 g) potatoes

1¼ cups (300 ml) water

5 cloves garlic, peeled

15 saffron threads, briefly roasted and
  crushed

2 red bird's-eye chilies, seeded and
  coarsely chopped

2 red bell peppers, roasted, skinned
  and diced

Juice of ½ lemon

1 cup (250 ml) olive oil

Salt and pepper to taste

½ cup (100 g) moghrabieh (giant
  couscous)

⅓ cup (80 ml) olive oil

2 large brown onions, diced

2 large leeks, white part only, diced

4 cloves garlic, sliced

10 saffron threads

1 teaspoon cumin

1 teaspoon fresh thyme leaves

2 tomatoes, seeded and diced

1 red finger-length chili, seeded and
  shredded

3 bay leaves

3 cups (750 ml) water

1½ lbs (700 g) whole porgy or sea
  bream, heads and tails removed, cut
  in half (or 1 lb/500 g fillets)

½ cup (25 g) coriander leaves (cilantro),
  coarsely chopped

Squeeze of lemon juice

To make the Hot Pepper Rouille, cook the potatoes in water with the garlic, saffron and chilies until the potatoes are soft and the water has nearly evaporated. Tip into a liquidizer with the peppers and half the lemon juice and whiz to a purée. With the motor running, dribble in the oil until it is all incorporated, then add the remaining lemon juice. Season with salt and pepper and adjust with extra lemon juice, if necessary. The Rouille will keep in a sealed container in the fridge for up to a week.

Put the moghrabieh in a saucepan with 1 cup (250 ml) water and bring to a boil. Lower the heat and simmer gently for 15 minutes until tender.

Meanwhile, heat the oil in a large heavy-based casserole dish. Add the onions, leeks and garlic and sauté for 4–5 minutes, until they start to soften, without coloring. Add the spices and thyme and sauté for a few more minutes. Then add the tomatoes, chili, bay leaves and moghrabieh and stir well. Finally, pour in the water and bring it to a boil. Lower the heat, cover the pan and leave to simmer very gently for 30 minutes.

Add the fish pieces, cover the pan and continue to simmer gently for 4–5 minutes, until the fish is just cooked. Ladle the stew into deep bowls, sprinkle on a few coriander leaves, add a squeeze of lemon and let everyone help themselves to a dollop of Rouille.

SERVES 8

SEARED SCALLOPS WITH ALMOND CRUMBS, HUMMUS AND CRISP ARMENIAN AIR-DRIED BEEF

It's important to use Arabic bread to make the crumbs for this recipe as they will be crunchier.

4 tablespoons olive oil

8 slices bastourma or air-dried beef, cut into thin shreds

12 fresh scallops

1 cup (40 g) watercress leaves

1 cup (100 g) frisée lettuce, coarsely torn

1 small purple onion, very finely sliced

Salt and pepper to taste

¼ cup (60 ml) Lemon Garlic Dressing (page 130)

¾ cup (200 g) hummus

Extra-virgin olive oil

Almond crumbs

Grated rind of ½ orange

2½ tablespoons olive oil

½ cup (80 g) whole blanched almonds

3 large cloves garlic, sliced

1–2 slices stale Arabic bread, diced

¼ cup (20 g) sesame seeds, toasted

Sea salt to taste

Make the Lemon Garlic Dressing by following the recipe on page 130.

Before you make the Almond Crumbs, dry the orange rind overnight or put in a very low oven for 30 minutes. This will intensify the orange flavor.

Put the oil in a small saucepan and when it is hot, fry the almonds for 1–2 minutes, until they just start to color. Add the garlic and pieces of bread and continue to fry, tossing everything around in the pan, so the mix colors evenly to a rich golden brown. Tip into a sieve to drain off any excess oil, then put into a food processor and blitz to smooth crumbs. Scrape the crumbs into a bowl and stir through the sesame seeds and orange rind. Season with a little salt.

Heat 2 tablespoons of the oil in a skillet and fry the bastourma slices until crisp. Remove from the pan and drain on paper towels. Wipe the pan and add 2 more tablespoons of oil. When it's smoking hot, add the scallops and let them sit in the pan for 45 seconds without moving them. Turn them over and leave them for 30 seconds. Now add the crumbs to the skillet and roll the scallops around to coat them in the mixture. Carefully remove the scallops from the skillet and put them on paper towels.

In a large mixing bowl, toss together the watercress, lettuce, onion and bastourma. Season lightly with salt and pepper, pour on the dressing and toss well.

To serve, spoon 3 walnut-sized blobs of hummus on each plate and place a scallop on top of each blob. Divide the salad between the plates, creating a little mound in the center of each plate. Drizzle with a little extra-virgin olive oil.

SERVES 4

GRILLED SARDINES WITH LENTIL TABBOULEH

We can't get enough of this tabbouleh. Not only does it look wonderful—all earthy browns and greens—but it tastes fantastic as well. Sardines are strongly flavored, especially hot off a charcoal grill, and the lentil tabbouleh is the perfect foil to their oiliness.

24 medium sardines, deboned

Olive oil

Salt and pepper to taste

Ground sumac

Lentil tabbouleh

½ cup (100 g) Puy lentils

Juice of 1–2 lemons

½ cup (20 g) mint leaves, coarsely shredded

2 cups (80 g) flat-leaf parsley leaves, coarsely shredded

3 shallots, finely diced

2 tomatoes, seeded and diced

1 teaspoon ground allspice

1 teaspoon ground cinnamon

Salt and pepper to taster

¼ cup (60 ml) extra-virgin olive oil

To make the Lentil Tabbouleh, put the lentils into a small pot and cover with twice their volume of cold water. Bring to a boil, then lower the heat and simmer for 25–30 minutes, or until the lentils are tender. Drain well and leave to cool.

Tip the lentils into a large mixing bowl and add all the other Lentil Tabbouleh ingredients. Toss well and leave for 10 minutes so the flavors mingle and intensify.

Preheat the oven broiler or barbecue as hot as possible. Brush the sardines with a little olive oil, season with salt and pepper and sprinkle lightly with sumac. Cook the sardines for a few minutes on each side—they won't take long—then serve them with the Lentil Tabbouleh.

SERVES 8 AS A STARTER OR AS PART OF A MEZZE SELECTION

RED MULLET GRILLED IN VINE LEAVES *sultan ibrahim*

12 red mullets (each about 4 oz/120 g)
12 vine leaves
Olive oil for frying

Chopped egg, coriander and lemon dressing
½ cup (125 ml) Lemon Garlic Dressing (page 130)
2 soft-boiled eggs, chopped
½ cup (25 g) coriander leaves (cilantro), coarsely chopped

Make the Lemon Garlic Dressing by following the recipe on page 130.

To make the Chopped Egg, Coriander and Lemon Dressing, toss the ingredients together and keep at room temperature until ready to serve.

To scale the red mullet, hold it under running water and use your thumb to run against the scales from tail to head—they come away very easily. Leave the fins and tail attached for presentation, but use a sharp knife to slice the fish along the underbelly. Hold the sides open and pull the insides away. Insert your finger into the reddish-colored gills and pull them out too. Rinse the insides of the fish under running water, paying special attention to rubbing away the dark blood line against the back bone. Pat dry.

If you are using preserved vine leaves, soak them well, then rinse and pat them dry. Fresh vine leaves should be blanched in boiling water for 30 seconds and then refreshed in cold water.

Arrange the vine leaves on your work surface, vein side up. Trim off the stalks and cut each leaf into a rectangle. Place a red mullet in the middle of each vine leaf and wrap it around the fish

Heat the oil in a large non-stick skillet and fry the fish in batches, for 2–3 minutes on each side. The vine leaves should be slightly blackened, but the fish will be tender, white and juicy. Serve right away with the Chopped Egg, Coriander and Lemon Dressing.

SERVES 4

CONFIT SALMON TARATOR WITH CORIANDER, WALNUTS AND TAHINI SAUCE

We love this slow-cooking technique for all sorts of fish and seafood. It works particularly well with salmon, as it has a tendency to dry out. Instead, you end up with a lovely, butter-soft piece of fish that almost dissolves in your mouth. You can, of course, slow-cook individual portions in this way, but using the whole fillet (tail end removed) turns an everyday meal into a "special occasion" dish.

1⅓ lbs (600 g) Atlantic salmon, cut from
   the center, skin on, pin bones
   removed
1 tablespoon Fragrant Salt (page 21)
2 onions, sliced
2 cups (500 ml) olive oil

Tahini sauce
⅔ cup (150 g) plain yogurt
3 tablespoons tahini, well stirred
1 clove garlic, crushed with ¼ teaspoon
   salt
Juice of 1 lemon
½ teaspoon pepper

Tarator
½ cup (60 g) walnuts
1 cup (50 g) coriander leaves (cilantro),
   finely shredded
1 small purple onion, very finely diced
1 red finger-length chili, seeded and
   finely diced
½ teaspoon ground sumac
Juice of 1 lemon
¼ cup (60 ml) extra-virgin olive oil
Salt and pepper to taste

Make the Fragrant Salt by following the recipe on page 21.

Dust the salmon all over with the Fragrant Salt and refrigerate for an hour to lightly "cure". Before cooking, rinse the salmon and dry it thoroughly.

You'll need a deep skillet or baking tray that is just large enough to hold the piece of salmon. Put the onions in the pan and carefully place the salmon on top, skin side up. It is important to raise the salmon off the bottom of the pan, or it will cook too quickly. Pour in the oil. Put the pan on the stove and heat gently to 140°F (60°C). Cook for 8 minutes then remove from the heat and let the salmon sit in the oil for another 2 minutes. Carefully lift the salmon out of the oil and place it on paper towels to drain. Allow it to cool slightly, then peel off the skin and gently scrape away the blood line.

To make the Tahini Sauce, whisk all the ingredients together until smooth and creamy.

To make the Tarator, preheat the oven to 325°F (160°C). Spread the walnuts out on a baking tray and roast for 8–10 minutes, shaking them around from time to time so they color evenly. Tip the nuts into a dish towel and rub vigorously to remove as much of their papery brown skin as possible. Chop the walnuts finely and put in a mixing bowl with the coriander leaves, onion, chili and sumac. Pour on the lemon juice and oil, season with salt and pepper and mix together well.

To serve the salmon, smear the exposed surface with a little Tahini Sauce, then pack on the Tarator topping neatly and evenly so it completely coats the fish. Serve at room temperature, with some extra Tahini Sauce on the side.

SERVES 6

CROSSING THE BORDER

POULTRY

IT IS VIRTUALLY IMPOSSIBLE FOR TOURISTS to take foreign-registered rental cars over the border from Lebanon into Syria, which meant that from Tripoli onwards we would have to deal with the extra hassle of organising service taxis or possibly buses—not the best option when one is loaded down with laptop computers, camera equipment and precious film.

We drove north to Tripoli along the coast road for the last time, passing Byblos with its quaint souks and Crusader castle, and coastal sprawl that became a line of luxury seafront resorts, each with its own private beach. In the north the countryside became rockier, with scrubby gorse-covered cliffs bordering the road. At one point a deep gorge gashed deeply into the landscape right by the highway revealed the crumbling remains of the sixteenth-century Moussalahyha Castle set low in its valley.

Tripoli is Lebanon's largest center after Beirut, so we had expected a certain level of business, but nothing had prepared us for the chaos of its late-morning traffic that Saturday. We fought our way through a hellish cacophony of blaring horns and fug of diesel fumes to Jamal Abdel Nasser Square, where the service taxis congregate, and after some brisk negotiations Amal had organized our transport to the Syrian port city of Lattakia. Our first challenge was sorted; our next task was to track down Tripoli's legendary sweet shop, Rafaat Hallab & Sons.

The first priority, though, was lunch, and a row of golden rotisserie chickens in a nearby café was all it took to tempt us inside. This was clearly not a Westerner's haunt, and we received a few strange looks from the waiters as we grabbed a table close to the barbecuing action. Our fellow customers were rough-looking men with lean, hawk-like faces, sucking on chicken bones, and the air was thick with chili-smoke that burnt our eyes, but the barbecued chicken was tasty with a pungent garlic sauce and plenty of warm Arabic bread to accompany it.

Back on the street we stopped a juice vendor to try a cup of inky black sousse—liquorice juice. We had been fascinated by the idea of liquorice as a drink, and were not disappointed. It wasn't sweet like other fresh fruit juices, and tasted faintly medicinal, but it was refreshing and curiously addictive.

Lebanon's most famous sweet shop turned out to be a rather unprepossessing café on the edge of the souk. That was outside; inside, the display of goods was spectacular. Cabinets and shelves groaned with baklava crammed with nuts and drenched in fragrant syrup and shredded kataifi pastry stuffed with thick clotted cream. We spotted the quaintly named znoud el sitt (ladies' forearms) and taj el malak (king's crown), and mounds of pretty ma'amoul biscuits. Ma'amoul are an essential part of the socialising that takes place during religious festivals in the Middle East and they were walking out the door during the current busy Easter-holiday period.

Just then Rafaat Hallab himself walked up to introduce himself as the grandson of the original Rafaat Hallab who had founded the business in 1881.

He related the Hallab family story with practised ease and urged us to taste one of the house specialties, faiselieh, a kind of baklava triangle stuffed with dark green pistachios, created especially by his grandfather for the state visit of King Faisal of Iraq in 1936.

While the pastries are still painstakingly made by hand in the double-storied factory behind the shop, the business has expanded beyond anything the original Mr Hallab could have imagined. These days Hallab & Sons export their sweets all around the world and churn out a staggering three tonnes of pastries every day—even more over the summer season and during festive seasons.

Our senses had been somewhat dulled by sugar and we'd completely lost track of the time. Bidding Mr Hallab a hasty farewell, we pelted through the busy streets to find our taxis and continue our journey north to Syria.

The bored immigration official looked confused by our presence at the checkpoint on Lebanon's northern border, as the majority of tourists crossing into Syria use the well-worn route from Beirut to Damascus. We waited a long frustrating hour for our passports to be stamped and returned, by which time it was late in the afternoon and our mood was black. Everything was bleaker and dirtier on the Syrian side of the border. Depressingly flat plains stretched to the horizon, interrupted only by mounds of rubbish, electricity pylons and scrappy banana plantations. We passed a miserable collection of Bedouin tents, the plastic sheets flapping in the wind. A few grimy children scrabbled in the dirt and a solitary barefoot woman in dusty black robes walked along the side of the road behind a donkey.

As we drove further north things improved; the countryside became greener and we passed pine forests, citrus orchards and olive groves. In the distance we could see the foothills of Jebel Ansariyya, the mountain range that separates the coastal plain from the Orontes Valley and the vast Syrian desert. This was Crusader country, and lurking up in the picturesque hills were their massive castles—Qala'at Marqab, Qala'at Salah ad-Din and the legendary Krak des Chevaliers.

A few miles outside our destination, Lattakia, we stopped by the roadside where an old peasant couple were baking mountain bread in a clay oven. They were pitifully poor, dressed in layers of shabby clothing held together with string. They were utterly

FAISELIEH, A KIND OF BAKLAVA TRIANGLE STUFFED WITH DARK GREEN PISTACHIOS, CREATED ESPECIALLY BY HIS GRANDFATHER FOR THE STATE VISIT OF KING FAISAL OF IRAQ IN 1936.

silent and an expression of despairing resignation was etched on their faces. We bought as much bread as we could and pushed some notes into the old man's work-worn hands.

Dusk was falling as we drove into Lattakia in the uneasy knowledge that we had made no arrangements for accommodation. Our driver made a suggestion, and after a series of protracted and loud negotiations with Amal it looked like something had been sorted out.

At first, things looked promising enough. We passed the bright lights of a beach resort and a Meridien hotel. "This very good beach," declared our driver, waving a hand through the open car window into the blackness. And then, at the end of a muddy pot-holed laneway, he bumped to a halt in front of a square concrete box. "Here is very nice villa. Come."

Filled with an impending sense of doom, we followed the manager up the steps to inspect our rooms. The villa was evidently only newly built but was already in a state of decay: floor tiles were cracked, light fittings had no bulbs, the linen was grubby and the toilet was leaking. We were too weary to even think about finding alternative accommodation, so we gloomily dumped our bags and decided to head straight out to find some dinner.

Several people had told us that a fish restaurant called Spiro's on the Corniche was the only place to go in Lattakia, which was otherwise limited in eating options. It was nothing fancy, we were told, but it served good, fresh grilled seafood.

It was certainly nothing fancy, just a long rectangular room with high ceilings and peeling paintwork. It was virtually empty and there were no other women in the place. However, there were white cloths on the tables and the waiters were business-like and courteous. We were escorted into the huge kitchen to inspect the fish and watched while our choice of plump little red mullets were scaled and gutted in front of us.

A short time later they arrived on the table. Grilled over charcoal, their flesh was succulent and sweet. The fish came with a tahini-based tarator sauce and a simple dressing made from lemon juice and garlic. We gorged ourselves and scooped up mounds of the accompanying za'atar salad with puffy rounds of Arabic bread.

Despite the horrors waiting for us back at the villa, out there in front of us was the Mediterranean, lapping against the shore. And behind us in the darkness was the rest of Syria; vast, unexplored and a whole new adventure.

AN OLD PEASANT COUPLE WERE BAKING MOUNTAIN BREAD IN A CLAY OVEN.

CHICKEN COOKED ON COALS, ALEPPO-STYLE, WITH CRUSHED WALNUTS, LEMON GRATED RIND AND MINT

We spent a lot of time in the souks of Aleppo following our noses towards the smell of grilling chicken. As well as chickens roasting on spits, we also found stalls where chickens were split, squashed between metal holders and barbecuing over glowing coals. A Weber barbecue (or another solid fuel barbecue) is ideal for cooking this recipe, and it will seem more authentic if you are cooking outdoors. Otherwise, use a ridged griddle pan in your kitchen. Be warned, though—it will create quite a lot of smoke! If you have a fold-over metal barbecue grill you'll find they're ideal for keeping the chicken flat. Otherwise, spear each chicken crosswise with a couple of long metal skewers. This will keep them flat.

2 free-range chickens (about 4 lbs/ 1¾ kgs total weight)
2 cloves garlic, crushed with ½ teaspoon salt
½ cup (50 g) walnuts, lightly toasted and chopped
Grated rind and juice of 1 lemon
1 red bird's-eye chili, deseeded and finely chopped
¼ cup (20 g) mint leaves, finely chopped

¼ cup (12 g) coriander leaves (cilantro), finely chopped
3 tablespoons olive oil
Salt and pepper to taste
Lemon wedges to serve

To prepare the chickens, cut them down the back and splay them open.

Mix the garlic paste with the walnuts, lemon rind and juice, chili, mint, coriander leaves and olive oil. Mix briefly, then pour onto the chicken and rub well all over. Set aside for 30 minutes or so.

When your barbecue is glowing (or your ridged griddle pan is smoking hot), cook the chicken for 10 minutes or so, turning it from time to time so it doesn't burn.

When the chicken is cooked, season with salt and pepper and remove from the heat. Cut into pieces and serve with wedges of lemon. Arabic bread and a chopped-leaf salad make good accompaniments.

SERVES 4

MARINATED AND GRILLED PIGEON WITH CRUSHED TOMATO AND POMEGRANATE

4 squabs or pigeons (about 14 oz/400 g each), or 8 quails (about 7 oz/200g each)

Marinade
1 red bird's-eye chili, coarsely chopped
4 sprigs thyme, coarsely broken
Grated rind of ½ lemon
1 clove garlic, coarsely chopped
3 tablespoons olive oil

Tomato and pomegranate crush
4 tomatoes, peeled and deseeded
1 tablespoon pomegranate molasses
2 tablespoons extra-virgin olive oil
1 shallot, coarsely chopped
1 clove garlic, coarsely chopped
½ teaspoon ground cumin

½ teaspoon ground cinnamon
Juice of ½ lemon
Salt and pepper to taste
Squeeze of pomegranate
2 tablespoons flat-leaf parsley, coarsely chopped

Prepare the Marinade by combining all the ingredients.

Trim the birds of their necks, claws and wing tips. Split them in half down the backbone, and neatly slice out the breastplate (sternum) in the middle. Be careful not to cut through the flesh and skin of the bird. Clean the birds and pat them dry. Place them in the Marinade, cover and leave for 6 hours or overnight.

To make the Tomato and Pomegranate Crush, put 3 of the tomatoes and all the other ingredients, except the parsley, into a food processor and pulse to a fine coulis-like consistency. Tip into a small saucepan and slowly bring to a boil. Remove the pan from the heat. Finely dice the fourth tomato and stir into the sauce with the chopped parsley.

When ready to cook the birds, heat a large heavy-based skillet to smoking hot. Fry the birds 2 at a time, skin side down, for 2 minutes until they color, then lower the heat to medium and cook for another 2 minutes before turning. Cook for 4 minutes or until a lovely deep golden brown all over. Remove the birds from the pan and cut each into quarters. Stack onto a large serving platter and serve with the Tomato and Pomegranate Crush on the side and accompanied by a watercress salad.

Serves 4

CRISP QUAIL WITH FRAGRANT SALT

While the spices in this dish are a classic Lebanese combination, the technique is a Chinese method which I learned during my time in Hong Kong. Dunking the birds quickly into boiling stock has the effect of tightening the skin, without cooking the flesh. Then when you fry or roast them, you get a wonderfully crisp, parchment-like skin. You can use this method with all poultry or game birds.

8 cups (2 liters) water

⅔ cup (150 ml) cider vinegar

8 large quails (about 7 oz/200g each)

2 teaspoons Fragrant Salt (page 21)

1 large thumb fresh ginger, peeled and sliced

4 star anise pods

1⅔ cups (400 ml) vegetable oil

Make the Fragrant Salt by following the recipe on page 21.

Put the water and vinegar into a large non-reactive pan and bring to a boil. When bubbling away, drop in a quail and leave it for 10–15 seconds. Remove and refresh the bird in cold water before patting dry. Repeat with the remaining birds, then put them in the refrigerator, uncovered, for at least 6 hours, to dry completely.

When you are ready to fry the quail, season them all over with the Fragrant Salt. Heat a medium-sized heavy-based pot. Add the ginger and star anise to the dry pot and move them around over the heat to release the aromatic oils. Carefully pour in the vegetable oil and heat to 350°F (180°C), or until a cube of bread sizzles to the surface. Drop in 4 of the quails, breast side down, and fry for 2–3 minutes. The quails won't be fully immersed in oil, so you'll need to gently shake the pan so the bubbling oil swirls around them. Once they start to turn golden, turn them over and fry for another few minutes.

Remove the birds from the oil and sit them on paper towels for a few minutes to absorb any excess oil. Repeat with the remaining 4 birds. Serve them right away as a starter, perhaps with a little watercress salad.

SERVES 4

BARBECUED FREE-RANGE YOUNG CHICKEN SCENTED WITH CARDAMOM AND THYME

18 cardamom pods

3 cloves garlic, coarsely chopped

½ tablespoon salt

2 tablespoons fresh thyme, chopped, or 2 teaspoons dried thyme

½ teaspoon ground sumac

⅓ cup (80 ml) olive oil

1 large free-range chicken (about 2½ lbs/1¼ kgs), or 4 chicken legs (marylands)

Freshly ground black pepper to taste

4 teaspoons Toum (page 20)

2 pieces Arabic bread

1 cup (40 g) flat-leaf parsley leaves, coarsely chopped

4 tomatoes, coarsely chopped

1 small purple onion, finely diced

1 Lebanese cucumber, coarsely chopped

Make the Toum by following the recipe on page 20.

Using a mortar and pestle, pound the cardamom pods to loosen the husks. Remove the husks and continue pounding to bruise the seeds and release their flavor. Add the garlic, salt, thyme and sumac. Pound for a few minutes, mixing all the ingredients together well. Add 3 tablespoons of the olive oil and stir in well. Continue to crush until you have a thick, smooth paste.

Rub three-quarters of the paste over the chicken, making sure you get into all the little creases and corners. Mix the remaining paste with the remaining oil and pour over the chicken pieces. Cover and leave to marinade for 4–8 hours, turning occasionally.

When ready to cook, heat your oven broiler or barbecue to its highest temperature. Season the chicken with plenty of black pepper and cook on a high heat for a few minutes until golden all over. Lower the heat and cook slowly for a further 10–15 minutes, until the chicken is cooked through. Turn the chicken pieces constantly to prevent them from burning. Towards the end of the cooking, brush the chicken pieces all over with the remaining marinade and a little Toum. Cook for a few more minutes.

Split each piece of Arabic bread in half. Arrange half a piece of bread on each plate and scatter on some parsley, tomato, onion and cucumber. Top with the chicken and serve with extra Toum if you're game!

SERVES 4

PARMESAN-CRUMBED QUAIL WITH EGGPLANT, GOAT'S CHEESE AND WALNUTS

This is an impressive dinner-party dish. Preparing the quails can be a bit fiddly, but it's not difficult once you know what you're doing. The result is well worth the effort: juicy pink quail in a crunchy, tangy coating. The parmesan-crumb coating also goes well with many fish, poultry and meat cuts—from humble lamb chops to firm white fish fillets. If you find the idea of boning quail a bit daunting, feel free to use halved chicken thigh fillets, pieces of veal escalope or even lamb cutlets.

4 large quails (about 7 oz/200g each)

Salt and pepper to taste

Dijon mustard

1⅔ cups (100 g) fresh breadcrumbs

3 tablespoons finely grated parmesan

1 teaspoon ground sumac

¾ cup (125 g) flour

2 eggs, lightly beaten with a little water

2 tablespoons olive oil

2 tablespoons clarified butter or ghee

Eggplant Salad with Soft Goat's Cheese
 and Walnuts (page 138)

Make the Eggplant Salad with Soft Goat's Cheese and Walnuts by following the recipe on page 138.

This process sounds involved, but what you're aiming to do is cut each breast and leg away from the bird's ribcage in one piece, so you end up with two partially deboned halves of quail. Using a sharp knife, start by trimming the quails of their necks and wing tips. Next, slice along each side of the breastbone, running your knife close to the ribcage and easing the breast meat away in one piece. At the neck end of the bird you'll encounter the wishbone, which is attached to the wing bone. You'll need to slice around it and down through the ball joint. At the other end of the quail you'll encounter the thigh bone, which is attached to the bird's backbone. Cut through the ball joint to free it from the carcass. Repeat this process with the other side of the quail. All being well, you should now have two halves of bird, each comprising a breast that is joined to a thigh and drumstick. For the sake of neatness, detach the drumstick from the thigh bone and discard it. Pat the birds dry.

Lightly season the quail pieces with salt and pepper and smear a little mustard on the flesh side. Mix the breadcrumbs, cheese and sumac together. Dust each piece of quail with flour, then dip into the egg wash and then the parmesan crumbs so it is well coated.

Heat the oil and clarified butter in a large skillet. Place the quail in the pan, skin side down, and fry for a minute on a medium-high heat. Turn and cook on the other side for a further minute. Then lower the heat, and cook for a minute more on each side.

Serve the quail right away on the Eggplant Salad with Soft Goat's Cheese and Walnuts, although you will probably want to eat them in your hands as they have an irresistible handle of bone to make it easy.

SERVES 4 AS A STARTER

QUAIL STUFFED WITH MA'AHANI AND BAKED IN KATAIFI WITH WHIPPED BULGARIAN FETA AND PAPRIKA OIL

You can buy spicy Lebanese sausages—known as ma'ahani or makanek—from many Middle Eastern butchers or delis. For this recipe you'll need to squeeze the meat out of the sausage casings. Otherwise, use the recipe for home-made Ma'ahani on page 55. As this is quite a rich dish, you'll probably only need to serve 1 each with a few salad leaves.

8 quails (about 7 oz/200g each)
Salt and pepper to taste
Mint leaves
10 oz (300 g) Ma'ahani Sausage Mixture (page 55)
6½ oz (185 g) kataifi pastry
⅔ cup (150 g) butter, melted
Salt and pepper to taste
Paprika Oil (page 21)
Ground sumac

Whipped Bulgarian Feta Sauce
¾ cup (200 g) Bulgarian feta
⅓ cup (100 g) Yogurt Cheese (Labneh—page 118) or plain yogurt
1 tablespoon Dijon mustard
Salt and pepper to taste

Make the Paprika Oil, Ma'ahani Sausage Mixture and Labneh by following the recipes on pages 21, 55 and 118.

To make the Whipped Bulgarian Feta Sauce, crumble the feta into a food processor and blitz to a smooth purée. Add the Labneh and mustard and process again until well combined. Season with salt and pepper and refrigerate until needed.

Trim the quail of their necks and wing tips, then split each bird in half down the backbone and neatly slice out the breastplate (sternum) in the middle. Be careful not to cut through the flesh and skin of the bird. Clean each bird and pat it dry.

Place the birds on the work surface, skin side down, and season lightly with salt and pepper. Arrange a few mint leaves on top of each quail, then add a heaped tablespoon of Ma'ahani sausage mixture. Fold each quail around the stuffing, which should be moist enough to stick the two halves together.

Unravel the kataifi pastry into 1 long skein and ease away one half. Return the rest to the packet, seal tightly and refrigerate or freeze for future use. Trim the pastry to a 8 in (20 cm) length, and carefully divide into 8 sections. Work with one section at a time, keeping the rest covered with a damp dish towel to stop it drying out. Bunch the strands together tightly and arrange in a strip along the work surface. Brush along the length of the pastry with the melted butter and season with salt and pepper. Place the quail at one end of the pastry and roll it up tightly to make a fat pastry cocoon around the body of the bird. Trim so any excess is tucked underneath. Repeat with the remaining quails and pastry. Cover with a damp dish towel and refrigerate for at least 30 minutes before baking.

Preheat the oven to 400°F (200°C). Place the quails on an oven tray lined with baking paper and cook for 15–20 minutes, until they are golden brown and crisp. Drain briefly on paper towels.

To serve, place a quail on each plate and pour the Whipped Bulgarian Feta Sauce around it. Drizzle a little Paprika Oil on the sauce and sprinkle with a little sumac.

SERVES 8 AS A STARTER

GRILLED FLAT CHICKEN WITH BROAD BEAN CRUSH

This flattened chicken dish is cooked under the grill and served smeared with the earthy and spicy broad bean crush. The crush is also delicious on toasted bread, served as a canapé with drinks before dinner.

2 free-range chickens (about 4 lbs/
  1¾ kgs total weight)
Salt and pepper to taste

Broad bean crush
1 clove garlic
½ teaspoon salt
1 cup (125 g) broad beans, podded,
  blanched and peeled
1 shallot, very finely diced
¼ cup (12 g) coriander leaves (cilantro),
  finely chopped
3 tablespoons extra-virgin olive oil
Pinch of ground red pepper

Freshly ground black pepper to taste
Juice of 1 lemon

Preheat your oven broiler to its highest temperature and line the tray of the broiler with foil to make cleaning up easier.

To prepare the chickens, cut them down the back and splay them open. Season them with salt and pepper and place them under the broiler, skin side down, making sure they are about 1¼ in (3 cm) from the heat source. Cook for 5 minutes, then turn and cook for a further 5 minutes, or until the skin starts to blister.

While the chickens are grilling, prepare the Broad Bean Crush. First, pound the garlic and salt to a smooth paste. Next, add the remaining ingredients to the mortar and pound them one by one or tip everything into a food processor. Either way, what you are aiming for is a sludgy, rough texture.

When the chickens are cooked, smear on the Broad Bean Crush and cook for a few more minutes. Serve with Arabic bread, lemon wedges and a soft leaf salad.

SERVES 4

PICKLED QUAIL WITH OLIVE BREAD

Although they are heart-breakingly tiny, rice birds are eaten with gusto as a mezze dish in Lebanon. On our recent trip, I was excited to find them so often on the menu. In one particularly memorable dish, the birds were fried before being pickled in a sweet-sour marinade with shredded vegetables. This is my attempt to re-create the experience, using quail.

Pickled quail
8 quails (about 7 oz/200g each)
Salt to taste
3 tablespoons olive oil
1 purple onion, finely sliced
1 green finger-length chili, deseeded
  and finely shredded
1 stick celery, finely shredded
1 clove garlic, crushed with ½ teaspoon
  salt
Grated rind and juice of 1 lemon
½ cup (125 ml) water
Extra-virgin olive oil
Olive Bread (page 206)

Spiced flour
½ teaspoon black peppercorns
½ teaspoon caraway seeds
½ teaspoon cardamom seeds
1 tablespoon flour

Make the Olive Bread by following the recipe on page 206.

To make the Spiced Flour, grind the spices in a mortar or spice grinder, then sieve to separate the husks. Stir this fine powder into the flour and reserve the larger husks to add to the pickling braise.

Trim the quail of their necks and wing tips, and cut them in half. Pat them dry, season with salt and dust with the Spiced Flour. Heat the olive oil in a heavy-based pan and arrange the quail pieces, skin side down. Cook on a medium heat for 2–3 minutes, until they start to color. Turn them and cook for a further 2–3 minutes. Add the vegetables, garlic paste, lemon juice and water to the pan and cook on a high heat for a minute. The vegetables should still be crunchy. Taste and adjust the seasoning, if necessary; the flavors should be nicely tangy.

Tip into a serving dish and leave to cool, then cover and refrigerate overnight. You can eat this dish chilled, or allow it to return to room temperature. Drizzle with extra-virgin olive oil and serve with Olive Bread and unsalted butter.

SERVES 4 AS A MAIN COURSE OR 8 AS PART OF A MEZZE SELECTION

DOUBLE-COOKED DUCK WITH CINNAMON, HONEY, CARDAMOM AND MASTIC

1 duck
1 tablespoon Cumin Salt (page 21)
¾ cup (200 ml) vegetable oil
Extra-virgin olive oil
Orange blossom water

Poaching Stock
16 cups (4 liters) chicken stock
2 cinnamon sticks
6 star anise pods
8 cardamom pods
1 whole head garlic, cut in half crosswise
⅓ cup (80 ml) honey
15 strands saffron
½ head celery, coarsely chopped
2 medium onions, coarsely chopped
1 leek, white part only, coarsely chopped
1 red bird's-eye chili, cut in half
5 mastic crystals, crushed with
  ½ teaspoon salt
6 extra cardamom pods

Make the Cumin Salt by following the recipe on page 21.

Remove the duck's neck and wing tips and tie its legs together. Pluck out any stubborn feathers. Rub the duck all over with the Cumin Salt and refrigerate overnight.

Put all the Poaching Stock ingredients, except for the mastic crystals and 6 extra cardamom pods, into a large stockpot and bring to a boil. Skim, then cook at a rolling boil for an hour until the stock reduces by a quarter. Strain the stock and add the crushed mastic and 6 more cardamom pods. Bring to a boil and carefully immerse the duck. Cover with a piece of baking paper trimmed to fit and simmer gently for an hour. Don't allow the stock to boil. After an hour, turn off the heat and leave the duck to sit in the hot stock for 5 minutes before taking it out and draining well. Invert the duck to ensure all the stock drains from its internal cavities. Leave it to dry overnight. The stock can be frozen and reused for poaching. Reserve a little to serve as a gravy with the duck.

When ready to cook, cut the duck into quarters. Preheat the oven to its highest temperature and heat the vegetable oil in a wok or large saucepan to 350°F (180°C) or until a cube of bread sizzles to the surface. Put the duck in the oil, skin side down, and cook until golden brown, shaking the pan gently to make sure the duck is covered in oil. It should take around 4–5 minutes to cook. Remove and drain briefly on paper towels.

Place the duck on a baking tray, dust with a little extra Cumin Salt and drizzle with a little extra-virgin olive oil. Put in the oven for 2 minutes until the oil starts to sizzle. Remove from the oven and splash on orange blossom water to taste.

Serve with Jewelled Cracked Wheat Pilaf (page 89) or a saffron pilaf. Warm a little of the stock to serve as a gravy.

SERVES 4

SPICY CHICKEN BAKED IN MOUNTAIN BREAD WITH SPINACH, CHICKPEAS AND PINE NUTS
musakhan

This dish is based on a Bedouin recipe, in which chickens are cooked on bread with lots of sumac and bitter wild greens. The idea is to eat the juice-soaked bread with the chicken—you'll definitely get your hands dirty.

2½ tablespoons olive oil

2 onions, finely grated

2 cloves garlic, finely chopped

1 teaspoon ground cinnamon

1 teaspoon ground nutmeg

1½ teaspoons ground sumac

3 bunches spinach leaves, blanched, squeezed and chopped

1 cup (150 g) cooked or canned chickpeas

1½ cups (300 ml) chicken stock

Juice of ½ lemon

1 cup (150 g) toasted pine nuts, coarsely crushed

4 large square pieces of mountain bread

Extra-virgin olive oil

Salt and pepper to taste

Spicy chicken

4 whole chicken legs

2 cloves garlic, crushed with ½ teaspoon salt

½ teaspoon ground cinnamon

½ teaspoon ground cumin

½ teaspoon freshly ground black pepper

2 tablespoons olive oil

Cut through the meat of the chicken legs to expose the thigh and leg bones. This will help them cook more quickly. Mix together the garlic paste, spices and olive oil and rub all over the chicken. Leave in a cool place to marinade for 1–2 hours.

Heat the oil in a large non-stick skillet and sauté the onions and garlic until they are soft and the liquid has evaporated. Add the spices and stir in well. Add the chopped spinach to the pan, then the chickpeas. Use a fork to lightly crush the chickpeas, then add half of the stock. Turn up the heat and boil for about 5 minutes, or until the stock has evaporated. Remove from the heat and add the lemon juice and pine nuts. Leave to cool, then refrigerate until needed.

When ready to cook, preheat the oven to 400°F (200°C). Cut 4 pieces of baking parchment roughly 1¼ in (3 cm) larger than the squares of mountain bread. Lay them on the work surface and place the bread on top. Spoon a dollop of spinach mixture onto the center of each piece of bread and place a chicken leg (maryland) on top.

Gather the edges of the paper (and bread) together above the chicken and tie with kitchen string so you have a little bag. Place on a baking tray and cover with foil to stop the paper getting crisp and the string from burning. Cook for 20 minutes. Carefully open the bag and check that the chicken is firm to touch. If necessary cook for a further 10 minutes.

Meanwhile, tip the remaining spinach mixture into a pot with the remaining chicken stock. Add a splash of extra-virgin olive oil and season with salt and pepper. Cook for 10 minutes on a gentle heat.

Present individual parcels for each person to unwrap at the table, and serve with bowls of the spinach stew.

SERVES 4

THE ARMENIAN INFLUENCE

MEAT AND GAME

IN THE DAWN LIGHT OUR VILLA AT LATTAKIA looked no more welcoming than it had the night before. The first glimmers of daylight threw the charmless place into stark relief, and even at this early hour the air smelt of rotting fish. Across the cold grey sands, past the mounds of driftwood and rubbish, a small group of men sat huddled around a charcoal brazier warming their hands and drinking tea. Lattakia was a miserable place and it was time to move on.

Things improved immediately once we hit the road, and as the port town's outskirts fell away behind us, so did our black mood. The drive north-east to Aleppo took us through hills thickly covered with oaks and pines, and past ancient olive groves that stretched far into the distant north to Turkey. Rivers and lakes watered lush valleys, and the fertile central plains of northern Syria were dotted with cherry orchards, their branches a fluffy mass of pink and white blossom.

We reached Aleppo with a renewed sense of optimism, cheered by the day's warm sunshine. Our hotel had been recommended to us and after negotiating our way through the narrow traffic-filled streets, we found it tucked away at the end of a laneway on the edge of the Old City. El Mandaloun was a delightful boutique hotel in a converted seventeenth-century merchant house, its rooms arranged in two storeys around a tranquil courtyard. Our rooms were an Orientalist's dream come true: the exquisite antique tiles were cool underfoot, ornately carved wooden shutters opened onto the courtyard below, and the wrought-iron beds were made up with crisp white linen and locally woven silk bedspreads. It was all we could do to drag ourselves away from the bliss of it all, but the lure of Aleppo's famous souks was stronger.

The hotel was located near Jdeideh, Aleppo's Armenian quarter, an area of flag-stoned laneways and honey-colored merchant houses. Intricately carved wooden balconies jutted out above the street and the metal signs of exotically named restaurants swung gently overhead. Central courtyards are a characteristic feature of Arab architecture, and every now and then an open doorway offered a tantalising glimpse of a secret world: a tinkling fountain and vine-laden trellises, a brief flash of colored robes as a young woman flitted behind half-open shutters, an old man snoozing in the sunshine and a skinny cat darting into the shadows.

Aleppo is Syria's second-largest city, and it has been a trading center since ancient times. Its history is drenched in blood, as its strategic position on the timeworn trade route between the Mediterranean and Asia made it subject to a series of invasions: Hittites, Egyptians, Assyrians, Persians, Greeks, Romans, Byzantines, Arabs, Mongols and Ottomans all seized Aleppo, practising increasingly monstrous acts of violence upon each other.

Today, most trading activity centers around the souks, as it has done for centuries. The rambling rabbit-warren of laneways and covered alleys extend through the Old City to the foot of Aleppo's great citadel, and before long our noses led us through the "meat quarter" to a shawarma stand. Clouds of garlic-scented smoke billowed out from the griddle and a queue of customers stood eagerly waiting for their lunch. Another vendor offered toshka, Armenian toasted cheese sandwiches made from puffy rounds of Arabic bread. Opposite, a man dished up steaming bowls of foul medames, a peasant dish of broad beans that is popular in many Middle Eastern countries. The Aleppan version was delicately spiced with red peppers as well as cumin, garlic and lemon.

And then we were in the souks, a whirling profusion of chaos and color under a high, vaulted corrugated-iron roof. Jostling crowds thronged past us, pushing in all directions. Young boys with trays of pastries balanced on their heads ducked neatly past groups of chattering *chador*-clad women; housewives fingered their way through mounds of lacy underwear and haggled over the price of soap powder; a shrunken old man pushed a donkey and cart piled high with scrap metal; and a teenager sorted

through a huge pile of pumpkin seeds. As one, and from all sides, shopkeepers urged us to inspect their goods. Did we want fresh dates or sheep's intestines? What about a very nice tablecloth?

"Come my friend. You are welcome in my shop!"

"You speak English? Come, I make you coffee."

"You want carpet. I have very good quality. You come on magic carpet ride with me!" This last uttered with a cheeky grin.

We stumbled out into the sunlight, blinking, to find we'd been deposited at the foot of the citadel that dominates the city of Aleppo. It rises high on a natural mound at the east of the souk and measures a staggering hundred and sixty-four feet (fifty meters) from the depths of the moat that surrounds it to the tip of the minaret on its peak. We strolled open-mouthed beneath the massive portal and wound our way along a dog's leg of dimly lit passages, through soaring stone chambers to the summit. It was curiously quiet above the relentless activity of the street life below and we paused for moment gazing out through the ramparts upon a montage of rooftops, minarets and domes, and

مقددات زينو

there in the distance, just beyond the edge of the city, gently belching factory chimneys.

"Come on. We're on a mission," announced Greg. We were off to visit one of Aleppo's famed sausage-makers. Many of these are Armenian, grandchildren of those refugees who survived the genocide committed against them by the Turks more than a century ago. Along with other minority Christian groups, Armenians were driven out of Anatolia and many thousands found refuge in Syria.

It is the Armenian influence that is responsible for the very different kind of flavorings found in Aleppan food. In particular, they make liberal use of dried ground red peppers—milder than chili peppers, but hotter than paprika—which add an exciting piquancy to many dishes. The city's Armenian butchers are famous for their small goods, in particular, bastourma and soujok. The former is a kind of pastrami—air-dried beef that is coated in a thick fenugreek spice paste. Soujok are highly spiced beef or lamb sausages, usually cut into chunks and fried, often with an egg on the side.

Nizar Abdou, the chef at the highly regarded Yasmeen restaurant in Jdeideh, had given Greg directions to his preferred butcher. We had no name, but a series of directions:

past the Planet Hotel … second set of traffic lights … petrol station on the right … take the one-way street … It wasn't promising, but somehow we ended up outside the front of the Awajet al Joub butcher, admiring the mounds of sausages strung up in the window. To the amusement of Zeno and Mahmoud the butchers, Greg was in heaven. They offered us tastes of bastourma and soujok at varying stages of maturity, and we also sampled an interesting kind of mortadella sausage made from chicken and stuffed with pistachio nuts.

Later than evening we ate at Beit Wakil, one of several old Arabic houses in the Armenian quarter that have been converted to restaurants and which had come highly recommended. As with many of the old merchant houses in Jdeideh, Beit Wakil is built on top of a series of stone cellars that run in an interconnecting labyrinth beneath the entire quarter. In addition to serving as a cool store, legend has it that they were also used as a place of hiding by Christian families fleeing from Arab persecution. Today they serve a more prosaic function, typically being converted into cosy bars where you can enjoy a weak Syrian beer before dinner or a fat post-prandial cigar.

Beit Wakil's building dates back to the sixteenth century and it has been immaculately and faithfully restored. The restaurant is hidden away down a narrow winding alley and from the front it is little more than a simple wooden door set into a tall stone wall. Inside, however, is a wealth of exquisite detail, from the arched Arab windows and their intricate laced stonework to the geometric marble floor tiles, and its courtyard dining area is perfumed with the seductive scent of jasmine and citrus blossom.

The menu offered plenty of Aleppan specialties. We tried a version of muhammara, a dip made from finely crushed walnuts and red peppers with a splash of tangy pomegranate molasses, as well as that curious mortadella-style sausage. Greg went into raptures over a lamb's tongue salad that came finely shredded with tangy pickles, parsley and tomato, and we both worked our way through Aleppan-style kibbeh nayee, which had a definite crunch from the bulgur or cracked wheat and a big chili and cumin hit—quite different from the Lebanese version. Next came a za'atar salad made from fresh wild thyme topped with shredded, mildly salty cheese, and soujok roulo—a kind of bread pinwheel spread with spicy soujok sausage. The only disappointment of the evening was that Aleppos's famous cherry kebabs were not in season, but we made do with another speciality of the house, lamb kebab al chama.

By now the restaurant was filling up and a short man with carefully styled hair got up to sing a repertoire that was restricted to old Nat King Cole numbers. It was our cue to head for bed.

LEMONY LAMB KEBABS

1¾ lbs (800 g) boneless lamb leg meat
2 purple onions, cut into large dice
Salt to taste
Squeeze of lemon juice

Marinade
Grated rind of 1 lemon
¼ teaspoon black peppercorns, finely
　crushed
½ teaspoon coriander seeds, finely
　crushed
1 clove garlic, crushed with ½ teaspoon
　salt
2 tablespoons olive oil

Combine the Marinade ingredients in a shallow dish. Cut the lamb into ¾-in (2-cm) cubes and add to the Marinade. Toss so the meat is well coated, cover and leave to marinade for at least 1 hour.

　When ready to cook, heat your barbecue or griddle pan as high as possible. Put 4 pieces of lamb on each skewer, alternating with pieces of onion. You should allow 2 skewers per person. Season very lightly with salt. Put the skewers on the barbecue or griddle pan and cook for a couple of minutes, turning from time to time, so they cook evenly and the onions start to caramelize. Just before removing them from the heat, squeeze on the lemon juice.

　Serve, Arabic style, in warm pocket bread with chopped tomatoes, onions, parsley and a dusting of sumac.

SERVES 4

DOUBLE LAMB CUTLETS WITH ALEPPO-STYLE SOUR CHERRY SAUCE

In spring, the northern part of Syria is covered with the white blossom of sour cherry trees. The fruit often features in dishes from this part of the world, and a meatball dish served in a sour cherry sauce is particularly renowned. This recipe is our interpretation, but it uses thick double lamb cutlets instead of ground lamb, which can be quite fatty. The addition of cream is, of course, utterly unconventional, but it creates a delicately sweet-sour sauce that is delicious. You need only some buttered rice as an accompaniment.

½ teaspoon ground cumin
½ teaspoon ground cinnamon
¼ teaspoon ground white pepper
4 extra thick lamb cutlets
Salt to taste
3 tablespoons olive oil

Sour cherry sauce
1 tablespoon olive oil
3 shallots, finely sliced
1 clove garlic, finely chopped
8 sour cherries, soaked in a little water
　for 1 hour
¾ cup (200 ml) chicken stock
¼ cup (60 ml) heavy cream
Juice of ½ lemon
⅓ cup (12 g) mint leaves, finely shredded

To make the Sour Cherry Sauce, heat the oil in a small non-stick skillet and sauté the shallots and garlic until they soften. Add the cherries and their soaking water to the pan with the chicken stock. Cover the pan and simmer very gently for 30–45 minutes, until the cherries begin to break down in the liquid. Once the cherries are very soft, remove the lid and raise the temperature. Bubble vigorously until most of the stock has evaporated and you are left with a thick sauce.

　Mix the spices together. Season the lamb cutlets with salt, then dust them lightly with the spice mix. Heat the oil in a large heavy-based skillet and cook the cutlets for 2 minutes on each side for medium–rare. Remove the lamb from the pan and leave it in a warm place to rest while you finish the sauce. Add the Sour Cherry Sauce to the pan with the cream and lemon juice. Simmer gently for a few moments, then stir through the mint leaves and pour over the cutlets as you serve them.

SERVES 4

SLOW-ROASTED LAMB WITH RED PEPPER AND POMEGRANATE PASTE

This dish was inspired by the popular muhammara dip from Aleppo.

5 lbs (2½ kgs) leg of lamb, bone-in

Red pepper and pomegranate paste
3 cloves garlic, peeled
1 small red bird's-eye chili, deseeded
1 teaspoon salt
½ teaspoon white peppercorns, crushed
1 tablespoon Red Pepper Paste
   (page 104)
3 tablespoons pomegranate molasses
2 tablespoons olive oil
1 teaspoon honey
½ cup (125 ml) cold water

Make the Red Pepper Paste by following the recipe on page 104.

To make the Red Pepper and Pomegranate Paste, crush the garlic and chili with the salt to a smooth paste. Pound the white peppercorns to a coarse powder and mix with the garlic and chili. Stir in the Red Pepper Paste, molasses, oil, honey and water. Rub the paste all over the lamb and leave to rest at room temperature for a couple of hours.

When ready to cook, preheat the oven to the highest temperature. Place the lamb in a roasting tray and put it in the oven. Cook for 15 minutes, then lower the temperature to 320°F (160°C). Roast for a further 15 minutes for each 1 lb (500 g) weight to cook the lamb pink. (Increase the cooking time to 20–25 minutes for each 1 lb (500 g) for better-cooked lamb.) When cooked, remove from the oven, cover loosely with foil and leave to rest for 20 minutes before carving. Serve drizzled with some of the pan juices.

SERVES 4–6

SLOW-COOKED SWEET AND SOUR LAMB *lahm bil khall*

This is a wonderfully rich and tasty dish to make in the early autumn when tomatoes are still plentiful, although it is just as good with canned tomatoes. This style of sweet and sour braise is popular throughout the Arab world. In Lebanon, it would usually be eaten with a cracked-wheat pilaf, but if you want to further the Arab theme serve it with saffron rice.

4–6 lamb chops
Flour, for dusting
3 tablespoons olive oil
8 pearl onions, halved and peeled
2 cloves garlic, finely chopped
⅓ cup (90 ml) white wine or cider
   vinegar
1 teaspoon sugar
One 14-oz/400-g can whole tomatoes
1⅔ cups (400 ml) vegetable or chicken
   stock
Few sprigs of thyme
1 teaspoon ground coriander
¼ teaspoon ground allspice
1 cup (150 g) cooked or canned
   chickpeas

Dust the lamb chops with the flour. Heat the oil in a large heavy-based casserole dish. Brown the chops all over, then remove them from the pan. Add the onions and garlic and stir them around in the oil for a few minutes, then raise the heat and add the vinegar and sugar. Let it bubble vigorously for a few minutes, then lower the heat and return the chops to the pan with the tomatoes, stock, herbs and spices. Stir well, then cover the pan, lower the heat and leave to simmer very gently for 1–1½ hours. About 10 minutes before the end of the cooking time, add the chickpeas.

SERVES 4

LAMB SHAWARMA

We can't count the number of times we cook this dish. It's a fail-safe dinner-party special, and popular at family get-togethers. It's best—and most authentically Middle Eastern—when cooked on a solid fuel barbecue (a Weber is ideal). The aroma of spiced meat grilling on charcoal never fails to send us both off into a souk-reverie! If you debone and butterfly the leg, it reduces the cooking time, and when you carve the meat you end up with thin strips of pink lamb—rather like a doner kebab—which makes it even more Middle Eastern. Serve with a soft herb salad, a bowl of labneh or tahini-yogurt sauce and plenty of warm Arabic bread so that people can roll their own pita sandwiches. For a slightly more formal meal, serve it with a big bowl of Lebanese Nut Rice (page 88).

1 leg of lamb (about 5 lbs/2½ kgs)
Spicy Marinade (page 21)
Lebanese Nut Rice (page 88)

Make the Spicy Marinade and Lebanese Nut Rice by following the recipes on pages 21 and 88.

Stab the meat all over with the tip of a sharp knife and place the lamb in a shallow dish or plastic container that it will fit into snugly. Pour over the Spicy Marinade and use your hands to rub it in well. Cover, refrigerate and leave to marinade overnight or up to 2 days.

When ready to cook, light your barbecue or heat your oven broiler to its highest temperature. The lamb takes about 45 minutes to 1 hour to cook medium-rare. Leave it to rest for 15 minutes before serving.

SERVES 6

SLOW-COOKED VEAL SHANKS WITH GIANT COUSCOUS AND WINTER VEGETABLES

A truly great, all-in-one winter dish.

⅓ cup (100 ml) olive oil
12 pearl onions, peeled and left whole
3 sticks celery, cut into ¼-in (5-mm) cubes
2 medium carrots, cut into ¼-in (5-mm) cubes
8 baby turnips, trimmed
3 cloves garlic, finely chopped
1 teaspoon cumin
1 teaspoon cinnamon
½ teaspoon freshly ground black pepper
1 tablespoon ground ginger
Salt and pepper to taste
1⅓ cups (200 g) flour
4 veal shanks
One 14-oz/400-g can chopped tomatoes

1 cup (150 g) cooked or canned chickpeas
4 cups (1 liter) chicken stock
1¼ cups (300 ml) white wine
¾ cup (150 g) uncooked moghrabieh (giant couscous)
1 cup (250 ml) water
⅓ cup (12 g) mint leaves
2 tablespoons blanched grated orange rind
2 tablespoons blanched grated lemon rind

Preheat the oven to 325°F (170°C). Heat half the oil in a large skillet. Sauté the vegetables and garlic gently until soft, but not colored, then sprinkle on the cumin, cinnamon and pepper and cook for a few more minutes, turning the vegetables well so that everything is nicely coated. Transfer the vegetables to a heavy-based casserole dish.

Mix the ginger, salt and pepper with the flour and dust the veal shanks thoroughly. Heat the remaining oil in the skillet and brown the shanks all over, two at a time. Place them on top of the sautéed vegetables in the casserole dish. Add the tomatoes, chickpeas and stock. Deglaze the skillet with the wine, simmer to reduce a little and then pour it into the casserole. Cover and cook in the oven for 1½–2 hours.

Put the moghrabieh in a saucepan with the water and bring to a boil. Lower the heat and simmer for 15 minutes until tender. Add the moghrabieh to the casserole about halfway through the cooking time.

When ready to serve, finely chop the mint leaves and mix with the citrus rind. Sprinkle over the shanks as you serve them.

SERVES 4

RABBIT HOTPOT WITH BLACK PEPPER, GINGER AND CINNAMON

2 farmed rabbits*

3 tablespoons olive oil

16 small tomatoes, halved

2 purple onions, cut into large dice

1 teaspoon coriander seeds, roasted and
    lightly crushed

2 lemon quarters

Few sprigs of thyme

2 tablespoons sherry

1 cup (250 ml) chicken stock

Marinade

2 teaspoons black peppercorns

2 cloves garlic, peeled

1 teaspoon coarse salt

1 teaspoon ground cinnamon

1 teaspoon ground ginger

2 tablespoons olive oil

Garnish

1 cup (150 g) blanched almonds

$\frac{1}{3}$ cup (80 ml) olive oil

$\frac{1}{2}$ cup (25 g) coriander leaves (cilantro),
    shredded

* *Make sure that you buy farmed
rabbits for this dish, as the wild ones
are much leaner and have a tendency
to dry out more quickly and become
tough.*

To make the Marinade, put the peppercorns into a mortar and grind to a coarse powder. Tip out and reserve. Next, put the garlic and salt into the mortar and pound to a smooth paste. Return the pepper to the mortar with the cinnamon, ginger and oil, and mix together well.

Remove the kidneys and fat from the rabbits and cut into pieces. Pour on the Marinade and rub well into all the rabbit pieces. Cover and refrigerate for 6–8 hours.

Preheat the oven to 400°F (200°C). Heat the oil in a large heavy-based casserole dish. Add the rabbit pieces and fry until colored all over. Add the tomatoes, onion, thyme and coriander seeds to the pot and stir well. Squeeze the lemon quarters and toss them into the pot as well. Add the sherry and bubble briefly on a high heat. Add the stock and bring to a boil. Cover the casserole dish and cook in the oven for 30 minutes.

Towards the end of the cooking time, fry the almonds in the oil until golden brown—be careful not to burn them.

To serve, garnish each portion with a sprinkle of fried almonds and coriander leaves.

SERVES 4

VENISON SHISH KEBABS WITH SYRIAN DESERT TRUFFLES AND PURPLE ONIONS

It was desert truffle season during our visit to Syria and they appeared on menus all over the country.

2 cups (500 ml) water

$\frac{1}{3}$ cup (100 ml) dry white wine

2 tablespoon extra-virgin olive oil

Juice of 1 lemon

2 cloves garlic, peeled and smashed

3 sprigs thyme

Pinch of salt

8 Syrian desert truffles or fresh
    portobello mushrooms

$1\frac{3}{4}$ lbs (800 g) venison topside, round
    or rump

$\frac{1}{2}$ teaspoon ground cumin

$\frac{1}{2}$ teaspoon ground cinnamon

$\frac{1}{4}$ teaspoon ground white pepper

2 purple onions, cut into large dice

3 tablespoons olive oil

Salt to taste

Squeeze of lemon juice

To prepare the truffles, put the water, wine, oil, lemon juice, garlic, thyme and salt into a saucepan and bring to a boil. Drop in the truffles and bring back to a boil. Remove from the heat and leave the truffles to sit in the hot stock for 10 minutes. When cool enough to handle, cut each truffle in half.

Cut the meat into $\frac{3}{4}$-in (2-cm) cubes and put it into a large mixing bowl. Mix together the cumin, cinnamon and white pepper and sprinkle over the venison. Toss to coat evenly.

When ready to cook, heat your barbecue or griddle pan as high as possible. Put 4 pieces of lamb on each skewer, alternating with pieces of onion and truffle. You should allow 2 skewers per person. Brush them with oil and season very lightly with salt. Put the skewers on the barbecue or griddle pan and cook for a couple of minutes, turning them from time to time so they cook evenly and the onions start to caramelize. Just before removing them from the heat, squeeze on the lemon juice.

Serve, Arabic style, in warm pocket bread with chopped tomatoes, onions, parsley and a dusting of sumac.

SERVES 4

THE DAILY KHOBZ

BREADS

THE NEXT DAY WE BREAKFASTED ON POACHED FRUIT, warm Arabic bread, fresh curd cheese, boiled eggs and tiny cups of thick bitter coffee before heading out into the brilliant early-morning sunshine.

The streets were coming to life as shop owners banged open their doors and shutters, ready for the day's trading. We squeezed our way between a street vendor wheeling his load of roasted black and red pumpkin seeds and a teenage boy squeezing fresh orange juice into plastic glasses with great aplomb. All around us stallholders were heaving crates of produce into position, trimming vegetables and arranging displays of strawberries, artichokes, green almonds and tiny broad beans. The ka'ak man was doing a brisk trade selling the popular sesame-encrusted breakfast breads, and from a nearby pastry shop a steady stream of men in business suits emerged clutching sticky cheese-stuffed pastries.

We turned into Al-Hattab Square and immediately spotted a long queue of people lined up along a wall. A bearded face appeared at a small window, followed by a hand thrusting a stack of Arab bread at the closest customer. An old man wearing long robes and a *keffiyeh* carefully slid his bundle into a shopping bag, strapped it onto the back of his bicycle and pedalled away. Another threw his pile deftly across a park bench like a casino croupier dealing a hand of poker. And all the while, the queue got longer. We were intrigued.

We knocked on the back door and were invited in to look around. Inside it was hotter than hell and the constant roar and clatter of machinery was almost unbearable. A

conveyor belt ran around the edge of the small room, delivering flat rounds of dough into the mouth of a roaring inferno which was fed by a massively muscled man shovelling coal into its depths. Another conveyor belt carried the cooked breads, puffed up like golden balloons, to their final destination, where they dropped over the edge and down onto the filthy floor.

Ahmad Hadi, the chief baker, paused to wipe the sweat from his brow. "This is nothing," he said to us between gasps. "You should see how hot it gets in summer. It reaches 56 degrees in here."

Ahmad's bakery is something of an institution in the Jdeideh neighborhood, and several generations of bakers have supplied locals with their daily khobz. Ahmad told us that they churn out around ten thousand rounds of bread on a typical day.

"Why does the bread drop on the floor?" we asked him.

"To flatten it." He smacked his hands together. "It has to cool down for a few moments, too. If you put it in a plastic bag when it is too hot, it becomes sticky."

We could bear the terrible heat and noise no longer so left them to it. As we departed, Ahmad thrust a package into our hands and we sat for a while in the middle of Al-Hattab Square in the sunshine, chewing on the warm, yeasty bread.

AROUND THE EDGE OF THE SMALL ROOM, A CONVEYOR BELT DELIVERED LITTLE BLOBS OF DOUGH INTO THE GAPING MOUTH OF A ROARING INFERNO.

Greg had spotted a curious little shop on the edge of the souk where they made kataifi pastry, and we went to watch the mesmerising process. First, a youth dropped a runny slop of white pastry dough into a wide triangular funnel that was positioned above a cast-iron griddle plate. This rotated and a neat pattern of concentric pastry circles formed within seconds upon its heated surface. Another lad deftly gathered the pastry strands together to form a long skein of pastry that was then twisted and stacked with others onto a tray ready to be dispatched to pastry shops around the neighborhood.

Ready for a break from food, Amal and I decided to take ourselves off to the fifteenth-century Hammam Yalbougha al-Nasry, one of Syria's most famous bath houses. Bath houses in the Middle East are strictly segregated, but luckily it was a "women's day", so we purchased our "all-inclusive" ticket and entered an extraordinary medieval world of stone and steam.

We walked through a labyrinth of dimly lit passages, getting hotter and hotter, until finally we reached the hellish steam rooms where we could dimly make out a couple of large women, flopped naked on the marble floor. We lay near them in a stupor, gazing through the impenetrable fug towards a tiny shaft of light in the high domed ceiling. Then someone grabbed my hand and I was led back through the gloom to a massage room where two women in wet petticoats pushed me down onto the slippery tiled floor, pummelled and prodded me and threw cold water in my face. Next, they briskly washed my hair and body with Syrian bay-leaf soap while crooning ancient lullabies in my ear. The encounter ended with the traditional three kisses and I was sent on my way.

Amal and I met up again in the rest area, where we collapsed in nervous exhaustion, puce in the face. All around us, groups of women and children were singing, dancing and clapping their hands. Most of them had brought a picnic and sat munching on chicken wings or sipping glasses of mint tea. We watched, fascinated, as a young Muslim woman got dressed. On went a lacy red bra and G-string; next, a nylon tracksuit and her *chador* robes; finally, a long belted raincoat and *hijab*.

"Forgive us for asking," we ventured, "but don't you get very hot in all those clothes?"

She sighed in exasperation. "Of course I do. But we have to wear it. It is what our husbands wish." She hesitated and then grinned cheekily at us. "As you see, what I wear underneath is my own business."

A NEAT PATTERN OF CONCENTRIC PASTRY CIRCLES FORMED WITHIN SECONDS UPON ITS HEATED SURFACE.

MANOUSHI BREAD DOUGH

Manoushi bread is the number one snack food all around Lebanon and Syria. Essentially, it is a sort of pizza although a little bit softer and more chewy than the Italian version. Use this dough as the base for any of the toppings suggested in the following chapter. Having tested numerous bread doughs, in all sorts of ovens and on all sorts of baking sheets, the one thing we can say with certainty is that this style of Middle Eastern flat bread is immeasurably improved by baking on a hot stone. Most kitchenware stores stock them—they're often called pizza stones. They're not expensive, and if your family are pizza fans they're especially well worth the investment.

2⅓ cups (355 g) flour
1 teaspoon dried yeast
½ teaspoon salt
¾ teaspoon sugar
¾ cup (175–200 ml) warm water
1 tablespoon extra-virgin olive oil

Sift the flour into a large mixing bowl and add the yeast and salt. Dissolve the sugar in the warm water and dribble it into the dry ingredients until they absorb enough to make a sticky dough. How much water is required will entirely depend upon your flour. Mix in the olive oil and use your hands—or the dough hook on your electric mixer—to knead the dough until it is smooth and silky. It will take about 10 minutes. Lightly oil the ball of dough and put it into a bowl. Cover and leave in a warm place to rise for 2 hours, by which time it should have at least doubled in size.

Knock the air out of the dough, then tip it out onto a floured work surface. Cut the dough into 12 portions, then lightly flour each one and put them on a tray, covered, for another 10 minutes. When ready to cook, roll each portion out to a 6-in (15-cm) circle and cover with the topping of your choice (pages 216–8).

MAKES 12 ROUNDS

ANISEED BREAD WITH WILD FIGS

We came across a number of different versions of hard aniseed breads in bakeries around Syria. This is our interpretation, and although quite different, it is utterly delicious—a hint of sweetness from the aniseed and figs, a lovely crumbly texture and melting crust. The bread is wonderful when it's served warm from the oven with lashings of cold unsalted butter or a dollop of tart jam, and it works equally well with the savory flavors of creamy blue cheese, Brie, a strong Cheddar with bite—or, if you want to stay Middle Eastern, a sharp, salty feta.

¾ tablespoon dry yeast
Pinch of sugar
¾ cup (180 ml) warm water
1⅓ cups (260 g) semolina
1½ cups (225 g) flour
1 tablespoon aniseed seeds, plus extra
   to sprinkle on top
1 tablespoon sesame seeds, plus extra to
   sprinkle on top
Dried wild figs, stalks removed and diced
½ teaspoon salt
¾ cup (180 ml) olive oil
1 egg, lightly beaten
1 egg yolk
1 tablespoon water

Dissolve the yeast and sugar in ⅔ cup (140 ml) of the warm water and set aside for 10 minutes until it begins to froth.

In a large mixing bowl, combine the semolina, flour, aniseed, sesame seeds, dried figs and salt, then rub in the oil. Stir the egg into the dry ingredients. Pour on the frothy yeast and use your hands to bring the mixture together to form a dough. Add the remaining warm water—plus a little more, if necessary. The dough should be firm, and not wet or sticky.

Use your hands or the dough hook on an electric mixer to knead the dough vigorously for 10 minutes, until it is smooth and shiny. Lightly oil the ball of dough and put it into a bowl. Cover and leave in a warm place to rise for 2 hours, by which time it should have doubled in size.

Knock the dough back, then shape it into a round that measures roughly 8 x 1¼ in (20 x 3 cm) and put it on a lightly oiled baking sheet. Whisk together the egg yolk and water and brush the top of the loaf. Sprinkle on ½ teaspoon aniseed and 1 teaspoon sesame seeds and leave in a warm place for another 45 minutes.

Preheat the oven to 400°F (200°C) and bake the bread for 20–30 minutes, until it is a lovely golden brown. It should sound hollow when you tap the bottom. Transfer to a wire rack and leave until completely cool before eating—if you can resist!

MAKES 1 LOAF

PULL-APART CHEESE BREAD DINNER ROLLS

Bread that's still warm from the oven is a real crowd-pleaser, particularly when it's full of softly melting cheese. Pop it in the middle of the table for everyone to pull apart.

Yogurt Bread Dough (recipe below)
½ cup (100 g) grated haloumi or mozzarella
3 tablespoons grated parmesan
1 teaspoon dried mint leaves
Olive oil

Make the Yogurt Bread Dough by following the recipe below.

After the bread has finished proving for the first 2 hours, knock it back and knead in the cheeses and dried mint leaves.

Preheat the oven to its highest temperature. Divide the dough into 12–14 walnut-sized balls and arrange them in rows on a greased baking tray. As they prove again, they will puff up and merge into one another. Brush with olive oil before baking for 15–20 minutes.

Tip onto a wire rack to cool slightly before serving.

MAKES 12–14 ROLLS

YOGURT BREAD DOUGH

A versatile dough that we use for making Olive Bread (recipe below), Pull-Apart Cheese Bread Dinner Rolls (recipe above) and Lebanon's famous lamb pizzas, Lahm bi Ajine (page 220).

2 cups (300 g) flour
½ teaspoon salt
¾ teaspoon sugar
1 tablespoon dried yeast
3 tablespoons warm water
⅔ cup (150 g) plain yogurt
3 tablespoons extra-virgin olive oil

Sift the flour into a large mixing bowl and add the salt. Dissolve the sugar and yeast in the warm water. In another small bowl, whisk together the yogurt and olive oil.

Pour the bubbling yeast into the flour with the yogurt mix. Knead for about 10 minutes, until the dough is smooth and silky. Lightly oil the ball of dough and put it into a bowl. Cover and leave in a warm place to rise for 2 hours, by which time it should have at least doubled in size

Knock the air out of the dough then tip it out onto a floured work surface. Proceed according to which recipe you are making.

OLIVE BREAD

Yogurt Bread Dough (recipe above)
½ cup (150 g) chopped green olives
1 teaspoon fresh thyme leaves
½ teaspoon dried chili flakes (optional)
Olive oil

Make the Yogurt Bread Dough by following the recipe above.

After the bread has finished proving for the first 2 hours, knock it back and knead in the olives, thyme and chili flakes.

Preheat the oven to 400°F (200°C). Shape the dough into a round and place on a greased baking tray. Leave in a warm place for another 45 minutes to prove again. Brush with olive oil before baking for 20–30 minutes, until it is golden brown. It should sound hollow when you tap the bottom. Transfer to a wire rack and leave until completely cool before eating.

MAKES 1 LOAF

DESERT KINGDOMS

SAVORY PASTRIES

WE LEFT ALEPPO IN THE STEELY LIGHT OF EARLY MORNING. We had a lot of country to cover before reaching Palmyra, our destination for the night. The suburbs merged into dusty fields, followed by vast plains of young green wheat that stretched out on either side of the road. Even at this early hour, groups of farm workers were busy picking oranges, tossing them straight into the back of waiting trucks. Bedouin women in richly colored peasant dresses were bent over rows of cos lettuces while their children waited nearby, buckets in hand. In the distance, scattered villages of soft cream limestone broke the horizon.

We broke the drive at the Roman ruins of Afamya, on a windswept mound overlooking the al-Ghab plain. Apart from a few cows meandering among its distinctive barley-sugar columns, the site was deserted. We walked the length of the cardo—the main street—guidebook in hand, reading about Afamya's remote history as an important trading post in the Roman Empire and its pre-eminence for breeding horses.

The next leg of our journey took us to Hama, famed for its *norias*, the medieval wooden water wheels which still draw water from the Orontes River to irrigate the surrounding fields. We found this hard to believe, however, as the Orontes was nothing more than a sluggish, muddy dribble. The *norias'* vast creaking wheels made an eerie moan as they turned, their spokes silhouetted starkly against the sky, and two young boys made a show of bravado by leaping into the putrid, litter-choked river.

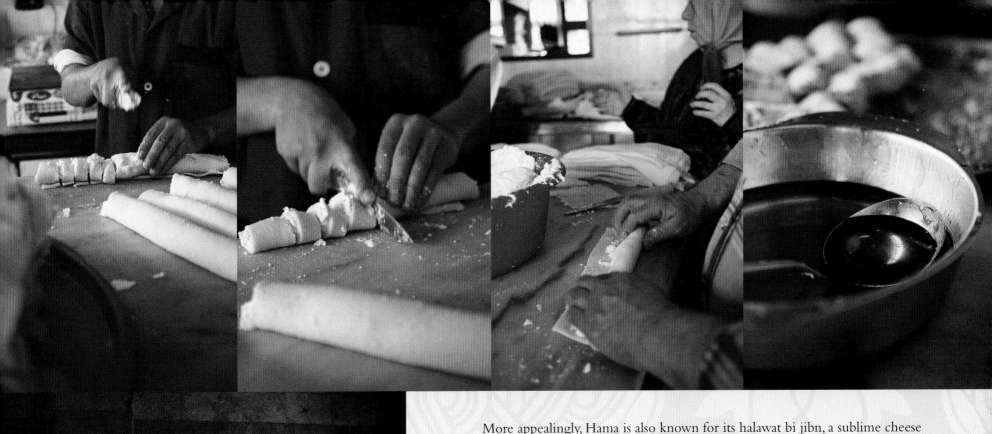

More appealingly, Hama is also known for its halawat bi jibn, a sublime cheese dessert, and our driver had promised we wouldn't be disappointed. We stopped in the centre of town at a busy café, and watched as one of the pastry chefs poured a great molten mass of cheesey-semolina onto a marble bench. He then proceeded to stretch and fold, stretch and fold, all the while sprinkling the mix with a thin, perfumed syrup. The paper-thin "pancakes" were then spread with thick clotted cream and rolled into a long sausage before being briskly cut into thick slices. We bought several portions, and while they were rich and creamy, they weren't as sweet as we feared.

T. E. Lawrence described the Krak des Chevaliers as "the most wholly admirable castle in the world." The well-preserved fortress stands high on a massive outcrop and was strategically built to dominate the Homs Gap, a break in the two mountain ranges that run the north-south length of Syria and Lebanon. From its lofty strategic position the castle controlled the flow of trade between the Mediterranean and inland cities, as well as trade between Asia Minor and the Holy Land.

The first fortress on the site was built in 1030 by the local Emir of Homs, but it was under the Knights Hospitaller that the Krak was expanded and rebuilt to become the largest Crusader castle in the Holy Land, and a key landmark in the territorial aspirations of Christendom.

The knights controlled the castle for 127 years as a garrison, storehouse and monastery, and it withstood repeated sieges and attempts by Muslim armies to take it. Its proud boast is that its defences were never actually breached, but by the late thirteenth century the Crusades had all but failed; Jerusalem was in Mameluke hands and the Christians were retreating. The castle's dénouement was rather sad: when the Mameluke sultan Beybars surrounded the Krak, the knights within it simply gave up, agreeing to leave peacefully. The Mamelukes further strengthened the Krak, but with time its greatness faded.

The day had become overcast by the time we approached the castle and a few drops of rain were falling, but our hearts lifted as it came into view, perched dramatically atop a windswept ridge that dropped away on all sides to the plain below. An incredible relic such as this would be crawling with tourists if it were anywhere else, but as in Lebanon there were surprisingly few other visitors around as we wandered through the inner fortress, passing a *hammam* (bathhouse), kitchens, warehouses and a large vaulted hall. The perimeter walls on the outer ramparts afforded magnificent views of low green hills, where a lone kestrel hovered and swooped, and the snow-tipped peaks of the Anti-Lebanon Mountains in the distance.

The longest section of our drive to Palmyra, the legendary desert kingdom of Queen Zenobia, was still to come. The great Syrian heartland was farmed with olive groves and almond orchards, crops of swiss chard, potatoes and lettuces. Then the fields and their villages of grey stone, each with their own elegant minaret, were replaced by barren wasteland which, in turn, became an endless expanse of scrubby desert.

We reached Palmyra just before sunset and headed straight up to Qala'at ibn Maan, a seventeenth-century citadel on top of a nearby hill. This was the best vantage point to watch the setting sun tinge Palmyra's sprawling ruins with gold.

Palmyra dates back to the second century BC and was once a key staging post for caravans traveling to and from the Mediterranean and along the old Silk Road from China and India to Europe. It was dubbed the city of palms after the Romans conquered Syria and was maintained as a handy outpost and buffer against incursions from the east.

The kingdom's most famous leader was Queen Zenobia, who ruled the desert like an Arab Boadicea, after her husband was assassinated in mysterious circumstances. She was reputed to have been a gifted linguist, politician and warrior, and, naturally, a great beauty, to boot. Ultimately, she was vanquished and carted off to Rome, where according to legend she went on a hunger strike that eventually finished her off.

Suitably impressed by our first sightings of Palmyra we headed to the prosaically named Pancake House in the nearby township, which turned out to be a surprisingly good

choice. Bedouin dishes dominated the menu and we were each presented with a complimentary lentil soup to begin our meal. It was tangy with lemon and fragrant with cinnamon, and just the thing on a cold night. Next we were served mansaf, a lamb and rice dish laden with cardamom, peanuts, almonds and chicken, poached in a light lemony broth with rice on the side.

Everyone we had spoken to had emphasised the importance of seeing the sun rise over Palmyra's ruins, but we were all a little reluctant to commit. It had been a long day and the desert air had made us weary, but the decision was made for me, at least, by the muezzin's call to prayer outside my bedroom window at four-thirty the next morning.

I had romantically imagined small groups of people, united in purpose, heading towards the ancient ruins, but a wonderful stillness pervaded Palmyra at that early hour. A few Bedouin hawkers on ancient motorbikes were getting an early start and one or two tourists were walking ahead of me in the distance.

A Bedouin on a small white camel came over and offered me a camel ride. I

thanked him politely, and told him truthfully that I'd left my money back at the hotel, but after a few minutes he came trotting back. "You come with me. I give you free ride," he insisted after I once again demurred. Was this to be my reward for the early start? He helped me up and tucked himself in behind me, arms clutched just a little too tightly around my waist, and we trotted off to tour the ruins in the peaceful dawn.

After taking me around the impressive amphitheatre and agora and along the vast colonnaded avenue that led to the Temple of Bel, he pulled a mobile telephone from beneath his robes and rang his uncle to say we were coming for tea. As the three of us sat in the shade of an ancient column, sipping on mint tea that was sweet and strong, the Bedouin picked up a lump of honey-colored limestone and rolled it between his hands.

"So many people come to see this place," he said quietly. "It is very magical. Very old. But for you it is a holiday. For us it is life. It is not so special."

With that, he let the stone fall to the ground and a little cloud of dust blew away in the desert air.

MANOUSHI BREAD WITH ZA'ATAR

Manoushi Bread Dough (page 205)
3 tablespoons za'atar
1 tablespoon ground sumac
⅓ cup (100 ml) extra-virgin olive oil

Make the Manoushi Bread Dough by following the recipe on page 205. Preheat the oven to the highest temperature.

Roll the bread out into rounds. Combine the topping ingredients and spread over the Dough. Bake for 3 minutes.

MAKES 12 ROUNDS

MANOUSHI BREAD WITH SPINACH AND CHEESE

Manoushi Bread Dough (page 205)
2 tablespoons olive oil
1 bunch spinach leaves
½ cup (125 g) grated mozzarella
¼ cup (60 g) grated haloumi or parmesan

Make the Manoushi Bread Dough by following the recipe on page 205. Preheat oven to highest temperature.

Heat the olive oil in a large skillet. Add the spinach leaves and stir briefly until wilted. Roll the bread out into rounds. Combine the topping ingredients and spread over the dough. Bake for 3 minutes.

MAKES 12 ROUNDS

MANOUSHI BREAD WITH TWO CHEESES

In Lebanon we ate a version of manoushi using a local cheese—ackawi—a soft, white cow's milk cheese which has a strong flavor, almost like blue cheese. Use any mild blue cheese to achieve a similar effect.

Manoushi Bread Dough (page 205)
Extra-virgin olive oil
⅓ cup (80 g) crumbled mild blue cheese
⅓ cup (80 g) grated mozzarella

Make the Manoushi Bread Dough by following the recipe on page 205. Preheat oven to highest temperature.

Roll the bread out into rounds and brush with olive oil. Combine the two cheeses and scatter over the dough. Bake for 3 minutes.

MAKES 12 ROUNDS

SYRIAN MOUNTAIN BREAD WITH CRUSHED CHILIES, GREEN ONIONS AND CUMIN

Manoushi Bread Dough (page 205)

1/3 cup (100 ml) extra-virgin olive oil

12 red finger-length chilies, deseeded and coarsely chopped

4 green onions (scallions), finely diced

2 leeks, white parts only, finely diced

Juice of 1 lemon

1 teaspoon black cumin seeds

1/2 teaspoon freshly ground black pepper

Sea salt flakes to taste

2 1/2 tablespoons crumbled fresh goat's cheese (optional)

Make the Manoushi Bread Dough by following the recipe on page 205 and leave it to rise for 2 hours in a warm place.

Heat the olive oil in a small saucepan. Add the chilies, onions, leeks and lemon juice. Cook gently for 12–15 minutes, until everything is tender. Add the spices and salt and stir well. Leave to cool and set aside.

Preheat the oven to its highest temperature. Knock the air out of the dough, then tip it out onto a floured work surface. Cut the dough into 10–12 portions, then lightly flour each one and roll it out as thinly as you can. You are aiming for rough circles, around 7 in (18 cm) in diameter. Cook each round on a baking stone for 1–2 minutes until its starts to blister and color slightly. Wrap the breads in a dish towel to keep warm while you bake the rest. When all the breads are ready, smear each with a dollop of the chili mixture. Roll them up and pack them into a baking tray. Warm them through briefly before serving with the goat's cheese, if using.

MAKES 12 ROUNDS

STUFFED LEBANESE PASTRIES WITH GROUND DUCK AND SPINACH *duck fatayer*

Traditionally, these pastries are shaped into a three-sided pyramid, which can be left slightly open at the top to reveal the filling or sealed to make a closed pie.

Dough

2 2/3 cups (400 g) self-raising flour

3 oz (80 g) cold butter, diced

1/2 teaspoon salt

Warm water

1 egg yolk

2 tablespoons water

Filling

3 duck legs, meat removed and ground

4 shallots, finely diced

2 cloves garlic, finely diced

1 Granny Smith apple, grated

1/2 teaspoon ground cinnamon

1/2 teaspoon ground nutmeg

1/2 teaspoon ground ginger

1/2 cup (25 g) coriander leaves (cilantro), finely shredded

1 tablespoon pomegranate molasses

1 bunch spinach leaves, blanched and chopped

1 cup (150 g) fried pine nuts

To make the Dough, put the flour, butter and salt into a food processor. Pulse to form coarse crumbs, then add just enough water to bring it together to a Dough. Tip out and rest for 30 minutes.

Mix the Filling ingredients together in a large mixing bowl.

When ready to make the fatayer, preheat the oven to 400°F (200°C). Divide the Dough into 12 pieces. Flour your work surface and rolling pin, and roll each piece of pastry into a circle around 4 in (10 cm) in diameter. Put a tablespoon of Filling in the center and bring three sides up and over the Filling to form a traditional pyramid shape. Moisten the edges and pinch the sides together to seal. Mix the egg yolk and water together to make an egg wash. Place the pastries on a lightly oiled baking sheet, brush with a little egg wash and bake in the oven for 8–10 minutes, or until golden brown.

MAKES 12 PASTRIES

GROUND LAMB PIZZA *lahm bi ajine*

Don't buy ground lamb from the supermarket for this recipe as it's far too fatty. You don't want the lamb to be too lean, however. Ask the butcher for leg lamb with some fat, but no sinews.

Yogurt Bread Dough (page 206)
½ lb (250 g) ground lamb, not too lean
1 tomato, deseeded and finely diced
1 small purple onion, finely diced
⅓ cup (15 g) flat-leaf parsley leaves, very thinly sliced
1 teaspoon ground allspice
1 red bird's-eye chili, deseeded and finely diced
1 teaspoon pomegranate molasses
Salt and pepper to taste

Make the Yogurt Bread Dough by following the recipe on page 206. Preheat the oven to its highest temperature.

To prepare the filling, place the ground lamb on a large chopping board and put all the other ingredients, except the salt and pepper, on top. Use a large knife to chop and mix everything together until well combined. It should be the consistency of a fine paste. Season with the salt and pepper.

Roll dough out into rounds of 4 in (10 cm) in diameter and brush with olive oil. Smear the mix thinly over the rounds and bake for 3 minutes.

MAKES 12 SMALL PIZZAS

SAMBOUSEK PASTRIES WITH CHEESE AND LEEK

Sambousek are crescent-shaped pastries popular around the Middle East.

⅔ cup (150 g) clarified butter*
3 leeks, white part only, finely diced
2 cloves garlic, finely chopped
¾ cup (200 ml) vegetable or chicken stock
1 bay leaf
½ teaspoon sugar
Salt and pepper to taste
½ cup (100 g) grated haloumi or cheddar
½ cup (100 g) grated mozzarella
1 teaspoon dill, finely chopped
Ground white pepper to taste
8 sheets filo pastry

* *It's important to use clarified butter with pastries. If you use normal butter, the milk solids can burn and you get little black burnt bits on your lovely golden pastries.*

Heat a tablespoon of the clarified butter in a skillet and sauté the leeks and garlic until they soften. Pour in the stock and add the bay leaf, sugar, salt and pepper. Cut out a circle of greaseproof paper that's large enough to cover the leek mixture (this will stop a skin from forming as it slowly cooks down), lower the heat and cook very gently for 25 minutes, until the mixture has reduced down to a melting-soft mass. Remove the pan from the heat, and allow the mixture to cool. When it is completely cool, stir in the cheeses and dill and season lightly with white pepper.

To make the sambousek, work with one sheet of filo at a time, and keep the others covered with a dish towel. Spread out a sheet of filo on the work surface and cut lengthwise into thirds. Each strip will make one sambousek. Take one strip and brush along its length with the clarified butter. Place a tablespoon of the filling across the corner at one end of the pastry. Fold this corner up and over on the diagonal to make a triangle shape. Fold the triangle over, and continue in this fashion along the length of the pastry. You should end up with a neat, triangle-shaped pastry parcel. Seal any open edges with more clarified butter. Repeat with the remaining pastry and filling until you have about 24 sambousek. At this stage you can freeze the pastries if you like; otherwise, cook them immediately.

Preheat the oven to 400°F (200°C). Line a baking tray with baking parchment and arrange the pastries on it. Brush each one again, lightly, with clarified butter then cook for 8 minutes, or until golden brown. Serve them as an appetizer.

MAKES 24 PASTRIES

GARDEN OF THE WORLD

ICE CREAMS AND SORBETS

AFTER THE EMPTY SILENCE OF THE DESERT, the traffic-choked streets of Damascus were an assault on the senses. The traffic was gridlocked, the blaring of horns and screeching brakes was incessant and the acrid clouds of black exhaust fumes made our eyes burn. "*Haram*, I hate this city," muttered our driver. "This is why I do not come here. Every week the traffic gets worse. This is madness." It was a complaint we were to hear frequently over the course of our stay in the Syrian capital. The proprietor of one hotel snorted when we timidly suggested that the traffic in Damascus was even worse than Beirut's. "Beirut!" she exclaimed. "Beirut is a paradise compared with Damascus."

It all seemed a far cry from the city's golden years as the center of the great Umayyad caliphate, when Damascus was known as the "Garden of the World". The faded billboards and modern high-rise office blocks that fringed the traffic-clogged multi-laned carriageway made it hard to believe that the great Barada River once cascaded freely from the nearby mountains to water the city's gardens and to fill its fountains. Or that under the patronage of the caliphs, the world's leading scholars, musicians and artists came to Damascus to study and to teach, while they delighted in its glittering mosaics and ornately carved sandstone palaces.

The jewel in the Ummayad crown was the great mosque, built on the ancient ruins of a Roman Temple of Jupiter. Even today it remains one of the holiest sites in

Islam, second only to Mecca and Medina, and is considered one of the most magnificent buildings of Islam. Its great courtyard, prayer hall, minarets and domes are a felicitous blend of Byzantine, Hellenistic and Arabic construction and decoration.

The mosque borders the eastern end of the Hammadiya souk, the beating heart of Damascus' Old City. We wandered along the souk's great length, stopping to peer through windows laden with gold jewellery or stacked high with bolts of damask cloth. While the Hammadiya souk and its environs are a popular tourist haunt, they are also the main area of local commerce, so amongst the rails of tawdry worry beads and poor-quality leather, you also find all the stuff of daily domestic business, from toys, plastic clothes pegs and hardware to shoes, *hijab* (headscarves) and all manner of ribbons, buttons and bows.

A loud group of giggling Bedouin women pushed past, their faces marked with black tattoos. Through their veils they were licking ice-cream cones from the legendary Bakdach ice-cream parlour, famous all over the Arab world since 1885 for its bouza, a pounded ice cream with an extraordinary elastic texture made with mastic and sahlab, a thickening agent made from the root of an orchid.

We squeezed in at one of the long formica-topped tables opposite a couple of Iraqi truck drivers who were taking spoonfuls of pistachio-topped ice cream from

dainty aluminum bowls. The place was packed with tables of women, young couples, solitary businessmen reading newspapers, large noisy families and darting waiters bearing aloft trays piled high with ice cream. And through the whirr of ceiling fans and the constant hum of Arabic chatter we heard the regular thudding beat of massive wooden mallets pounding ice cream in cold metal tubs.

Mansour Rifai, one of the ice-cream makers, told us that Bakdach pounds its way through ten tonnes of ice cream every week. "In the old days," he explained, "we had to cool the ice cream with ice that was brought down from the mountains. It used to take several hours to freeze a pound (half kilo) of ice cream; now it takes about ten minutes." He introduced us to two ice-cream pounders, who paused from their efforts to show us their hefty wooden mallets before throwing them up in the air for dramatic effect and giving us a cheeky grin as they resumed their labors.

The main Hammadiya souk is surrounded by a maze of tiny alleyways, some of which lead to the Bzouriyya souk—the seed bazaar—where mounds of pistachios, cashews and almonds share space with tubs of glacé fruit, coffee and spices.

Just off the Bzouriyaa souk is the Azem Palace and we wandered into its shady

THROUGH THE WHIRR OF CEILING FANS AND THE CONSTANT HUM OF ARABIC CHATTER WE HEARD THE REGULAR THUDDING BEAT OF MASSIVE WOODEN MALLETS POUNDING ICE CREAM IN COLD METAL TUBS.

garden, away from the maelstrom of the souks. Built in the 1700s as the governor's private residence it has been beautifully restored to show off the distinctive ablaq stonework, banding black basalt and sandstone. The displays inside varied from the fascinating (tiny grains of rice carved with verses from the Koran), to the beautiful (exquisitely inlaid musical instruments) and the downright bizarre (cosy domestic scenes featuring costumed mannequins).

It was now after six o'clock and the square in front of the Ommayad Mosque was sinking into shadow. Plenty of people were out and about and the shops were doing a brisk early-evening trade. We followed a narrow winding street lined with carpet and antique shops that took us to Bab Touma, the city's Christian quarter.

One result of the Syrian government's increased support of entrepreneurship has been the restoration of the Old City's unloved khans—or merchant houses—into upmarket restaurants. We had dinner that night at Elissar, one of the more established of these restaurants and a perennial favorite with politicians, diplomats and tourists. It fills a converted eighteenth-century khan, and has the typical covered central courtyard and over-the-top décor—gaudily tiled walls, wooden panels dripping with gilt and a central marble fountain. It was packed, and customers dressed up in their evening finery were still pouring in when, towards midnight, we made our way back to our hotel in the cool night air.

LEBANESE LEMONADE SORBET

10 whole lemons
¾ cup (150 g) superfine (caster) sugar
2 cups (500 ml) water
1 tablespoon Turkish apple tea
    (optional)
Splash orange blossom water, to taste

Sugar syrup
⅔ cup (120 g) superfine (caster) sugar
¾ cup (200 ml) water

To make the Sugar Syrup, put the sugar and water into a small saucepan and heat gently, stirring occasionally until the sugar dissolves. When the syrup is clear, increase the heat and bring to a boil. Lower the heat and simmer gently for a few minutes, then remove from the heat and leave to cool.

Wash the lemons well, cut each one into eight and place the pieces in a large mixing bowl. Pour on the sugar and massage the lemons, rubbing the sugar into the skin. The abrasive action releases the lemon oils. At the same time squeeze out as much juice as possible from the flesh. After about 5 minutes the sugar should have dissolved into a thick syrup. Cover the bowl with plastic wrap and chill in the fridge for around 4 hours.

Add the water and 1 cup (250 ml) of Sugar Syrup and return to the fridge to chill overnight. Strain and discard the lemons then add the tea, if using and the orange blossom water. Pour into an ice cream machine and churn, according to the manufacturer's instructions.

MAKES A LITTLE OVER 4 CUPS (1 LITER) OF SORBET

BLACKBERRY AND HALAWA SALAD WITH WATERMELON AND ROSEWATER SORBET

It is also nice to add small pieces of watermelon to the blackberries and strawberries.

2 baskets blackberries
1 basket strawberries
⅓ cup (12 g) mint leaves, finely
    shredded
⅔ cup (100 g) crumbled pistachio
    halawa
Watermelon and Rosewater Sorbet
    (page 236)
½ cup (80 g) unsalted pistachio nuts,
    coarsely chopped and sifted

Vanilla sugar syrup
½ cup (100 g) superfine (caster) sugar
⅓ cup (100 ml) water
1 vanilla pod, split and scraped
Peel of 1 lemon

Make the Watermelon and Rosewater Sorbet by following the recipe on page 236.

To make the Vanilla Sugar Syrup, put the sugar, water, vanilla pod and lemon peel into a small saucepan. Bring to a boil, then simmer gently for about 5 minutes. Remove from the heat. When cool, remove the vanilla pod; this can be washed and reused to flavor your canister of sugar.

Put the blackberries, strawberries and mint into a mixing bowl and pour on half the Vanilla Sugar Syrup (use the rest in another dessert). Toss gently, then divide between 4 shallow bowls. Crumble on the halawa and place a large spoonful of sorbet on top. Garnish with the pistachio nuts.

SERVES 4

ICE CREAM BASE

This very useful Italian-style ice cream mixture can be used as the base for all sorts of flavorings. Play around with a variety of molds, or make cones using greaseproof paper.

1¼ cups (250 g) superfine (caster) sugar
1 vanilla pod, split and seeds scraped
1 cup (250 ml) water
10 egg yolks
4 cups (1 liter) heavy cream

Put the sugar, vanilla seeds and water into a small saucepan and dissolve over a gentle heat, stirring occasionally. (Use the scraped pod to perfume your sugar canister.) When the syrup is clear, increase the heat and bring to a rolling boil.

Meanwhile, put the egg yolks into an electric mixer and whisk until thick, pale and creamy. With the motor running, slowly pour the sugar syrup onto the egg yolks. Continue whisking for about 5 minutes, or until the mixture cools. You will see it dramatically bulk up into a soft puffy mass. Fold in the cream and chill in the refrigerator.

Pour the chilled mixture into an ice cream machine and churn, according to the manufacturer's instructions.

MAKES AROUND 3 PINTS (1½ LITERS) OF ICE CREAM

TOASTED ALMOND ORANGE PRALINE ICE CREAM

You only need half the amount of praline for this ice cream recipe, but it is tricky to make in smaller quantities. Freeze the rest and use it as a garnish for this ice cream or other desserts.

Grated rind of 2 oranges
1 cup (200 g) superfine (caster) sugar
2 tablespoons water
1⅓ cups (200 g) blanched whole
    almonds, lightly toasted
1 portion Ice Cream Base (recipe above)

Make the Ice Cream Base by following the above recipe and chill in the refrigerator.

Preheat the oven to 210°F (100°C). Dry the orange rind for 3 hours, then grind to a fine powder.

To make the praline, put the sugar and water in a saucepan and heat slowly until the sugar dissolves, stirring occasionally. Bring to a boil and cook for about 5 minutes, until the syrup reaches the thread stage (when a drop of syrup falls from a wooden spoon in a long thread) at about 225°F (110°C).

Stir in the almonds. The syrup will crystallize and harden as the oils are released from the nuts. Lower the heat and stir patiently until it redissolves to a smooth caramel. This will take 10 minutes or so.

Carefully pour the caramel onto a baking tray lined with baking paper. Smooth it out, sprinkle the ground orange rind over the praline and then leave it to cool and harden. When the praline is completely cold, bash it with a rolling pin to break it into chunks, then pound it to crumbs in a mortar and pestle. The praline should be the consistency of coarse breadcrumbs.

Pour the chilled Ice Cream Base mixture into an ice cream machine and churn, according to the manufacturer's instructions, until nearly set. Add half the almond and orange praline towards the end of the churning time.

MAKES AROUND 3 PINTS (1½ LITERS) OF ICE CREAM

HONEY CARAMEL ICE CREAM

Honey caramel
½ cup (100 g) superfine (caster) sugar
⅓ cup (100 ml) honey
⅓ cup (100 ml) water
1 teaspoon ground ginger
Ice Cream Base (page 230)

To make the Honey Caramel, put the sugar and honey in a saucepan with 3 tablespoons of the water. Bring to a boil, then lower the heat and simmer gently until it starts to darken and caramelize. Add the rest of the water and continue simmering until everything dissolves back to a smooth caramel, then whisk in the ground ginger.

Make the Ice Cream Base by following the recipe on page 230, substituting Honey Caramel for the syrup. Whisk until mixture is cool. Chill then pour into an ice cream machine and churn, according to the manufacturer's instructions.

MAKES AROUND 3 PINTS (1½ LITERS) OF ICE CREAM

FIG BARBERRY ICE CREAM

¼ cup (60 g) dried figs
¼ cup (40 g) barberries, dried sour cherries or currants
2 tablespoons Cointreau liquer
1 portion Ice Cream Base (page 230)

Soak the figs overnight in enough warm water to just cover them. Soak the barberries overnight in enough orange juice to also just cover them.

Put the figs and their soaking water into a small saucepan and bring to a boil. Lower the heat and simmer gently until they are very soft. Add the Cointreau and stir well. Tip into a liquidizer, blend to a smooth purée and leave to cool.

Make the Ice Cream Base by following the recipe on page 230 and chill in the refrigerator. Add the cold fig purée to the chilled base mixture, pour into an ice cream machine and churn, according to the manufacturer's instructions. Towards the end of the churning time, add the drained barberries and let the machine stir them in thoroughly.

MAKES AROUND 3 PINTS (1½ LITERS) OF ICE CREAM

LIQUORICE ICE CREAM

5 sticks (7 oz/200 g) black liquorice candy
1¼ cups (300 ml) water
Ice Cream Base (page 230)

Cut the liquorice into small pieces and put into a saucepan with the water. Heat slowly, stirring from time to time, until the liquorice dissolves to a smooth paste.

Make the Ice Cream Base by following the recipe on page 230. Stir around a third into the melted liquorice, a bit at a time, so that it is incorporated gradually and remains smooth. Tip back into the remaining base mixture, stir and chill in the refrigerator. Pour the chilled mixture into an ice cream machine and churn, according to the manufacturer's instructions.

MAKES AROUND 3 PINTS (1½ LITERS) OF ICE CREAM

ROSE OF DAMASCUS

Turkish delight ice cream
2½ cups (625 ml) milk
2½ cups (625 ml) heavy cream
1⅔ cups (320 g) superfine (caster) sugar
10 egg yolks
⅓ cup (80 ml) rosewater
Splash of red food coloring (optional)

Filo pastry flowers
10 sheets of filo pastry
¾ cup (200 g) clarified butter, melted
¾ cup (100 g) confectioner's (icing) sugar
⅓ cup (100 ml) honey, warmed

Toffeed strawberries
1 basket strawberries
Superfine (caster) sugar
Dried rose petals (optional)

To make the Turkish Delight Ice Cream, put the milk and cream in a large, heavy-based pan and heat gently. Meanwhile, put the sugar and egg yolks in a large mixing bowl and whisk by hand until thick and pale. Pour on the hot cream and whisk in quickly. Tip the custard mix back into the pan and heat gently until it thickens to coat the back of a spoon. Remove from the heat immediately and cool in a sink of iced water. Stir to help it cool down quickly. When cool, stir in the rosewater and enough food coloring to tint it a pale pink.

Pour the chilled mixture into an ice cream machine and churn, according to the manufacturer's instructions, until nearly set. Line a ¾-in (2-cm) baking tray with plastic wrap. Tip the ice cream into the tray and smooth the surface. Transfer to the freezer until ready to assemble the dessert.

To prepare the Filo Pastry Flowers, preheat the oven to 320°F (160°C). Line and butter 2 baking trays, each about 10 in x 12 in (25 cm x 30 cm).

Lay a sheet of filo on your work surface and brush liberally with clarified butter and dust with icing sugar. Repeat with 2 more layers, drizzling a little warm honey on the third sheet of filo. Continue stacking and brushing with 2 further layers of pastry. On the top (5th) layer, brush with butter, but do not sprinkle on icing sugar

Repeat this process with the remaining 5 sheets of filo pastry. You should now have 2 stacks of filo pastry, each comprising 5 pastry layers.

Use an 3½-in (8-cm) flower-shaped pastry cutter to cut 12 flowers from each pastry stack—24 in total. Carefully transfer the pastry "flowers" to the prepared baking trays and lay a sheet of baking parchment on top of each tray. Weight down lightly with another tray, which will keep the flowers flat as they cook. Bake for 8–10 minutes, or until golden. Remove from the oven and leave to cool.

To prepare the Toffeed Strawberries, preheat the oven broiler to its highest temperature. Hull the strawberries and cut them in half. Dust them all over with caster sugar then place them under the broiler until the sugar caramelizes, turning once. Alternatively, use a blow torch.

When ready to assemble, remove the ice cream from the freezer. Turn the block out onto a chopping board and peel away the plastic wrap. Use the 3½-in (8-cm) flower-shaped pastry cutter to cut out 12 flowers of ice cream.

Place a pastry flower on each plate and top with a flower of ice cream. Add another pastry flower and ice cream flower, and finish with a top layer of pastry. Dust each Rose of Damascus with icing sugar and serve with the Toffeed Strawberies, and dried rose petals if you're feeling particularly exotic.

MAKES 6

MUSCAT ICE CREAM

2½ cups (600 ml) muscat
⅓ cup (55 g) sultanas or raisins
⅓ cup (100 ml) water
½ cup (100 ml) glucose syrup
¼ cup (50 g) superfine (caster) sugar
6 egg yolks
2 cups (500 ml) whipping cream

Put the muscat in a heavy-based saucepan with the sultanas and bring to a boil. Lower the heat and simmer until reduced to ⅓ cup (100 ml). Strain through a fine sieve and reserve both the sultanas and the intense, syrupy muscat.

Put the water, glucose and sugar into a heavy-based saucepan and bring to a boil.

Meanwhile, put the egg yolks into an electric mixer and whisk until thick, pale and creamy. With the motor running, slowly pour the sugar syrup onto the egg yolks. Next, pour on the muscat and continue whisking for about 5 minutes, or until the mixture cools. You will see it dramatically bulk up into a soft puffy mass. Fold in the cream and chill in the refrigerator.

Pour the chilled mixture into an ice cream machine and churn, according to the manufacturer's instructions. Towards the end of the churning time, add the sultanas and let the machine stir them in thoroughly.

MAKES AROUND 1½ PINTS (850 ML) OF ICE CREAM

SOUR CHERRY MASCARPONE SORBET

¼ cup (50 g) dried sour cherries
1 cup (250 ml) water
¼ cup (50 g) superfine (caster) sugar

Mascarpone sorbet
2 cups (500 m) water
½ cup (125 ml) corn syrup
1 cup (215 g) superfine (caster) sugar
1 vanilla pod, split and seeds scraped
¼ cup (60 ml) lemon juice
2¾ cups (700 g) mascarpone

Coarsely chop the cherries and place them in a small pan with the water and sugar. Simmer gently until the cherries are soft and the liquid is syrupy. Remove from the heat and cool.

To make the Mascarpone Sorbet, put the water, corn syrup, sugar, vanilla seeds and lemon juice into a heavy-based saucepan and heat gently, stirring occasionally until the sugar dissolves. When the syrup is clear, increase the heat and bring to a boil. Remove from the heat and leave to cool.

When the syrup is completely cold, stir it into the Mascarpone Sorbet and chill. Pour the cold mixture into an ice cream machine and churn, according to the manufacturer's instructions. Towards the end of the churning time, add the cherries and let the machine stir them in thoroughly.

MAKES A LITTLE OVER 2 PINTS (1 LITER) OF SORBET

CHOCOLATE AND CINNAMON SORBET

2 cups (500 ml) water
1 cup (250 ml) milk
½ cup (100 g) superfine (caster) sugar
3 tablespoons glucose syrup
2 cinnamon sticks
7 oz (200 g) best-quality dark chocolate
1½ tablespoons cocoa powder

Put the water, milk, sugar, glucose and cinnamon sticks into a large saucepan and slowly bring to a boil.

Break the chocolate into pieces and put it in a mixing bowl with the cocoa powder. Pour on the boiling milk mixture, stirring until the chocolate and cocoa have melted and dissolved.

Cool, stirring from time to time. Strain the mix to remove the cinnamon sticks, then pour into an ice cream machine and churn according to the manufacturer's instructions.

MAKES A LITTLE OVER 4 CUPS (1 LITER) OF SORBET

WATERMELON AND ROSEWATER SORBET

5 cups (1¾ lbs/800 g) chopped
    watermelon
1 cup (200 g) superfine (caster) sugar
¼ cup (70 ml) glucose syrup
¾ cup (200 ml) water
Juice of 2 limes
Splash of rosewater

To make the sorbet, chop the watermelon into large chunks and discard the seeds. Whiz to a purée in a food processor and sieve.

Put the sugar, glucose and water in a saucepan and bring to a boil over a medium heat, then lower and simmer for 5 minutes. Mix the fruit purée with the syrup and allow to cool. Add the lime juice and rosewater. Pour into an ice cream machine and churn according to the manufacturer's instructions.

MAKES A LITTLE OVER 2 PINTS (1 LITER) OF SORBET

THE STORYTELLER OF DAMASCUS

PUDDINGS AND SWEET PASTRIES

TRUFFLES ARE NOT THE SORT OF THING YOU NORMALLY ASSOCIATE WITH THE MIDDLE EAST, but we were on a mission to track down Syrian desert truffles, known locally as chama. This variety has been considered a great delicacy since the early days of civilisation; cuneiform tablets excavated from Mesopotamian sites around the Euphrates River depict baskets of desert truffles being sent to the palace for the pleasure of the king. Chama were also considered a delicacy by medieval Arabs, and early culinary manuals contain references for preparing and cooking with truffles.

Of course, this is a different kind of truffle from the European ones that are rooted out by snuffling pigs underneath certain kinds of trees in France and Italy. Syrian truffles grow in the desert, and most prolifically around the oasis town of Palmyra. Hunting for truffles in the desert might seem a thankless task, but the Bedouins have been doing it for centuries. They know the signs: the particular little weed that grows nearby and the tiny bumps that disturb the sand like little blisters.

At a vegetable stall near Martyrs' Square in Damascus we spotted them: a strange kind of funghi piled high in black rubber baskets. They had been delivered that morning and were still encrusted with desert sand. The old stallholder lovingly plucked one from a basket and handed it to us to inspect. It looked like a cross between a chestnut and a small round potato. A pile of them were soaking in a tub of water and a young man was carefully lifting them out, one at time, and scrubbing them clean with a stiff brush.

The old man showed us that as with European truffles, there are two varieties of desert truffles: black and white. Similarly, the black ones are considered superior, but both are milder and less pungent than their European cousins. The most popular way of cooking chama is to skewer them and grill them over charcoal, and in fact we had enjoyed a very similar dish at Elissar the previous night. The truffles had a delicate mushroomy flavor and an interesting texture, something between water chestnuts and tinned mushrooms. The stallholder told us that his favorite way of eating them was sliced and fried with garlic in clarified butter. Sadly, this was not a treat he could often enjoy as, while not quite in the same league as European truffles, chama are expensive. At the start of the season one could pay around US$16 per 2 lbs (1 kilo) for white truffles and US$20 for the black variety—a hefty slice of the housekeeping budget for most Syrians.

We were standing near a row of pastry shops, each with impressive multi-tiered displays of sticky golden pastries in the window, and a stream of customers were stocking up on supplies for the weekend. We followed a delivery boy to an alleyway at the rear of the shops and explained our interest in seeing the pastry chefs at work. He good-naturedly gestured for us to follow him into a tall, narrow building and then up the stairs, where we found ourselves in a dimly lit, low-ceilinged room. Two burly men in white chef's jackets

THE OLD STALLHOLDER LOVINGLY PLUCKED ONE FROM A BASKET AND HANDED IT TO US TO INSPECT. IT LOOKED LIKE A CROSS BETWEEN A CHESTNUT AND A SMALL ROUND POTATO.

were rolling out wafer-thin sheets of pastry in a cloud of flour. In a series of graceful movements, one of the men draped the inside of a massive circular tin with layer upon layer of translucent pastry. Then he scattered on a fragrant, sugary mass of chopped nuts, followed by more pastry layers, and with surgical precision he marked the surface with diamond-shaped incisions using a long sharp knife.

As each tray was filled it was hurled onto the floor, where a boy ladled on a great lake of golden ghee. The air felt dense and sticky with oil and sugar, and within minutes we were covered in a fine dusting of flour. Our delivery boy picked up his tray and we followed him downstairs to the ovens, where we were each given a tasting of baklava, warm from the oven.

By now, dusk was falling and we were in need of a caffeine jolt. Damascus is famed for its coffee houses, and one of the best known is An Nafura, in a laneway near the Ummayad mosque. We were just in time for the evening's "main event," for inside the smoke-filled room the TV had just been turned off and Mr Rashid ab Shadi had taken up his position, center stage.

By day Mr ab Shadi is a grocer; come early evening, he dons an embroidered waistcoat and fez, and reads to the assembled crowd. He's a hakawati—a traditional Arab storyteller—and every night, for one hour, he holds his audience spellbound with the legendary exploits of ancient heroes like Sultan Beybars or the epic love tale of Antar ibn Shadad and the beautiful and virtuous Abla. These are tales familiar to every Arab schoolchild and the listeners know them almost by heart.

THE AIR FELT DENSE AND
STICKY WITH OIL AND SUGAR
AND WITHIN MINUTES WE
WERE COVERED IN A FINE
DUSTING OF FLOUR.

Mr ab Shadi stopped and peered at us over his reading glasses as we took our seats at a tiny round table, and then continued. The largely male audience were getting into the spirit of things, reciting the familiar verses with Mr ab Shadi and interjecting comments of their own. In his right hand the storyteller held a large sword that he waved in the air and thrust towards the audience to demonstrate a point. Every now and then he slammed it down on the table for dramatic effect.

And then, from somewhere outside, we heard the loudspeaker from the nearby mosque crackle into life. It was the signal for Mr ab Shadi to put down his sword and close his large leather-bound book. A man at a nearby table summoned the nargileh waiter to load up his pipe with a fresh coal, and the sweet scent of apples filled the air as he puffed.

Mr ab Shadi folded up his reading glasses and tucked them into his waistcoat pocket. He shook the proprietor by the hand and shuffled off, leaving his story unfinished.

ALISON'S PEACH YOGURT PANNACOTTA WITH ORANGE BLOSSOM PEACH CARAMEL

Orange blossom peach caramel

1 cup (200 g) superfine (caster) sugar

3 tablespoons water

⅓ cup (100 ml) fresh orange juice

1 tablespoon peach schnaps

Splash of orange blossom water

Peach purée

1½ cups (300 g) superfine (caster) sugar

2 cups (450 ml) water

1 lb (500 g) ripe yellow peaches

Pannacotta

2 tablespoons superfine (caster) sugar

1¼ cups (300 ml) of the peach poaching
    syrup

4 x 1.6 g sheets of gelatin, or 1½
    teaspoons gelatin powder

1⅓ cups (325 ml) whipping cream

1⅔ cups (400 g) plain yogurt

1½ cups (350 ml) of the Peach Purée

1 tablespoon peach schnaps

1 tablespoon walnut oil

Garnish

Fresh peach slices (optional)

Fresh blueberries, halved (optional)

Persian fairy floss (optional)

To make the Orange Blossom Peach Caramel, put the sugar and water in a saucepan. Bring to a boil, then lower the heat and simmer gently until it starts to darken and caramelize. Add the orange juice, peach schnaps and the orange blossom water, and continue simmering until everything dissolves back to a smooth caramel, then remove from the heat.

To make the Peach Purée, put the sugar and water into a saucepan with the whole peaches. Cover with a circle of greaseproof paper to ensure the peaches are submerged. Simmer gently in the syrup until they are tender. Remove the peaches, reserving the syrup. When the peaches are cool enough to handle, rub away the skins and cut the flesh away from the pit. Tip the flesh into a liquidizer and whiz to a smooth purée.

To make the Pannacotta, put the sugar and peach poaching syrup in a saucepan and heat gently to dissolve the sugar. Soak the gelatin in a little cold water for a few minutes until it softens, then squeeze well. Remove the peach syrup from the heat and add the gelatin. Stir well to dissolve and leave to cool a little.

In a large bowl, stir together the cream, yogurt and Peach Purée. Add the cool syrup mixture and stir to combine thoroughly. Lightly oil dariole molds with the walnut oil. Strain the Pannacotta mixture through a fine sieve and pour into the molds. Refrigerate until they set.

To serve, unmold the Pannacottas and serve drizzled with the Orange Blossom Peach Caramel. Garnish with fresh peach slices and blueberries and, if you like, a little mound of Persian fairy floss.

SERVES 8–10

KURT SAMPSON'S WHITE CHOCOLATE SOUR CHERRY PUDDING

1 cup (250 g) unsalted butter, softened

1 cup (200 g) superfine (caster) sugar

2 eggs

1⅔ cups (400 g) self-raising flour

Salt to taste

1 teaspoon vanilla extract

1 cup (250 ml) milk

½ cup (100 g) dried sour cherries,
    chopped into small pieces

½ cup (60 g) white chocolate, chopped
    into small pieces

Preheat the oven to 350°F (180°C). Cream the butter and sugar until smooth, then add the eggs, one at a time.

Sift the flour and salt together and stir the vanilla extract into the milk. Gently fold the flour into the creamed mixture, alternating with the milk. Finally, gently fold in the chopped cherries and chocolate pieces, taking care not to overwork. Stir everything.

Lightly grease a pudding basin or small dariole molds and pour in the pudding mixture. Cover each mold or the basin with silicon baking paper and seal tightly with a layer of foil. Put into a deep baking tray and pour in enough boiling water to come halfway up the sides of the molds or pudding basin. Bake for 30–40 minutes if using molds, 40–50 minutes if you're using a pudding basin. Test, by inserting a skewer, which should come out clean when the puddings are cooked.

SERVES 8–10

LEBANESE DOUGHNUTS WITH LEMON SYRUP

Once the dough has proved and doubled in bulk, you can transfer it to the fridge, where it will keep quite happily for up to 4 days.

Lemon syrup

1½ cups (300 g) superfine (caster) sugar

⅓ cup (100 ml) water

2½ tablespoons lemon juice

1 tablespoon corn syrup

1 vanilla pod, split and seeds scraped
   (optional)

Doughnuts

2 teaspoons (10 g) dried yeast

4 cups (600 g) flour

A pinch of salt

⅓ cup (70 g) superfine (caster) sugar

1¾ cups (440 ml) milk

⅓ cup (70 g) unsalted butter

3 eggs

1 egg yolk

Candied grated lemon rind (optional)

To make the Lemon Syrup, combine all the ingredients in a large heavy-based saucepan and heat gently, stirring to dissolve the sugar. Bring to a boil, then remove from the heat and leave to cool.

To make the Doughnuts, mix the yeast, flour and salt in a large mixing bowl. Put the sugar and milk in a saucepan and heat gently to dissolve the sugar. Do not boil. Pour onto the butter and stir to melt. Leave until it cools to lukewarm, then whisk the eggs and egg yolk into the liquid. Pour the liquid into the flour and stir in by hand, until the batter is smooth. Cover the bowl and leave in a warm, draught-free spot for 1 hour, by which time the dough should have doubled in size.

Shape the Doughnuts into a little quenelles using 2 spoons, or put the dough into a piping bag and use a pair of scissors to snip off little dollops.

Heat the oil to 350°F (180°C) or until a cube of bread sizzles to the surface. Drop the Doughnuts into the oil and fry for 4–5 minutes, until golden brown. Sit the hot Doughnuts in the syrup and leave for a few minutes to soak before serving. They are particularly good with a tart ice cream; try the Fig Barberry Ice Cream (page 231) Sour Cherry Mascarpone Sorbet (page 236) or a good quality purchased vanilla or lemon ice cream. For an extra lemon hit, garnish with candied lemon rind.

MAKES 24 SMALL DOUGHNUTS

LEBANESE MILK PUDDING WITH PASSIONFRUIT *passionfruit muhallabeya*

Muhallabeya

⅔ cup (130 g) superfine (caster) sugar

4–5 grains mastic, ground with 1
   teaspoon superfine (caster) sugar

½ cup (50 g) cornstarch

4 cups (1 liter) milk

1 cup (250 ml) water

3 tablespoons orange blossom water

Passionfruit sauce

2 cups (500 g) passionfruit pulp

½ cup (100 g) superfine (caster) sugar

¼ cup (60 ml) glucose syrup

To make the Muhallabeya, put the sugar, ground mastic and cornstarch in a bowl and add ⅓ cup (100 ml) of the milk to make a paste.

Put the rest of the milk and the water in a large saucepan. Add the paste and stir well. Bring to a boil, whisking continuously. Once it boils, remove the pan from the heat and stir in the orange blossom water. Strain into a jug. Leave to cool slightly, then pour into attractive serving glasses. Seal each glass with plastic wrap to prevent a skin forming.

To make the Passionfruit Sauce, put the passionfruit pulp into a food processor and blend for a minute to break it down. Strain through a fine sieve, reserving the juice. Add the juice to the sugar and glucose in a small pan. Bring to a boil, then lower the heat and simmer for 10 minutes to make a thick yellow sauce.

Just before serving, drizzle a generous amount of Passionfruit Sauce over the top of each glass.

SERVES 6–8

SESAME TART WITH BERRY ROSE MOUSSE

The various components of this dessert can all be prepared ahead of time so that it just needs to be assembled quickly before serving. It is a lovely light summer tart, perfect when berries are in season—and so pretty, like a soft pink cloud. You'll only need half the amount of pastry for this tart, but it can be tricky working with smaller quantities of the nuts and seeds. Freeze the rest for another occasion.

Almond and sesame pastry

1 cup (150 g) blanched almonds, roasted

½ cup (65 g) sesame seeds, lightly roasted

⅔ cup (130 g) superfine (caster) sugar

3 cups (450 g) flour

1 teaspoon cinnamon

⅓ teaspoon salt

Grated rind of ½ lemon

1½ cups (335 g) unsalted butter

2 eggs

Splash of vanilla extract

Berry rose mousse

1½ cups (350 g) fresh berries (such as blackberries, raspberries, blueberries and boysenberries; reserve a few for a garnish)

⅔ cup (130 g) superfine (caster) sugar

2 x 1.6 g sheets of gelatin, softened in water or ¾ teaspoon gelatin powder

Splash of vanilla extract

Splash of rosewater

1¾ cups (375 ml) heavy cream

Berry sauce

1 cup (250 g) fresh berries (such as blackberries, raspberries, blueberries and boysenberries)

⅓ cup (100 ml) Vanilla Sugar Syrup (page 229)

Make the Vanilla Sugar Syrup by following the recipe on page 229.

To make the Almond and Sesame Pastry, put the almonds and sesame seeds into a food processor with the sugar and pulse to fine crumbs. Be careful not to overwork, as the oils will start to come out of the nuts and make the pastry oily.

Add the flour, cinnamon, salt and lemon rind to the mixture and pulse quickly to combine. Next add the butter, and pulse to form crumbs. Add the eggs and vanilla and pulse until the pastry just comes together in a ball. Push it together with your hands and remove from the food processor. Shape into a round, wrap in plastic wrap and chill for at least 1 hour.

After chilling, roll the pastry out thinly onto a well-floured work surface. Lift onto an 11-in (28-cm) tart ring and gently press into shape. Trim the edges and return to the refrigerator for another hour.

When ready to blind-bake the tart, preheat the oven to 350°F (180°C). Line the tart with foil, fill with baking beans and bake for 15 minutes. Remove the foil and beans and bake for another 15 minutes, or until the pastry has turned golden. Remove from the oven and cool on a wire rack.

To make the Berry Rose Mousse, put the berries into a liquidizer and whiz to a purée. Push through a fine sieve to remove the seeds then divide the purée in half. Put half into a small saucepan with the sugar and warm gently until the sugar dissolves. Add the gelatin sheets, stir to dissolve and leave to cool. Add to the rest of the berry purée and stir in the vanilla and rosewater. Whip the cream to stiffish peaks. Fold into the berry purée, then chill.

To make the Berry Sauce, put the berries into a liquidizer with the Vanilla Sugar Syrup and blitz to a smooth purée. Pour into a saucepan and bring to a boil, then remove from the heat and leave to cool.

When ready to serve, spoon the Berry Rose Mousse into the tart and scatter on the reserved berries. Serve each slice with a generous drizzle of Berry Sauce.

SERVES 6–8

FILO PILLOW PIES STUFFED WITH MASCARPONE AND ALMOND ORANGE PRALINE

These little pastries are based on a popular Lebanese pastry called znoud el sitt, (ladies' elbows), and are the perfect combination of crisp, sweet pastry, and an unctuously rich, cream filling. The semolina filling can be made ahead of time but the mascarpone filling should be made on the day of serving.

½–1 cup Toasted Almond Orange
    Praline (page 230)
8 sheets filo pastry
¾ cup (200 g) unsalted butter, melted

Semolina custard filling
4 cups (1 liter) milk
1 tablespoon orange blossom water
Grated rind of 1 lemon
Grated rind of 1 orange
8 egg yolks
2 eggs
1⅛ cups (220 g) superfine (caster) sugar
⅓ cup (90 g) fine semolina
¼ cup (60 g) unsalted butter, softened

Mascarpone filling
¾ cup (200 g) mascarpone
2 eggs, separated
¼ cup (50 g) superfine (caster) sugar

Make the Toasted Almond Orange Praline by following the recipe on page 230.

Preheat the oven to 320°F (160°C). To make the Semolina Custard Filling, put the milk, orange blossom water, and citrus rind into a large saucepan and slowly bring to a boil. Lower the heat and leave to cool a little.

In a mixing bowl, combine the yolks and eggs, sugar and semolina and beat until smooth. Strain the hot milk onto the egg mixture, stirring continuously. Pour the custard back into the cleaned-out saucepan and cook over a low heat until it thickens. Add the butter and stir in thoroughly. Tip the mixture into a shallow ovenproof dish and cover with foil. Put the dish into a larger roasting tin and pour in enough boiling water to come half-way up the sides of the dish. Bake for 60–70 minutes, until the custard sets firm. Remove from the oven and allow to cool. Store, covered, until ready to assemble.

To make the Mascarpone Filling, put the mascarpone and egg yolks into an electric mixer and whisk until firm. Whip the egg whites with the sugar until they form firm peaks. Fold this meringue mixture into the mascarpone and chill until required.

When ready to assemble the little pies, preheat the oven to 400°F (200°C) and remove the two Fillings from the fridge. Cut the custard into rectangles, about the size of a deck of cards.

Working with 1 sheet of filo pastry at a time, lay it on a work surface and brush with melted butter. Scatter a little Toasted Almond Orange Praline over one half of the pastry and fold the other half on top. Butter again, then cut the pastry into a diamond shape. Place a slice of the Semolina Custard in the center of the diamond and dollop a spoonful of Mascarpone Filling on top. Fold the points in and over the filling to form an envelope. Butter well then turn and butter the top. Repeat the process with remaining sheets of filo until you have 8 little pies.

Bake for 6–8 minutes until the pastries are golden brown. Serve them straight from the oven, either dusted with icing sugar or drizzled with caramel—perhaps flavored with orange. They are delicious served with fresh stone fruit such as peaches, nectarines, apricots or cherries.

MAKES 8 PIES

THE LAST DANCE

SWEET TREATS AND BEVERAGES

IT WAS THE LAST LEG OF OUR JOURNEY, following the road from Damascus back to Lebanon. A mere fifteen minutes on the road and we had left the congested city outskirts, passing a Palestinian refugee camp bristling with satellite dishes, and had reached the border crossing. After our frustrating experience entering Syria, getting out was a breeze. At a drive-through tollbooth, our passports were collected and stamped, and we were on our way again.

Eleven years ago this same border crossing had been little more than an untidy collection of fibro huts. It had grown into a gleaming great retail development where travelers could spend hours agonising over the vast array of duty-free spirits, perfumes and cigarettes.

We sped off through the countryside towards a looming dark bank of cloud before taking the turn-off to Zahlé, where Greg's family originate. We had visited the village on our honeymoon and remembered it as a comfortable, red-roofed place in the foothills of Mount Sannine above the Bekaa Valley. It's a popular summer resort and its main attraction is the Bardouni River which tumbles down from the hills through the heart of the city. The promenade along the Bourdani is lined with open-air restaurants, and in the summer months it teems with visitors.

It was raining when we drove into Zahlé and the streets were emptying fast. A street vendor was wheeling his ka'ak stand down the deserted street, the sesame-speckled horseshoes of bread dripping in the grey drizzle. The Bardouni promenade was empty and the shops were closing their shutters. We ducked into the one restaurant that was still open and took grateful refuge in the cavernous, brightly lit dining room. The restaurant's speciality was ice cream, so despite the weather, ice cream we were going to have.

The proprietor proudly showed us his display of tempting flavors—mulberry, orange, apricot, pistachio, lemon and rosewater—and we chose the famous stretchy mastic ice cream that we remembered so well from our previous visit to Zahlé. We were now thoroughly chilled, both inside and out, and could stand it no longer so we headed straight to Zahlé's Grand Hotel Kadri for a night of warmth and comfort.

The next day we woke to blue skies and sunshine, and what had seemed dismal and dreary the previous day was now charming and quaint. It was easy to accept Zahlé's alternative name of "Bride of the Bekaa".

By midday we were winding along a familiar dusty road to Massaya for a winter vineyard luncheon, at the invitation of co-owner Ramzi Ghosn. "Our cook is a local village woman and she makes very different food from the fare you normally find in Lebanese restaurants," he'd told us on our previous visit to the winery.

We basked in the sunshine in a spectacular setting, surrounded by mountains still capped with winter snow and vines that were just starting to sprout delicate

OLD MEN SAT ALONG THE
WATERFRONT, THEIR
LONG FISHING RODS
DOING A DELICATE
DANCE OVER THE WAVES.

fronds. Lunch was a procession of truly delicious dishes: a Lebanese-style bruschetta on chewy brown bread; a green herb salad of chervil, mint and chives; tangy silver beet in a creamy tahini-lemon dressing; crunchy potato kibbeh and fassoul—a comforting stew of slow-cooked red beans. Plump quails and marinated lamb cutlets were cooked over the coals of an open fireplace in the rustic 'rest house' and, of course, it was all washed down with liberal quantities of some of the vineyard's best offerings.

On our last evening in the Middle East we went for a final stroll along the Corniche to watch the sunset. A few old men sat along the waterfront, their long fishing rods doing a delicate dance over the waves. Dusk was falling and the street vendors were opening their stands for the evening. And then, out of the darkness, the muezzin started up. The doors to the mosque opened to admit the faithful, and a pool of golden light spilled out onto the pavement.

We chose a pavement café on Rue Maarad in Downtown for our last supper. It was a warm night, and the streets were busier than they'd been over the course of our four-week stay. It was nine thirty—early by Beirut standards—but the cafés around us were full.

At a nearby table a group of touring Spanish musicians spontaneously produced their instruments and began to play. They were interrupted by the restaurant's 'real' entertainment, an Arab clarinettist, who started his set with a Fehruz classic. A Muslim woman at the table next to us got up and did a belly dance, all sinuous hips and shy, seductive smiles through her lowered lashes. The tempo moved upbeat and a couple started a spontaneous 'dabka', the national folkdance of Lebanon.

The party atmosphere escalated with a string of traditional Arab folksongs. The maître d' was beside himself, clapping and laughing and exhorting us all to have a good time. And then, the clarinettist paused for a moment and the crowd looked up expectantly. As the first few notes of his next tune began, there was silence. One by one, people got to their feet and I saw a young man behind me brush a tear from his eye as, old and young, men and women, Muslim and Christian, they started to sing Lebanon's national anthem. And for a few precious moments it was as if the whole of Lebanon was united in one voice.

KAHLUA SWIRL COOKIES *Ma'amoul*

Ma'amoul are nut- or date-filled cookies that are popular in Middle Eastern communities around the world. They are an essential part of the round of socialising that takes place during religious festivals such as Easter and Eid al-Fitr, the Muslim post-Ramadan celebration. Traditionally, ma'amoul are made in decorative wooden molds. This is a slightly different way of preparing them, but looks very pretty with its swirly, spiral effect.

Filling

¾ cup (200 g) Medjool dates, pitted and chopped

2 tablespoons water

1 tablespoon superfine (caster) sugar

1 tablespoon Kahlúa coffee liquer

Cookie Dough

3⅔ cups (540 g) flour

1⅓ cups (300 g) unsalted butter

½ cup (60 g) confectioner's (icing) sugar

3 tablespoons olive oil

⅓ cup (90 ml) milk

1 egg white, beaten

Confectioner's (icing) sugar for dusting

To make the date Filling, blanch the dates in boiling water, then quickly immerse in cold water to loosen their skins. Peel and pit the dates, then put them in a saucepan with the water and sugar and bring to a simmer. Cook over a low heat, stirring continuously, until the dates soften and melt to a smooth, sticky mass. Remove from the heat and, when cool, stir in the Kahlúa. Blitz to a smooth paste with an electric hand-blender.

To make the Cookie Dough, sift the flour into a large mixing bowl. Add the butter and rub in with your fingers until it's the consistency of fine crumbs. Add the icing sugar and mix in well. Make a well in the center of the Dough and add the oil and milk, then work in until you have a smooth Dough.

Dust your work surface with flour. Divide the Dough into 3 portions and roll each one out to a large rectangle, about ⅛ in (3 mm) thick. Divide the Filling into thirds and smear onto each rectangle of Dough, leaving a clear margin along one long edge. Brush each clear edge with a little egg white and roll each piece up to form a long log, sealing well at the edge. Gently but firmly, roll each log back and forth to make it longer and thinner. Refrigerate for 20 minutes to firm up.

Preheat the oven to 325°F (160°C). Remove the chilled cookie logs from the fridge and slice on the diagonal to about ½ in (1 cm) thick. Arrange on a greased baking tray and cook for 10 minutes. Lower the temperature to 275°F (140°C) and cook for a further 10 minutes. Remove from the oven and cool on wire racks. The cookies should not color, but should remain pale and delicate. When cool, dust liberally with icing sugar.

MAKES AROUND 40 COOKIES

POMEGRANATE CORDIAL

To make a refreshing summer drink, put 2 tablespoons of pomegranate cordial in a tall glass. Add crushed ice and fresh mint leaves and top up with still or sparkling water.

6 large pomegranates (to yield around 1½ cup/375 ml juice)

¾ cup (180 g) sugar

Juice of 1 lemon

Line a colander with muslin and set it over a large bowl to catch the juice. Roll the pomegranates on your work surface to loosen the seeds. Cut the fruit in half crosswise and squeeze out all the pips and juice into the muslin. Gather the 4 corners of the muslin together and twist and squeeze to extract as much juice as you can. Bash with a rolling pin and twist and squeeze again.

Put the pomegranate juice and sugar into a non-reactive pan and heat gently to dissolve the sugar.

Raise the heat and bring to a boil. Skim away the froth, then lower the heat and simmer for 10 minutes. Stir in the lemon juice, then remove from the heat and cool slightly. Pour into sterilized bottles and seal. When completely cold, store in the fridge. It will keep for up to 2 weeks.

MAKES 1½ CUPS (350 ML)

TURKISH DELIGHT FLORENTINES

2½ tablespoons (50 g) unsalted butter
½ cup (125 ml) whipping cream
⅔ cup (125 g) superfine (caster) sugar
1 lb (440 g) flaked almonds
⅓ cup (60 g) flour
10 oz (300 g) best-quality dark
   chocolate
8 pieces rosewater Turkish delight,
   finely chopped

Preheat the oven to 320°F (160°C). Grease and line 2 baking trays with parchment.

Put the butter, cream and sugar in a small heavy-based saucepan and bring to a boil. Remove from the heat. Allow to cool slightly then stir in the almonds and flour.

Drop teaspoonfuls onto the baking trays, leaving plenty of room between each one for spreading. Flatten slightly with a wet fingertip. Bake for 8–10 minutes, until the biscuits are a light golden-brown. If you like, at this stage you can cut the biscuits into neat circles with a pastry cutter, before returning them to the oven to finish cooking. Bake biscuits for a further 8 minutes until they are a deep golden-brown.

Remove from the oven and, while they are still warm, scatter with the pieces of Turkish delight. (Alternatively, scatter the Turkish delight onto the melted chocolate before it sets.) Once the biscuits are cool and firm transfer them to a wire rack. Melt the chocolate and brush a thick coat onto the flat sides of the biscuits. Use a fork to create the traditional wavy pattern.

MAKES AROUND 15 BISCUITS

RASPBERRY TURKISH DELIGHT TRUFFLES

10 oz (300 g) dark chocolate
¾ cup (200 ml) whipping cream
8 pieces raspberry Turkish delight
Cocoa powder, for dredging

Heat the cream in a small saucepan and pour it onto the chocolate. Stir until the chocolate melts, then leave it to cool.

Chop the Turkish delight into small pieces and stir it through the chocolate cream. Allow it to cool completely, then scoop into little balls and roll twice in the cocoa powder.

MAKES 30 TRUFFLES

ROSEWATER SYRUP

Known as sharab al-ward in Arabic, this is a sweetly perfumed syrup that makes a lovely chilled summer drink. Put 2 tablespoons into a tall glass, add crushed ice and top up with still or sparkling water.

2 cups (400 g) sugar
1 cup (250 ml) water
1 tablespoon lemon juice
⅓ cup (75 ml) rosewater
A few drops of grenadine (optional, for
   color)

Put the sugar and water into a non-reactive pan and heat gently, stirring from time to time, until the sugar completely dissolves. Add the lemon juice and simmer for 10 minutes without stirring. Skim off any froth. Add the rosewater and grenadine, if using, stir, and simmer for a further 2 minutes. Remove from the heat and cool slightly. Pour into sterilized bottles and seal. When completely cold, store in the fridge. It will keep for up to 3 months without losing its intensity.

MAKES AROUND 2½ CUPS (600 ML)

CRUNCHY SESAME PISTACHIO COOKIES *barazek*

Housewives all over Lebanon and Syria buy these popular cookies by the pounds from souks—they might appear simple, but they are meltingly short and crunchy, and wickedly addictive.

¼ cup (40 g) soft brown sugar

⅓ cup (45 g) confectioner's (icing) sugar

⅔ cup (150 g) unsalted butter, softened

1 teaspoon vanilla extract

1 egg

1⅓ cups (200 g) self-raising flour

⅓ cup (50 g) pistachio nuts, cut into slivers

½ cup (60 g) sesame seeds, lightly toasted

Put the sugars and butter in a large bowl and cream together well. Mix in the vanilla extract and egg, followed by the flour. The dough softens easily, so transfer it to the fridge for 30 minutes before baking.

Preheat the oven to 350°F (180°C). Grease and line 2 baking trays.

Take little pieces of dough and roll them between the palms of your hands into small marble-sized balls. Flatten gently to form little discs around ½ in (1 cm) thick. Line up 2 dishes, one with the pistachio slivers and one with the sesame seeds. Press one side of the dough into the pistachios, then turn and press the other side into the sesame seeds. Carefully brush off any excess and place on the prepared baking sheets, allowing about 2 in (5 cm) between them for spreading.

Bake for 10–12 minutes, or until golden brown. Transfer the cookies to a wire rack and leave to cool.

MAKES 25–30 COOKIES

BITTER ORANGE CORDIAL

Use Seville oranges for a sourer, slightly less sweet cordial. To serve, put 2 tablespoons into a tall glass, add crushed ice and top up with still or sparkling water.

2 cups (500 ml) freshly squeezed orange juice

3 cups (600 g) sugar

Juice of 1 lemon

Put the orange juice and sugar into a non-reactive pan and heat gently, stirring from time to time, until the sugar completely dissolves. Bring to a boil, then lower the heat, add the lemon juice and simmer for 10 minutes without stirring. Skim off any froth. Remove from the heat and cool slightly. Pour into sterilized bottles and seal. When completely cold, store in the fridge. It will keep for up to 3 months without losing its intensity.

MAKES AROUND 3¼ CUPS (800 ML)

TURKISH COFFEE

Turkish or Arabic coffee is best made in small quantities in the traditional long-handled pot called a rakweh, but a very small saucepan will also do. Serve with baklava or Turkish delight.

1 cup (250 ml) water
3 heaped teaspoons Turkish coffee powder
2 teaspoons superfine (caster) sugar (optional)
Pinch of ground cardamom

Put the water into a rakweh or small saucepan and bring it to a boil. Add the coffee, sugar and cardamom, and bring back to a boil. As soon as the froth begins to rise, remove the pot from the heat. When the froth settles, return the pot to the heat and bring back to a boil. Repeat this process twice.

Serve the coffee immediately, taking care to give everyone a share of the hashweh (froth). Let the coffee settle in the cup for a moment before sipping.

SERVES 4

CAFE BLANC

Many Lebanese prefer a soothing café blanc to the caffeine jolt of strong Turkish coffee—especially at night time. Known as kahwa beida in Arabic, it is simply hot water flavored with a few drops of flower water, and sweetened to taste.

1 cup (250 ml) water
Sugar to taste
1 teaspoon orange blossom or rosewater

Bring the water to a boil and stir in the sugar, if using. Remove from the heat and stir in the flower water. Sip slowly.

SERVES 4

RECIPE INDEX

ACKNOWLEDGEMENTS

Our heartfelt thanks to the many people we met on our travels around Lebanon and Syria who welcomed us so warmly into their shops, businesses, cafés and homes, who fed us, told us their stories and showed us time and again the true meaning of Arabic hospitality.

Additionally, we wish to thank the following for their help on our journey:

First and foremost, we thank Cramer Ball, general manager of Gulf Air in Australia, the airline's Australian public relations consultants David Baker & Associates and all the Gulf Air staff. Their generosity ensured that our journey to and from the Middle East was seamlessly efficient and exquisitely comfortable and reminded us that long-distance flying can be enjoyed, rather than simply endured.

In Lebanon and Syria, we would like to thank the following people for looking after us and offering us advice: Salim and Véronique Hammod and the Hammod family, Hneine Khouri and her children Hany and Mimi, Shakib and Marie Baroud, Houda Bouri and Hady Zeidan. We would particularly like to thank Sami and Lilianne Maftoum for being a constant source of information, for helping us find cars and drivers and for so generously lending us their house in Halat sur Mer.

Thanks, too, to our traveling companions, Matt and Linda Harvey. Linda's good nature and cheery disposition made her a joy to be with and helped dispel the inevitable tensions and challenges of traveling in unknown territory. Matt's creativity and talent as a photographer is clear on every page of this book, and he has captured the beauty and extraordinary diversity of the region in a way that mere words never could.

We could not have undertaken the journey at all without the support and assistance of Greg's sister-in-law, Amal Malouf, our tireless tour guide, translator and trouble-shooter. We are deeply grateful for her assistance in our preparations for the trip and for organizing so much while we were there to ensure things ran smoothly. Thanks for all the introductions and for sharing your family with us along the way!

In Melbourne, many people helped by lending equipment and treasured personal possessions to enhance the food photography, most notably Aeria Country Floors, Market Import, Cranfields, Ex Libris, La Baraka, Wheel and Barrow, Fran Berry and Merran Evans. We are also very grateful to the A1 Middle Eastern Food Store, Ocean Made Seafood and The Vegetable Connection for supplying us with ingredients for the recipe testing and food photography. Thanks also to Caroline Velik who helped style the food shots so beautifully.

Greg would like to thank Dean and Geremy Lucas and the MoMo team for ensuring things ran smoothly during his many long absences. And Lucy would especially like to thank George and Oscar for their support, forbearance and understanding during the long months of recipe testing and photography when the house was taken over by strangers.

We both wish to thank Mara Szoeke and Alison Wall for their hard work during the photo shoot. Particular thanks are due to Alison, pastry-chef extraordinaire. Not only is she responsible for converting many of Greg's wild imaginings into sweet realities, but many of the desserts in this book are her own exquisite creations. Her contribution has been invaluable and we owe her a huge debt of thanks.

There are many other people who helped us transform our scribbled notes and drawings into a beautiful book. Thanks to Janet Austin for her eagle editor's eye and to Klarissa Pfisterer and Hamish Freeman for hand-drawing the map. We owe a very special thank you to Gayna Murphy, whose sumptuous and original design has made this book so much more than we could ever have hoped for.

We would like to express our gratitude to Sandy Grant and Julie Pinkham at Hardie Grant Books, for having the confidence in us to write yet another book. Their team have always been a pleasure to work with, and this experience has been no different. And so we reserve our final and most whole-hearted thanks to the wonderful Mary Small, associate publisher, whose clear vision has seen the book through from beginning to end. At all times—and particularly in the face of absurd deadlines—she has demonstrated a serenity, thoroughness and dedication to the task that goes way beyond the normal call of duty. Thanks for making the whole experience so joyous!